Henry James Coleridge

The Sermon on the Mount

Henry James Coleridge

The Sermon on the Mount

ISBN/EAN: 9783744659666

Printed in Europe, USA, Canada, Australia, Japan

Cover: Foto ©Lupo / pixelio.de

More available books at **www.hansebooks.com**

Quarterly Series.

TWENTY-SEVENTH VOLUME.

———

THE LIFE OF OUR LIFE.

ROEHAMPTON:
PRINTED BY JAMES STANLEY.

(All rights reserved.)

THE LIFE OF OUR LIFE.

PART THE SECOND.

THE PUBLIC LIFE OF OUR LORD JESUS CHRIST.

IV.

The Sermon on the Mount.
(*Concluded.*)

THE SERMON ON THE MOUNT.

(FROM THE END OF THE LORD'S PRAYER.)

BY

HENRY JAMES COLERIDGE,

OF THE SOCIETY OF JESUS.

A NEW EDITION.

LONDON:
BURNS AND OATES,
1882.

✠

DOMINE · JESU · CHRISTE · CLEMENTISSIME
FAC · ME · PER · ARCTAM · VIAM · JUSTITIÆ
ET · ANGUSTAM · PORTAM · PŒNITENTIÆ
INTRARE · AD · AULAM · SALUTIS · ET · VITAM · GLORIÆ
DOCE · ME · VITARE . DECEPTORUM . FALLACIAM
ET · DA · MIHI · IMITARI · SPIRITUALIS · OVIS · SIMPLICITATEM · ET · INNOCENTIAM
FAC · ME · RADICEM · CORDIS · CŒLO · NON · TERRÆ · AFFIGERE
NEC · IN · FOLIIS · VERBORUM · TANTUM
SED · POTIUS · IN · FRUCTIBUS · BONORUM · OPERUM · FIDELIS · MEREAR · INVENIRI
FAC · UT · VOLUNTATEM · PATRIS · CŒLESTIS · FACIAM
ET · VERBA · TUA · AUDIENS · OPERE · IMPLEAM
UT · IN · TE · FIRMATUS
NULLIS · A · TE · SEPARER · TENTATIONIBUS
AMEN.

(Ex Ludolpho.)

PREFACE.

As much as two years has passed since the appearance of the last two volumes of the work, a further instalment of which is now laid before the public. I then broke off the continuous publication of the series on the Public Life of our Lord, in order to make way for the general and compendious sketch of the whole work which is contained in the volumes called *The Life of our Life.* This was done in order that the accidents of health and sickness might in any case not prevent the completion of at least some outline of the whole Life our Lord, with explanations sufficiently clear to render the general plan intelligible. The greater part of the present volume was almost ready for publication a year ago, when ill-health obliged me for some months to lay it aside, as well as the next volume of the *Public Life*, a considerable part of which is finished. This following volume will appear, I hope, within a few months, and the remainder in due time, if God allows me the great privilege of health and strength to continue the work to the end.

The present volume needs little by way of special preface. The commentary on the Sermon on the Mount, which is here concluded, is in some respects the most arduous part, or at least one of the most arduous parts, of the whole undertaking, and I cannot pass from it without feeling still more deeply than before the utter inadequacy of the slight paraphrases and scanty illustrations which are here offered of words and instructions so divine and yet so simple. It is very little to say that I have had to write without ever being able to lay aside other, and sometimes very distracting, occupations. There have been holy and learned commentators on Sacred Scripture who have not thought it too much to give it to a single book of that Divine Volume the labours of a great number of years. The student of the Sermon on the Mount will easily understand how the whole of a life might be profitably expended in the illustration of these three chapters of one of the Gospels. In default of the commentary which might be desired on so singularly important and pregnant a monument of our Lord's teaching, it may be something to have endeavoured to stamp on the mind of the reader the impression which I am sure will grow deeper and deeper on all who devoutly study it—the impression of its unapproachable sublimity and majesty, its wisdom and adaptation to human needs, its intense tenderness and condescension, the ineffable authority which shines in its every word. One could almost wish that, as the Church has a special Festival in honour of our Lord's Prayer in the Garden, so also she had another special Festival in thanksgiving for the Sermon on the Mount. But, in truth, the precepts of this Sermon live on, as the Personal Example of our Lord lives on, in all ages of the Church, in all that is perfect and beautiful and heavenly in the thoughts and words and actions of her children. St. Paul speaks of his converts as his 'Epistle of commendation'—'the Epistle of Christ, ministered by us, and written, not with ink, but with the Spirit of the living God, not in tables of stone, but in the fleshy tables of the heart.'[1] And it may truly be said, that the best commentary on the Sermon on the Mount will be that history of the workings of Divine grace in the hearts of the most perfect Christians, the contemplation of which will be one of the chief elements of the ineffable beatitude of the Saints.

H. J. C.

London, Feast of the Holy Innocents, 1878.

---

[1] 2 Cor. iii. 2, 3.

CONTENTS.

CHAPTER I.
The Law of Mortification.
St. Matt. vi. 15—18; *Vita Vitæ Nostræ*, § 33.

	PAGE
Benefits of mortification	1
Instructions, positive and negative	2
What external show is to be avoided	3
Positive rules	4
Order in the instructions as to the three great works of piety	5
Almsgiving a divine virtue	7
As also prayer	8
Mortification, the virtue of a fallen state	8
Connected with the Fall	9
The Fall and man's original state	11
Losses of the Fall	11
Restoration by means of mortification	12
Beauty of its effects	13

CHAPTER II.
The Range of Mortification.
St. Matt. vi. 15—18; *Vita Vitæ Nostræ*, § 33.

	PAGE
Great range of mortification	15
How to begin it	16
Custody of the tongue	17
Self-love	17
The Apocalyptic dragon	18
Acts of Self-love	19
Weapons against it	20
Taming of the will	21
Of the intelligence and judgment	21
Thoughts and imaginations	22
St. Bernard's doctrine	23
Reasons for mortification	24
Its power with God	25
Connection with prayer	26
With the obtaining of favours	28
How God inflicts it	29
His various methods with souls	31
Advantages of passive mortification	32
Rapid advance in perfection	33
Results of this doctrine	34

CHAPTER III.
Fasting.
St. Matt. vi. 16—18; *Vita Vitæ Nostræ*, § 33.

	PAGE
Fasting and the natural law	35
Meditation on its fruits	36
Four facts in the purgative way	38
Four in the illuminative	39
Four in the unitive	40
Great needs of our time	41

CHAPTER IV.
Our Father in secret.
St. Matt. vi. 15—18; *Vita Vitæ Nostræ* § 33.

	PAGE
Injunction as to secrecy	44
Instances of saints giving a wrong impression	44
Precept of cheerfulness	46

	PAGE		PAGE
Self-affliction to be hidden	46	What makes the heart good	
Our Father in secret	48	or bad	81
The eye of God	49	Perversion of the mind	82
His knowledge of us	50	The 'light of the body'	83
As our Father	51	Truth and the intelligence	84
He is hidden in Creation	51	Man's original illumination described by Ecclesiasticus	85
Practice of His Presence	53		
Recollection	54	Possible ignorance as to the natural law	87
Why it is difficult	55		
We should live and work in His Presence	57	Perversion of reason	88
		The light of faith	89
		Effect of its perversion	90
CHAPTER V.		Of the darkness of false religion	92
Treasure in Heaven.			
St. Matt. vi. 19—21; *Vita Vitæ Nostræ*, § 34.		Of modern 'science'	93
		The light of conscience	94
Connection of the Sermon	58	Conscience when perverted	96
Chain of instructions	59	Our Lord's words applied to intention	97
Hope of reward	60		
Freedom from human respect	61	Doctrine of intention	98
Imagery of our Lord	62	Actual, virtual, habitual	98
Expanded by Him later on	63	How intention is spoilt	99
Use of earthly treasure	65	Several kinds of good intention	100
What is implied in the accumulation of wealth	66		
		Intention of servants, mercenaries, friends	100
Contemplations of holy writers	67		
Value of grace	68	Three kinds of the latter	101
Value of time	69	The rules of St. Ignatius	104
Rules as to use of sacraments and means of grace	71	His contemplation on the love of God	105
Sacrifice of the Mass	72	Dangers pointed out by our Lord	106
Union of our actions with those of our Lord	73		
Industries as to prayer	74	CHAPTER VII.	
Use of the intercession of the saints	75	*Single Service.*	
Their great power	76	St. Matt. vi. 24; *Vita Vitæ Nostræ*, § 34.	
The treasure and the heart	77		
Our Lord's knowledge of men	78	Connection of the passage	107
		Man the servant of God	108
		The two masters	108
CHAPTER VI.		God defending His servants	109
The Eye of the Soul.		Gentleness of the argument	110
St. Matt. vi. 22, 23; *Vita Vitæ Nostræ*, § 34.		Dominion of God	111
		We can serve no one else	112
The treasure of man	79	The usurper	113
It is twofold	80	Nature of the service of God	113

	PAGE
Complete and engrossing	. 114
Character of the Master .	. 116
The alternatives . .	. 117
Hardness of the service of Satan	. 118

CHAPTER VIII.

Confidence in God.

St. Matt. vi. 24—34; *Vita Vitæ Nostræ*, § 34.

Contemplation of our Lord	. 120
The audience on the Mount	. 121
Comparison of the 'Two Standards'	. 122
God and Mammon .	. 125
'The life more than the meat'	126
'Adding to our stature' .	. 128
Peculiar condition of God's servants . . .	. 129
'Consider the lilies' .	. 130
The heathens' case .	. 131
The Kingdom of God and His Justice . . .	. 133
Solicitude for the morrow	. 134
Our Lord insisting on this point	. 135
Extent of the precept .	. 136
Our Lord does not condemn necessary care . .	. 138
But 'solicitude" . .	. 139
Example of the Christian poor	140
Danger of want of confidence	142
How far this is of precept or of counsel . . .	. 143
All are sometimes bound to it	144
Special cases . . .	. 145
Tenderness of our Lord .	. 146

CHAPTER VIII.

The day and its evil.

St. Matt. vi. 34; *Vita Vitæ Nostræ*, § 34.

Connection of this passage with the Lord's prayer	. 147
Dominion of God . .	. 148

	PAGE
Petitions of the Prayer .	. 149
'All these things shall be added ' . . .	. 149
Solicitude for the morrow	. 151
Monotony of our life relieved by divisions of time .	. 152
Providence shown in the arrangement of days and nights	. 153
Continuity of our life .	. 154
What is meant by 'evil '	. 156
Each day has its appointed share	. 157
Preparation is not forbidden	. 159
Far-reaching enterprizes of the saints	. 161
Their magnanimity .	. 163

CHAPTER IX.

Judge not.

St. Matt. vii. 1, 2; *Vita Vitæ Nostræ*, § 35.

Connection explained .	. 164
In another way . .	. 165
In a third way . .	. 165
What judgment is forbidden	. 167
Our want of jurisdiction .	. 167
How far we may judge .	. 168
Rules as to rash judgment	. 170
Severity of ascetical writers	. 171
Reasons of Father Lancicius	. 172
Other reasons. . .	. 174
Recommendations . .	. 175
St. Catharine of Siena .	. 175
Her doctrine on this point	. 176
Two parts of this passage	. 177

CHAPTER X.

Motes and Beams.

St. Matt. vii. 3—5; *Vita Vitæ Nostræ*, § 35.

' Motes in our brother's eye '	. 179
Reasons of rectitude and decency against correction	. 180

xvi   *Contents.*

	PAGE
Doctrine of fraternal correction	181
The duty not barred by our own faults	182
Faults in those who are to correct others	183
Our Lord's rules	184
How we may hope for God's help	185

CHAPTER XI.
Pearls and Swine.
St. Matt. vii. 6; *Vita Vitæ Nostræ,* § 35.

	PAGE
Connection of the passage	187
Images used by our Lord	188
The dogs	189
The swine	191
St. Paul on virginity	192
What are the pearls	192
Incapacity for sublime truths	195
The sacraments	198
'Trampling under foot'	200
Fallen nature in revolt	201
Authority of the Church	203
Powers of evil	204

CHAPTER XII.
The Precept of Prayer.
St. Matt. vii. 7—11; *Vita Vitæ Nostræ,* § 35.

	PAGE
Connection of the discourse	205
Prayer in God's Kingdom	207
Great demands on our spiritual strength	208
The threefold exhortation	209
Prayer is enjoined unconditionally	210
Prayers not apparently answered	211
Conditions of prayer	212
Prayers indirectly granted	214
The Kingdom of God the kingdom of prayer	217
All things to be gained by it	219
Its immense privileges	220

CHAPTER XIII.
The Law and the Prophets.
St. Matt. vii. 12; *Vita Vitæ Nostræ,* § 35.

	PAGE
Our duty to one another summed up	222
Connection with the foregoing precept	223
Our Lord speaking of the two great commandments	224
Love of God includes love of our neighbour	225
Duty to our neighbour summed up in the precept of charity	226
Society of the angels in Heaven	227
Original society of man	228
Tradition of the human race after leaving Paradise	229
The Law of Sinai	229
The Prophets	230
The Law and the Prophets as to the two great traditions of man	231
Difference between the Jews and other nations	232
Our Lord's sayings as to the law of charity	233
Negative and positive precepts	234
Importance of this teaching in the Epistles	234
To the Thessalonians and Galatians	235
To the Romans	236
To the Corinthians	237
The Epistles of St. Peter and of St. John	238
The lives of the Apostles	240
Charity in the Church	241

CHAPTER XIV.
The Narrow Gate.
St. Matt. vii. 13, 14; *Vita Vitæ Nostræ,* § 36.

	PAGE
Change of tone on our Lord's words at this point	242

	PAGE
Notes of warning	243
Our Lord's habit of looking beyond the immediate occasion	245
Prophetical aspect of our Lord's words	246
Comparative failure of the Gospel teaching	248
Even in religious institutes	248
And in single souls	250
Our Lord's warnings	251
The narrow gate	251
St. Paul's doctrine about the prize	252
How is the gate to life narrow?	253
Full theological meaning of 'life'	254
And of 'destruction'	255
Truth of our Lord's words in this sense	256
Another sense of destruction	256
Redemption possible under all dispensations	257
Yet missed by the majority	258
Effect of our Lord's coming	259
And of the Catholic Church in the world	260
Cause of the failure of the multitude	260
Questions which may be asked	261
Our Lord speaks practically	262
Different senses of 'salvation' and 'perdition'	263
Some 'saved' in one sense and 'lost' in another	264
Salvation in the Church	265
She seldom can do her utmost	266
Many saved by repentance and the sacraments	266
Evil effects of general opinion and practice	267
Even in religious communities	268
Importance of lessons to us	269

CHAPTER XV.

The False Prophets.

St. Matt. vii. 15—20; *Vita Vitæ Nostræ,* § 36.

	PAGE
Our Lord's second warning	270
The false prophets	271
Application when He spoke	272
Opposition to His teaching	273
Future assaults on faith	274
Our Lord looking to the future	274
Prophetical character of His words	275
Excommunication of the man born blind	276
The false teachers in the times of the Apostles	277
Mention of them in the Epistles of St. Paul	278
St. John in the Apocalypse	279
Second Epistle of St. Peter	280
Epistle of St. Jude	282
Truthfulness of our Lord's description	284
Great variety of the false teachers	285
Image of the wolf	286
Desire of personal influence	288
The sheeps' clothing	289

CHAPTER XVI.

Trees and Fruits.

St. Matt. vii. 16—20; *Vita Vitæ Nostræ,* § 36.

	PAGE
Test given by our Lord	292
His description of the good and bad trees	292
Use of the same image elsewhere	294
Deep meaning of the image	29
The Holy Ghost the source of fruitfulness	296
The doctrine founded on the Divine Nature	297
Difficulties as to the test	298
It applies to sanctity as well as to doctrine	299

	PAGE		PAGE
But chiefly to doctrine	300	Great dangers of inattention to God	323
Words of St. John	300		
'Dissolving Jesus'	301	Case of the Scribes and Pharisees	324
False doctrine does this	302		
The test true in a further sense	302	Great pains taken by our Lord	324
Keen instinct as to the practical effect of doctrine	304	His teaching by Parables	325
		Principle of reserve	326
Illustrations	305	Language of St. James	327
Sentence on the useless tree	305	Our great need of strength	328
How this is executed	306	Trials for the faithful	329
Summary of the doctrine	307	The two classes in the Church	330
		Greatness of the fall	331

CHAPTER XVII.
Profession and Practice.
St. Matt. vii. 21—23; *Vita Vitæ Nostræ*, § 36.

		Two punishments here spoken of	331
The last two warnings	309		

CHAPTER XIX.
Teaching with authority.
St. Matt. vii. 28; *Vita Vitæ Nostræ*, § 36.

Profession without practice	310		
Connection of the warnings	310		
Our Lord speaks as the Object of worship	311	Wonder of the people at our Lord's manner of teaching	333
He speaks of a true profession of faith	312	Meaning of the Evangelist	334
Doctrine of St. Paul and St. James	312	Contrast between our Lord and other authoritative teachers	335
External character of the prevalent Jewish religion	313	Other instances of our Lord's 'authority' (note)	336
Nominal Christians	314	Examples in the Sermon on the Mount	336
Second part of the warning	315		
Our Lord the Judge	316	The Beatitudes	337
Possessors of *gratiæ gratis datæ*	317	Explanations of the Law	337
		Treatment of the question of divorce	337
St. Paul's words	318		
Meaning of the sentence of our Lord	319	Precept as to works of religion	338
		The Lord's Prayer	338

CHAPTER XVIII.
The Two Foundations.
St. Matt. vii. 24—27; *Vita Vitæ Nostræ*, § 36.

		The counsels and warnings	339
		The Church following our Lord's example	340
Case of those who hear and do not	321	Separated communities rejecting 'authority'	341
Parabolical language of our Lord	322	Why the teaching of the Sermon must rest on authority	341
The rock and the sand	322	Comparison with doctrines of faith	342

APPENDIX.

Harmony of the Gospels.

From *Vita Vitæ Nostræ*, § 29—36.

Sect. 29.—Beginning of the preaching in Galilee, and call of four disciples . . 344
Sect. 30.—The Sabbath at Capharnaum . . . 345
Sect. 31.—The Eight Beatitudes and the Light of the World 348
Sect. 32.—Evangelical Justice 349
Sect. 33.—Alms, Prayer, and Fasting 351
Sect. 34.—Confidence in God our Father 352
Sect. 35.—Against judging others, and of confidence in prayer 352
Sect. 36.—The narrow way to life 353

1

CHAPTER I.

The Law of Mortification.

St. Matt. vi. 15—18; *Vita Vitæ Nostræ*, § 33.

OF the three great works of devotion and satisfaction, almsgiving, prayer, and fasting, one still remains to be treated of in the legislation of the Sermon on the Mount. Our Lord's injunctions concerning fasting are exactly parallel to those which He has already given as to almsgiving and prayer. He does not directly enjoin either of these works, but He speaks of them all as if it were a matter of course that His disciples would practise them, and so be in need of instructions from Him to regulate the manner and spirit in which they were to be practised. As almsgiving may and ought to be understood, in reference to our Lord's precepts concerning it, as including all the works of corporal and spiritual mercy, and as prayer, in like manner, embraces a large range of acts of the mind and of the will and affections besides the direct pouring forth of vocal supplications to God, so must we understand that under the head of fasting we are to include all the various kinds of corporal mortification, and, indeed, the whole practice of that great virtue, whether external or internal, as far as our Lord's words can apply thereto. There is, perhaps, no other virtue as to which it is more necessary to rouse the minds of Christians than this. The subtle heresy of the day, which denies practically that man is fallen and in need of restoration, prepares the way for the rejection of mortification. Then the virtue itself is looked upon as something penal and vindictive only, as a violation of the rights of nature, and almost as a treason against her Maker. The truth of its remedial and elevating character, of the place which it occupies in the providence of God, of its natural dignity in consequence of the Passion and of the redemption of the world thereby, the beauty of the sacrifice which it involves, and the heavenly blessings which reward it, here on earth and in the next world, both as to the persons who practise it and the society in which they live—all these are forgotten, and the result is that a soft childish effeminacy creeps over even Catholic countries, far removed indeed from the pure robust virtue, as well as from the severity, of the ancient ages, which are the glorious periods of the history of the Church.

In this case, as in the case of the other two virtues already spoken of, our Lord's instructions are both negative and positive—what we are to avoid and what we are to do. He has before Him the character and example of the men to whom His hearers would naturally have looked as patterns if He had not warned them not to do so. The Pharisees were the most outwardly religious of all classes among the Jews. Their very profession was to practise the law of God with the utmost strictness, but all that they did was vitiated by the one dominant sin of hypocrisy, from which our Lord takes the name by which He calls them—wishing, perhaps, not to speak of them so much as priests, or even as Pharisees, when He is pointing out their faults. It is also clear that He is insisting very mainly here upon the interior religion with which He wishes His children to honour the Father, and to which the precepts which He is about to give relate. He is about to speak of laying up treasure in Heaven, purity of intention, singleness of service, freedom from solicitude, reliance upon Providence, abstinence from judgment of others, and the like. All this shows the fitness of His warnings against hypocrisy as the special danger for His disciples. The negative part of His instruction is summed up in the warning against hypocrisy—not that there might not be other faults by which the practice of this or any other good work might be infected, but because this is the interior flaw which may destroy all the merit of such works before God, even when they are to outward appearance performed in the most perfect manner.

The fasts of Christians, then, are not to be external displays of self-affliction and sorrow. 'When you fast, be not as the hypocrites, sad, for they disfigure their faces, that to men they may appear fasting'—they seek their reward in the esteem of men, who can see the outside, and so can appreciate the severity and strictness which are involved in the physical suffering of fasting, but who cannot enter into the intentions and motives which actuate those who fast. 'Amen, I say to you, they have received their reward,'—they have had the payment which they desired, and no other recompense remains for them at the hands of God, Who cannot reward what was not done for Him. This, then, is the negative side of the teaching of our Lord on this point. All outward show is to be avoided when we fast, for then it will be certain that we do not seek the esteem or applause of men, who cannot honour what does not meet the senses. It is clear that the outward show against which our Lord warns us is that kind of display for which we, like the hypocrites of whom He speaks, may receive personal honour and credit. The lesson, therefore, applies to austerities and observances which are voluntary, and not to those which are then and there commanded to all as a matter of obligation. No one can be specially honoured for obedience to a general law, which it would be a scandal not to obey—and in the case of such a matter of precept, it may be a duty which we owe to the law to let it be seen that we do not neglect it. Our Lord, therefore, is speaking of fasts and other austerities of private devotion, as to which He bids us be careful to make no display, and even, as we shall see, to be at pains to hide them, and avoid the very suspicion that we are practising them.

We come thus to the positive part of our Lord's instructions as to fasting. He teaches us not only to make no display of any such mortification which we may practise, but absolutely to hide it under an outward appearance which implies rejoicing and gaiety instead of suffering and mourning. 'But, thou, when thou fastest, anoint thy head and wash thy face, that thou appear not fasting to men, but to thy Father Who is in secret, and thy Father Who seeth in secret will repay thee.' The respect which men pay, by a sort of instinct, to the very appearance of self-mastery and severe virtue is so great, and the danger of vainglory in such matters so subtle and powerful, that we are to do even more to avoid it in this case than in the case of prayer or almsdeeds. It seems as if nothing but the most perfect virtue could be safe under the temptation of which we speak, and that, on account of the instinct which men have as to the difficulty of true self-conquest and mortification, it is especially dangerous in regard to the appearance of those virtues. Nor, indeed, has any virtue been more frequently aped by the professors of false religions, and the wolves in sheep's clothing, of whom our Lord speaks a little further on. Thus we are to do a little more here than to hide our fasting. We are to do what may positively mislead the thoughts of men concerning us. We are to seem the very contrary of what we are. But this is not all that our Lord has to tell us on the matter. At the very time when we are concealing our austerities from the eyes of men, under an appearance of gaiety, we are to keep the eyes of our heart fixed on the everwatchful and penetrating gaze of our Father, of Whom our Lord, in this part of the Sermon, speaks, not as our Father in Heaven, as before, but as our Father Who is in secret—close at hand, though invisible, and discernible to faith as certainly as if we saw Him. To Him all our thoughts and works and intentions are to be addressed, our life is to be a continued exercise of His presence, as it is termed by spiritual writers, whether we speak to Him directly in our thoughts and prayers, or work on in silence, as it were, under His eye, attending with all our power to the occupations on which we are engaged for Him. And our Lord does not bid us hope for no reward—on the contrary, He tells us expressly that we shall have the approval of our Father instead of the praise of men which we have foregone, and that His approval will in due time manifest itself in a reward such as He alone can give : first, for the work itself, whether of prayer or mortification, which we address to Him, and then for the pure and faithful and childlike intention with which it has been directed to His eyes alone. The hypocrites have their reward already, that which they seek; and we shall have our reward hereafter, that which we seek—and not hereafter only, but now and here, in the increase of grace and of familiarity with Him, and in the many other blessings which are attached to the interior exercises of the soul and heart.

There is something which is worthy of notice in the order in which our Lord has arranged His teaching as to these three principal works of piety of which we have been and are speaking. If we are to consider the order in which they may be placed as to their power of satisfying the judgment of God, we may remember that, as has been said above, St. Thomas teaches that almsdeeds satisfy more completely than prayer, and prayer than fasting. On the other hand, if we consider what it is that is offered to God in each of these works respectively, our souls are more worthy of God than our bodies, and our bodies are nearer to us than our temporal goods. In this order, prayer is the highest of the three, fasting the next, and almsgiving the last. There is however, another principle of arrangement, which has already been observed in the order of the Beatitudes, and which may also be illustrated from the passage before us. We saw that in the Beatitudes our Lord began with virtues which might have been practised in a state of innocence, and then passed on to those which belong to a state of conflict and penance. The Beatitudes end with the virtue of suffering for the sake of justice—a virtue which implies a state in which evil principles are so powerful as to dominate the whole of human society, and our Lord adds to that Beatitude a direct address to His disciples, in which He speaks as if that were to be the great characteristic virtue in which they were to be expressly tried. Now, if we turn to these instructions as to almsdeeds, prayer, and fasting, we find some traces of a similar order, as if it were natural to our Lord first to think of what might have been in a happy state of human innocence, and then of the virtuous works which would not have been at home there, but which are necessary and natural in a fallen race whose restoration has to be worked out, painfully, though most meritoriously, by the cooperation of the will and exertions of man with the wonderful graces of which God has been so lavish in the scheme of redemption. For our Lord's theology, if we may so speak, was not like ours, which dwells but little on the great realms of God's government which lie outside our immediate ken, or on the beautiful provisions of His wisdom and love which have been supplanted, as it were, by others, in consequence of the actual history of His creation. The whole plan of the Kingdom of His Father lay open before Him, and His Sacred Heart took delight in glorifying Him for every part of the scheme which He had devised for the blessedness of His children.

It is worth while to draw out a little more fully the thought which is here suggested. It is God's character, and the nature and faculties with which He has enriched his reasonable creatures, that give to the virtues of which we are speaking the prerogatives which they possess. For almsgiving or bountifulness is a Divine virtue—a virtue of which God has shown the most stupendous instance in the whole realm of His creation and providence, a virtue the principle of which is found to rule the ineffably blessed life of the angels in Heaven, who are arranged in hierarchies in which there is a wonderful gradation of gifts, and in which the higher spirits are commissioned to impart what they have received from the bounty of God to those who are not so near to Him. And the whole heavenly host is occupied, not only in the loving adoration and enjoyment of God, in Whose presence they dwell, but also in administering His merciful and beneficent providence to the whole of the inferior creation. Nor can we doubt that in a state of innocence the law by which God has given 'to every man a command concerning his neighbour,' would have prevailed as much as in our present condition, in which His scheme for the government of the world is, we may almost say, dependent for its success on the principal of mutual charity and assistance, both as to spiritual needs and temporal needs, and in which He seems to permit a number of material evils and miseries, for the relief of which He has made this principle the chief provision.

If it be true that almsgiving is thus, in a manner, a Godlike and heavenly virtue, the same may also be said, as is evident, of prayer. Prayer is the exercise of the highest of our faculties, those which belong to us by virtue of our spiritual and intellectual nature. In this respect there is no difference between our poor prayers and the most fervent and intense acts of love which the seraphim can frame. All prayer is essentially the intercourse between the heart of the creature of God and God Himself, and no more is needed to show that in the exercise of prayer we are practising a virtue which would have had the largest possible exercise in a state of innocence, as it will be the great occupation of the children of God in the eternal kingdom of Heaven. In the sense in which we are speaking of them, neither Paradise nor Heaven would be what they ought to be without the exercise of these virtues. But the case seems quite different when we come to the exercises of mortification. Mortification is essentially the virtue of a fallen and restored state; it is medicinal, corrective, penitential, preventive of relapse, and satisfactory for sin. In our present condition the other two virtues of which our Lord here speaks share with fasting the quality of satisfaction; but this quality is primary in the case of mortification, and only secondary in the case of almsdeeds and prayer. Fasting, in the restricted sense of the word, not only shares with the other exercises of mortification this quality, which seems to look back so directly to the fall of man, but it is in a manner of its own a direct reference to the history of that Fall itself, which was occasioned by the yielding to a temptation addressed to that appetite which is mortified, even in its lawful indulgences, by those who fast. We thus find our Lord, in this instance also, passing on to the regulation of the practice of a virtue which might never have found a place either in His own example or in the life of His children but for the fallen state in which mankind usually exists. There is something of the same order in the petitions of the Lord's Prayer. There, also, the first things that we are taught to ask of our Father in Heaven are such as might be prayed for if there were no such thing as sin upon the earth, while the later clauses speak of our trespasses and of those of others against us, of the dangers which surround us on every side from the temptations which beset us, and of the evils of all kinds to which we are exposed.

This connection of the necessity of mortification, and of the Christian teaching concerning it, with the fact and doctrine of the fall of man, may be considered as explaining the peculiar irritation which many men feel and show when such precepts are brought home to them as matters of practice. The unregenerate man seems to turn upon them, as if there were in them something especially derogatory to the dignity, and hostile to the liberty, of human nature. The men who are so angry at the idea of mortification, and of fasting in particular, are not all slaves to their belly, as the Apostle speaks.[1] They are often men of cultivation, refinement, and much self-restraint, who can understand that sensuality is something very degrading, and that the true life of man must consist in the exercise of the higher classes of the faculties with which he is endowed. But they are not free from the natural pride which revolts at the doctrine of a fallen state and of all its consequences. And the Christian teaching and practice concerning mortification are continual protests, not only as to the true

[1] Romans xvi. 18.

needs of our condition, but also as to the truth, what that condition really is. And so we have the warning of many saints, that we are not to believe, even on the evidence of miracles, any teacher who might lay down that the necessity of mortification no longer exists under the new Kingdom of the Gospel. Nor is there any point as to which the examples of the saints, wonderful as they are in their variety and adaptiveness to all callings, all characters, all states and conditions of life, or age, or sex, all degrees of strength or kinds of employment or occupation, are so uniform, as this point of the necessity of mortification, and of the thoroughness with which it must be applied to the whole man.

Our Lord, therefore, was not only following an order and a line of thought of which we have other examples in the most important parts of His teaching, when He added directions as to the practice of fasting to those which He had already given as to almsdeeds and prayer. He was touching in this case also one of the great foundations on which our right and perfect discharge of our duties as the children of God must rest. The law of prayer is founded on our spiritual nature and our relations to God. The law of mercy is founded on the position in which we are placed in His Kingdom, and on the commission which His Providence has intrusted to us with relation to one another. The law of mortification binds us, in consequence of the fallen nature which we inherit, of the change which that fall introduced in our condition, and of the means which God has adopted and enacted for our restoration. The whole history of humanity, and the whole condition of things in the world around us, as well as that of our own souls, must be one great riddle without the doctrine of the Fall. And the doctrine of the Fall cannot be understood without some acquaintance with Christian theology as to the condition in which man was originally placed before he fell.

The beauties and excellences of the original condition of mankind are the measure of the depth from which we have once more to rise, by cooperation with the grace of God which is brought home to us in our Lord. We believe that the first man was clothed with grace, filled with the knowledge of God and of His creatures, from the highest angels down even to the lower range of being. He knew both the mysteries which God had revealed to him concerning Himself, and the less hidden truths which are written for all intelligent beings to discern on the face of the creation which is His work. He knew his own end and the conditions on which it was easy for him to secure it. His soul was endowed with supernatural charity, with the panoply of justice and the virtue of religion. In himself he had no conflict or rebellion; the lower faculties and appetites were obedient to reason and conscience, his body, gifted with the capacity of immortality, perfect in all natural health and vigour and beauty, was the obedient and faithful instrument of the soul which governed it in absolute tranquillity and peace. Such was man, the docile child of God, lord of himself, and the appointed and acknowledged king of the creation in the midst of which he was placed. On his fall he lost, not any part of his nature, but the beautiful peace and harmony in which it had been constituted, when he received it from the hand of his Maker, a harmony and a peace of which Divine grace had been the crown and bond. His spiritual life died with the loss of grace, his mind became darkened, his will perverted, disorder became the normal state of his interior kingdom, the flesh began to rebel, appetite to rise up against the law of reason, the passions were let loose from the control of conscience, as man had attempted, as far as in him lay, to emancipate himself from the submission which he owed to God. The effects of the Fall reached beyond the soul. The body became liable to death and the thousand miseries which are, as it were, the shadows and the forerunners of death. The earth became a howling wilderness instead of a beautiful garden, and the lower creation no longer obeyed man, nor shared in that tranquil felicity which was the characteristic of his innocent existence in Paradise.

It is the decree of God that all that man has lost should be restored to him, and that he should gain, in the dispensation of his reconciliation, far higher boons than any that he had lost by his fall. But the means which God has appointed for this reconciliation are such as to make it necessary for man to bear his own part in the process, and his part may be summed up in the virtue of which we are speaking. The disorder under which he fell is not swept away by a violent exertion of Divine power, and although the healing of his ills is primarily the work of grace applied to his soul by the merits of Jesus Christ, although he has the fruits of the Passion, and the gifts of the Holy Ghost, and a whole system of life-giving sacraments provided as the instruments of his restoration, still that restoration essentially consists in the destruction, or as St. Paul constantly terms it, the death of the old Adam in him and the formation or creation of a new man after the image of our Lord. The first Christian sacrament is Baptism, of which the Apostle so constantly speaks as a spiritual death. This death, which is figured and effected in Baptism, has to be carried on and perfected throughout the whole of life, by the various exercises of mortification. It is one thing to purge away the stain of original sin, to implant the gifts of the Holy Ghost and what are called the infused virtues, and quite another to change the conditions under which man at present exists and has existed since his fall. Our state of warfare continues, though we have a whole array of most powerful weapons furnished to us to make it a warfare in which victory is easy. As long as we are in a state of conflict, so long will mortification, which is but another name for conflict with ourselves, be the essential condition of our existence. The pardon of our sins, which we receive in Baptism or in Penance, does not destroy the power of past habits, or the strength of the concupiscences, or the rebelliousness of the lower appetites, or the attractions of false pleasures, or the seductiveness of the world, or the malice, or the activity, or the might, of the evil spirits all around us. Our part in the conquest of all these enemies is summed up in the duty of mortification. Nothing but this will secure us in the grace which we have regained, and if there were no other reason for it, it would remain on this account incumbent on us, in the measure and degree in which we value our salvation, and are bound to provide ourselves with an escape from the eternal punishments which await the rebellious angels and the men whom they may seduce.

It is not the motive of fear only which is the principle on which we are to found our love and practice of Christian mortification. It is not only that by means of this death of the old man within us we escape the terrors of the eternal sufferings which await the enemies of God. Mortification, as we have said, is the restoration of order, the establishment of peace, the imposing of law, but it is also, or rather it is because of this that it is, the unfolding of the moral powers and spiritual energies, the implanting and nurturing of virtues, the cutting off of the hindrances which prevent the growth and vigour of the manly character. And thus it is the true life and development of humanity. The soul of man is the most beautiful of the works of God in the order to which it belongs, and it is intended to give Him honour and glory more worthy of Himself than that rendered by the physical universe all around us. It is to do this by fruitfulness in spiritual energy and beauty, a teeming magnificence of acts of virtue, interior and exterior, a loyal ready childlike service freely rendered to its Father and Lord, which are more precious than the homage of the visible creation, because they are spiritual and because they are free. What is so much to the glory of God is the only true happiness and nobility of man. In the original plan of His Providence, God was to receive this beautiful service from His creature in a way, it may be, which would have cost less pain and been attended with fewer difficulties. Now that it costs more, and is a more arduous warfare, it is not the less the true blessedness of our nature, which can still find no rest or peace or life except in the obedience to the law of its being. The merit is greater in proportion to the difficulty, and the crown of glory answers to the merit. We cannot give to God of that which costs us nothing, but the cost is light indeed, when we have the grace and the example of our Lord to aid us, and the ineffable happiness of a pure conscience as well as the hope of Heaven to cheer us in the conflict.

CHAPTER II.

The Range of Mortification.

St. Matt. vi. 15—18; *Vita Vitæ Nostræ*, § 33.

AFTER having said so much on the general necessity of the law of mortification, we may proceed to a brief sketch, such as may suffice in a work like the present, of the subject-matter to which that law has to be applied in practice. In the case of other virtues, such as patience or mercy, there may be times and positions in which there is but little scope for their exercise. But, in the case of mortification, we can hardly say that any part of our being at any time is exempt from its obligation. The field of Christian mortification is immensely wide, inasmuch as we have to correct and bring into subjection every sense and every faculty. All have been disorganized by the Fall, and if our life has been for any length of time one of disorder or self-indulgence, there will be habits and inclinations which have acquired a sort of possession which it requires continual exertion to counteract. But the teachers of the spiritual life do not urge us to attack every point at once. Although the chief root of our danger lies in the subtle and ingrained self-love, which is the most difficult of all our enemies to reach and exterminate, still, they tell us, in the process of mortification, to begin with the more external phases of the evil, and to set in order the use which we make of our senses before we go on to the exercises of interior abnegation. The eyes, the ears, and the senses of taste, of touch and smell, are to be first regulated, and the many faults of the tongue are then to be corrected. After this we may proceed to the various manifestations and devices of self-love in the proper sense of the name, and to the complete conquest of the will and the judgment.

The writers to whom we refer may be consulted as to the details of the conflict in each of these cases.[1] It need hardly be said that our mortification is to begin with the faults that involve direct danger to the soul, but it is not to stop with them. Thus, for instance, the mortification of the eye must begin with such a guard of looks as may avoid all objects that are in themselves provocative of evil desires, but it must go on to the denial of even innocent sights, when they are merely objects of curiosity or natural pleasure, such as may feed pride or ambition or worldliness, or when they are things with which we have nothing to do, such as the affairs of others, or when they are simply dissipating, and so hostile to the spirit of prayer and recollection. The same rule is found as to the use of the ear, and of the senses of touch, taste, and smell. In all these cases there is a wide field for abnegation, as to which it cannot be said that indulgence is a direct incentive to sin, but where the discipline of the soul and heart requires the sacrifice of much that might interfere with recollection and generate worldliness. In the treatment of the body, in particular, the practice of mortification has from the first been carried out to the extent of austerities and penances which have had hardly any limit, except that of the capacity of endurance with which human frames have been endowed. But especial importance has always been attached, in this warfare against self-

[1] See Alvarez de Paz, *De Extermin. Mali*, c. ii. pp. 1—3.

love, to the taming of the tongue, as to which St. James has said such striking things in his Catholic Epistle.[2] The catalogue of failings of which we may be guilty in the use of the tongue is a long one indeed. It begins with the sins against charity and veracity, such as detraction, however slight, and every kind of conscious inaccuracy, and goes on to duplicity, contentiousness, boasting, the discovery of secrets, even when not directly injurious, scurrility, idle talking, as to which our Lord has left us so strong a warning, and all imprudence, or thoughtlessness, importunity, irreverence of the slightest shade, and that faulty use of the tongue which consists in silence when it is our duty, or at least well, that we should speak. A momentary glance in thought at the wide range of subjects thus opened to us will be enough to show that the labour of external mortification entails on us a lifelong struggle, and can never be laid aside. And yet this part of the virtue of which we are speaking is the most easy. The external demeanour, the use of the senses, and even of the tongue, may be reduced to the rule of reason, and there may yet remain the conquest of the interior man, without which the labour already spent may be of little avail. The passions of the soul, the judgment, and the will, the thoughts and imagination, are still more difficult to tame than the outward senses, and yet there can be no perfect mortification till these also have been subdued. In a state of innocence, and in the happy state in which the Blessed will enjoy God for ever in Heaven, all these parts of human nature would be in perfect order and subordination, but in our present condition we are so disordered that we must do violence to ourselves if we are to be free from revolt.

The root of all our interior disorder is self-love. It is

[2] St. James iii.

remarkable how St. Paul seems to have meant to put his finger on this spiritual truth, when, in his description of the evil state of the world in the latter days, he begins by the prediction that men shall be lovers of themselves, and then goes on to speak of the various vices in which this one great root of mischief will make itself manifest. They shall be covetous, haughty, proud, blasphemers, disobedient to parents, ungrateful, and the like.[3] But the Apostle here speaks, if we may so say, as a theologian. An inordinate love of self deranges the whole system of human life as it was intended to be by God. Man is not created for himself, or to be his own end, but for God, and he is bound by the law of his creation not to love or use anything but with regard to God and for the end for which God made him. Self-love is a continual rebellion against this law of creation. It makes man his own end. It makes him think and desire and imagine and speak and act from morning to night for himself and not for God. The whole intention and aim of life are perverted, and in consequence all man's acts, internal and external, are diverted from their lawful aim. The corruption of intention makes the whole practice, even of apparent virtues, worthless in the sight of God, and the self-love from which it flows makes a man averse to the exercises of faith, hope, holy fear, mercy, beneficence, justice, meekness, humility, and the other virtues, all of which suppose a heart set in a contrary direction. Nor can the holy spirit of prayer reign in a soul which is thus occupied.

One of the holy writers, whom we have often followed in these pages, tells us that self-love is like the dragon mentioned in the Apocalypse, which had seven heads and ten horns.[4] He then draws out his interpretation in

---

[3] 2 Timothy iii. 2.
[4] Alvarez de Paz, *De Extermin. Mali*, l. ii. p. 2, c. iii. ; Apoc. xii. 3

the following manner. The seven heads are these: first, self-esteem, by which a man sets down to himself whatever good or fine qualities he may have received, and is full of his own excellence. The second is the desire to be loved and honoured for his own sake, from which proceed many faults, such as anger with those who do not admire us, complaints at their injustice, dissatisfaction at their esteem of others, and so on. In the third place, we have the fear of contempt and of the disfavour of men, not because it may injure God, but because it deprives us of the honour which we think that we deserve. The fourth of these defects is shame at our natural defects, and a desire to hide them, though they are not our fault. After this comes the care taken to hide our faults from the eyes of men, and this not from the desire not to give scandal, but only because if they are known we lose the good opinion of others which we do not at the same time deserve. Next comes the great care which some people take with the works which are to see the light of publicity, while on the other hand those which are to be seen by God alone are shamefully neglected and slurred over. Thus some men prepare with the utmost diligence and anxiety their speeches or lectures or sermons, or other things which are addressed to the public gaze, while their prayers and their interior exercises are performed in the most careless and perfunctory manner. The natural companion of this defect is another, which he makes the seventh of the dragon's heads—the defect by which things which are either duties, or at least useful and expedient to be done or said, are omitted, out of the fear that they may displease men.

It will be enough very shortly to enumerate the acts of self-love which the writer whom we are now following points out as the ten horns of the Apocalyptic dragon. First he puts the three desires which may spring up in such hearts as those of which he is speaking : the desire of things which are good for the body, the desire of unnecessary or even unlawful pleasures, and the desire of honour and pre-eminence. Then come three inordinate attachments : to external and sensible things, to persons, whether relations or friends, the thought of whom may be a great source of distraction and dissipation, and to our own work or ways, our peculiar exercises of devotion, the things in which we find consolation, and the like, in consequence of which inordinate love we are not willing to give them up in a moment for the good of others. And on these three attachments follow four kinds of bitterness—sadness when our desires are not carried out, envy at the gifts of others, and a desire to obscure them that they may not obscure us, the bitterness of impatience when any one is an obstacle to our wishes, and the bitterness of scruples which often are the chastisement of self-love.

The weapons which are to be used in this great warfare against our self-love are more or less implied in the statement which has been made as to the ways in which that love developes itself. The soul which desires to make itself perfect in self-conquest must master the use of the great principle of diffidence in self and confidence in God. It must pray earnestly for its victory, it must be frequent in the use of acts of love, of the direction of intention purely to God, and in the corresponding acts of self-hatred, acknowledgment of its own vileness, avoidance of singularity or prominence of any kind, the refusal of any love or homage from others which may feed pride, the acceptance of contempt, the ready manifestation to others of its own natural defects, and even of faults, where this can be done without danger to others, the mortification of all human respect, of affection to any created thing, honour, pleasure, popularity, and the like,

The Range of Mortification.

chastisement of the body, which has a great effect in humbling the soul, liberty of spirit in any good works or labours to which it may give itself, and the banishment of all bitterness.

The will, the understanding, and the judgment are all to have their own part in the discipline of mortification. The taming of the will is mainly the work of the practical application of the principle of the sovereignty of the will of God, and the allegiance which is owing to Him. Thus, it is an imperfection of the will to seek what is good or to avoid what is evil for our own advantage rather than for God. We must regulate our desires and pursuit or avoidance of various things, good and evil, by the standard of their relative position as to the perfect will of God, loving and seeking lesser goods less, and greater goods more, things that are neither good nor bad in themselves, only for the sake of the practice of virtue which they may make easy to us, and even goods in themselves, such as virtue, for the sake of the purity of our soul and our union with God. The will of God must be enough to make us give up, without repugnance, the works and occupations in which we have been serving Him with interest and success. What we see to be to our own good must be stamped as it were with the seal of His approbation, as far as we can discern it, before we endeavour to gain it. What we pray for must be asked with a direct and pure intention for His sake, and we should, as a general rule, fear our own choice in anything, considering it a great blessing to be guided as far as may be in all things by the will of others, as representing to us the will of God.

In the same way we must undertake the subjugation, so to speak, of the intelligence and understanding, the judgment and the passions of the soul, and the very thoughts of our minds. All are to be brought into captivity, according to the expression of the Apostle. The intelligence is liable to the vice of indolence, as when men remain in ignorance of their duties, or of what they ought to know in order to their right discharge, out of slothfulness; and, again, to the fault of useless activity and curiosity, occupation on things which do not become our position or age, as when an old man or a priest spends his time in studies which belong to children or to secular persons. Even things which it is useful for us to know must be studied with purity of intention, under authority and obedience, if possible, and in due time and measure. Again, the perfect use of the understanding requires the habit of doing nothing of any moment without previous deliberation, and the regulation of our whole conduct by the application of reason. It is a fault of an unsubdued intelligence to attempt to teach what we have not learnt, and to study and pass judgment on the lives and manners of others. The judgment may show singularity and independence, as in matters of doctrine, in choosing opinions which have no sanction among the wisest and most Catholic children of the Church, or, in the case of religious persons, in want of respect to the decisions of authority, or of the great body of our particular congregation, or, again, in disregard for the opinion of others, which the most mortified men are in the habit of seeking, even when not obliged to it, for the guidance of their own conduct in matters of even smaller importance. In the same way a want of mortification may be shown in the impetuosity and passionateness with which any good is sought or any evil avoided, or in an excess of joy or of sadness, when a good has been gained or an evil suffered.

Finally, the warfare of which we are speaking has to be carried into the very thoughts and imaginations of the heart. Without this, the peace of the soul cannot be

The Range of Mortification. 23

secured, nor that tranquillity restored to man which he enjoyed before the Fall. It is not in our power to be free from evil and useless thoughts altogether, but by the help of the grace of God we are able to meet them by a constant resistance, to reject them, and even to diminish gradually their number and importunity. Just as bad habits and unlawful desires can be broken down and driven away by constant perseverance, especially in the formation of contrary acts and desires, so also can vain and foolish thoughts be reduced in number and power by carefully feeding the mind upon wholesome and useful reflections. The importance of this discipline for the peace and purity of the soul cannot be too highly rated. Our ordinary thoughts tell us what we love and so what we are, and as our Lord declares in His famous words about the things which proceed out of the heart and defile the man,[5] all sins are first born in the thought. The law of grace requires a perfect purity in the eyes of God, Whose special attribute it is to read the heart.

St. Bernard[6] tells that there are three sorts of thoughts which are to be resisted and banished, first, all impure thoughts, leading to sins of the flesh or to any other serious sins; then, idle, curious, and useless thoughts, which feed as it were upon wind, and wander without restraint over the whole world; and, lastly, the thoughts which our Lord forbids when He tells us not to be anxious for the morrow, about food and raiment and other things without which our life cannot continue. Our mind can never be without its stream of thoughts, either good or bad, and the native unsteadiness and fickleness which belong to it, or the unmortified concupiscences which infect the soul, or the unguarded manner in which we use our senses, from which our conceptions are derived,

---

[5] St. Matt. xv. 19.
[6] Serm. *De Triplici Genere Cogitationum.*

or even the malice of our spiritual enemies who are allowed to assail us for our trial or as a punishment of our negligence, keep up a constant supply of the thoughts against which we have to contend. The weapons of our warfare in this case are very like those which we are to use in others like it—prayer to God for purity of heart, resistance at the very beginning of the evil thought, the remembrance of the presence of God, to Whom all our thoughts are open, custody of the senses, manifestation of our thoughts to our spiritual guide, avoidance of idleness, the occupation of the mind on good and useful things, and the desire and practice as far as we are able of familiarity with God as a Father Who loves us as children, and desires us to converse with Him in our hearts.

The large claims which are thus made upon our resolution and courage in the way of mortification, can only surprise us if we forget the original truth on which the whole doctrine of this virtue is founded. It is not that God requires of us to be cruel to ourselves, and to destroy or enfeeble the nature which He has given us. He designs us for an angelical life with Himself in Heaven, and the attainment of this is impeded by the disorder in which the Fall has left us, while the restoration of our moral ruin and the development of the virtues by means of which we are to gain our crown, are to be the fruits of a manly vigorous conflict with ourselves, just as the development of the natural resources and the unlocking of the treasures of some rich soil depend on the hard and persevering labour of the industrious race to whom it has been allotted by Providence. 'In the sweat of our brow we are to eat the bread' of virtue. The first covenant of God with the favoured race of Abraham was granted on the condition of circumcision, and that painful rite has always been understood as

The Range of Mortification.   25

figuring the spiritual circumcision which is the condition of all Christian graces and of the friendship of God. Our Lord, Who presents Himself to the Blessed in Heaven in all the unspeakable and entrancing radiance of His glory, sets Himself before us, here and now, with His head crowned with thorns and hanging on a cross. There is no other way of forming in ourselves the image of the Crucified in His interior perfection than that of the copying the lineaments of His Passion. Without this, our virtue can be only apparent—we shall be following our own will in all that we do, denying our senses nothing that is pleasant, and living an essentially natural and carnal life, in which there is no spiritual health, no peace of the heart, and so no familiarity with God.

On the other hand, nothing wins the heart of God like self-conquest. He is a most loving Father, and desires, with the intensity of which He alone is capable, to raise His children to the blessed state of close intercourse with and possession of Himself which He has designed for them, and which yet cannot be acquired by them save at the price of that restoration of health and peace to the soul of which mortification is the condition. So that, when we mortify ourselves, we gladden the Heart of our Father, and satisfy His greatest longing in our own regard. All His heavenly gifts depend upon mortification. Not that He exacts it as a severe taskmaster, but that He cannot pour them into the soul which is not prepared for them. The old man must die in us before we can be renewed after the image of the second Adam. The life of grace and of justice, perseverance and perfection, requires the removal of the impediments which forbid its implanting or stifle its growth. The clouds of earthly desires and cares darken the mind, and the heart which is the home of unrestrained concupiscences can never be at rest. But the gifts of God must find the eye of the intellect clear, and the heart at peace. Spiritual writers go on in the same way to show how the natural fruit of mortification is the lessening of faults and the doing away with the pain which we owe to the justice of God for the faults already forgiven as to their guilt, how it enables us to conquer temptations and to acquire virtues. But it will be enough in this place to say a few words on two more points connected with this virtue in general, before proceeding to that particular exercise of fasting which is the direct subject of our Lord's instruction in the Sermon on the Mount.

In the first place, it is well to note the immediate connection between the spirit and practice of mortification and the gift of prayer. Prayer is so closely connected with the virtues as on that account only to be dependent on mortification. But it is further true to say that, on account of its own special character and requirements, it is more dependent on mortification than are the virtues themselves. It is surely a matter of surprise when we think that, as far as can be known from what appears, the gift of prayer is not as common in the Church as it might have been expected to be. It is not uncommon to live a good life, to pass years without serious sin, to practise corporal austerities, to give much time and labour to works of mercy and to the exercise of the moral virtues. And yet there are but few in comparison who have the gift of prayer, and who are united with God in spirit and truth. The reason can be no want of condescension on the part of God, Whose delights are to be with the children of men, and Who has Himself become Man to satisfy His love for our nature. It cannot be that men any longer, as the Israelites of old, are too much afraid to wish to draw near to God, for this difficulty about the gift of prayer is a cause of great complaint and sorrow to many who would fain receive it. Nor can it be that the holy converse with God, in which prayer consists, is found to be bitter and wearisome to those who know it, for no one who has tasted the sweets of prayer but is full of hunger and thirst to enjoy them again. The reason lies therefore in the absence of the disposition which is necessary for this wonderful gift. That is, there are so few men of prayer, because there are so few men who are fitted for the exercise of prayer, and for the heavenly delight of which it is full. For prayer, under which name we here speak of all the exercises of contemplation, and of intimate familiarity with God, requires above all things a great and unwearied practice of mortification. Prayer is called by one of the ancient writers of the Church a virtue of extreme purity. Just as to gaze on the works of God here below, so as to take in their full beauty, to penetrate their delicate organization, and to pierce the depths of space in which they are set, the eye must be filled with light, and free from the slightest speck of dust, and be itself in perfect health, with no noxious humour in it to weaken its action, so must the soul which is to see and converse with God be open to the divine light by withdrawal from earthly desires and interests, it must be pure from the dust of worldly and foolish thoughts, and it must be at peace in itself with the tranquillity which can only be gained when the affections and desires are all in order, and when the sensual emotions, which are like winds which ruffle the sea, are calmed down and tamed. All this is the work of mortification and abnegation, which are as constantly rewarded by the gift of devotion and consolation in prayer, as the contrary fault of self-indulgence is punished by aridity and the feeling that God is at a distance from us. Thus St. Nilus says, that whatever we suffer with patience in any way is repaid to us in prayer, and when St. Ignatius heard a man commended as a man of great prayer, he corrected the speaker and said, 'A man of great mortification.'

It is certain that the tranquillity and serenity of mind and heart which are the fruits of the mortification and abnegation of which we speak, are blessings sufficiently desirable in themselves to be well worth the slight though continued labour which their acquisition costs. But their value in the spiritual life is wonderfully enhanced when we come to consider them as the means to the attainment of the gift of prayer.

And we must also remember that the mortification which purchases them for us has also the power with God of obtaining for us the favours which we ask, as well as the sweet delights of consolation in the act itself of prayer. For the saints tell us that God is too tender a Father not to be moved when He sees His children, not only asking Him in faith and with earnestness, but also afflicting themselves and putting themselves to pain in order to gain their petition. Thus it is commonly said, that when penance is joined to prayer the effect is almost irresistible with God. And, as those who will not give up earthly and material delights for the sake of union with God are ordinarily left to be the sport of distractions and desolation when they ask anything of Him, so, on the other hand, those who keep their senses and affections and thoughts under continual discipline, are rewarded by the gifts of compunction and consolation. These are the recompense of the souls who refuse, even in time of desolation, to turn to creature consolations and to seek for any joys short of those which are heavenly. 'My soul refused to be consoled,' says the Psalmist, 'I was mindful of God and I was delighted.'[7] This whole doctrine of the effect of mortification on the spirit of prayer is full of instruction as to the folly of an

[7] Psalm lxxvi. 4.

unrestrained soul in any condition and profession of life, if it has any desire at all of being near to God in prayer. But it applies more especially to those whose vocation and condition of life obliges them to deny themselves the ordinary comforts and joys which are allowed to secular persons. Visible and temporal things have a certain kind of passing happiness to confer on those to whom they are not forbidden, but men whose profession devotes them to the work of the sacred ministry and the service of the altar, men whose interests and occupations oblige them to live for the good of souls and the service of God, and thus to touch and handle daily the realities of the spiritual world and the issues of the everlasting conflict in which eternity is lost or won, are inexcusable indeed, and as miserable as inexcusable, if they let the trifles on which self-love can fasten, the childish toys of vainglory, or the pettinesses of comforts, or the small gains of self-interest, draw their thoughts away from the lofty and pure atmosphere in which alone prayer can be the true occupation of the soul. The loss which such men incur is immense, and it is not to be reckoned by what they themselves alone forfeit, inasmuch as the good of others for whom they labour is bound up in the Providence of God with their own union with Him. And the trifles which are the causes of so great a misery to themselves and others, are too contemptible to be capable of satisfying them.

Another remark which may be made here is this. God is so great a lover of mortification, not because He likes to see us suffer, but because He knows so well the immense value and power in the spiritual order of such sufferings as we are capable of, that He is not content to let even His most perfect servants lose this peculiar and special merit. Thus it often happens that when a soul has carried self-conquest and abnegation to the utmost limit, when the passions and senses are subdued, and reduced to order, when the thoughts and affections and imaginations have been tamed, and, as far as can be seen, the work of mortification has been faithfully accomplished, He takes it up Himself, and carries it on by means of the external providence to which He subjects those whom He loves. Our Lord's sufferings considered as mortifications were of this kind. He denied Himself in every way, but all through His Life, and especially in His Passion, He received far more from the hands of His Father by means of His enemies than He inflicted on Himself. This passive mortification, as it is termed, is more valuable in God's sight, and more secure, than the afflictions of various sorts which have no author but ourselves. For this reason, perhaps, it was that our Lord speaks of the Passion as the chalice which His Father gave Him, although it was of His own freewill that He drank it. The beauty of this mortification was enhanced by the prayer which He made in the Garden, that the chalice might pass from Him. It is not only suffering, but humble submission thereto, from whomsoever it came, that is the great characteristic feature in the Passion of our Lord. The image in which the prophet delights who has painted it in the most delicate and minute detail, is that of the sheep in the hands of her shearers, and the lamb that opened not her mouth.[8] Thus we have our Lord as the great example of this last and most precious form of mortification. Some holy writers see an allusion to this doctrine in His words to St. Peter about the form of his martyrdom, where He tells the Apostle that when he was young he used to gird himself, and walk where he would, but that when he was old, he should stretch forth his hands, as if in resignation to God's providence, and another should gird him

[8] Isaias liii. 7.

The Range of Mortification. 31

and lead him forth whither he would not.[9] That is, the beginnings of self-conquest, and of the restoration of the soul to the beauty and dignity which it has lost by the Fall, are the work of our own efforts in voluntary mortification, but when we become old in the service of God and in the practice of self-discipline, He subjects us to another kind of treatment, and exercises us in the higher ways of resignation and patient submission to the mortifications which come to us from without, and even against our will.

As God is so wonderful and inscrutable in His ways, it is not possible for us to lay down any certain law as to the method in which He treats the souls whom He loves, after they have purged themselves from their sins, and renewed the image of their Creator in themselves by mortification of the kind of which we have before spoken. In this, as in other departments of His government, He delights, if we may so say, in showing alike the freedom of His choice of means and the inexhaustible variety of His resources. We cannot argue from the experience of one saint, to the manner in which He will deal with the soul of another. Sometimes He leads the soul which has become docile in His hands along a path of light and peace, kindling in it the affections of tender charity and flooding it with consolations. Sometimes He deals with it in a manner altogether opposite. Instead of light, He covers it with darkness, He keeps it in a state of dryness and desolation and temptation, sadness reigns within, and it is exposed to persecutions, calumnies, or the discipline of sickness and physical sufferings of many kinds without. Thus St. Paul writes at one time of the supernatural consolations, the unspeakable words which he heard when caught up into the third heaven and the like,[10]

[9] St. John xxi. 18.   [10] 2 Cor. xii. 4.

and at another of the 'combats without, fears within,'[11] and of the great tribulations of every kind which he had to suffer. It is by such discipline as this that the soul is trained to patience, to resignation under any afflictions, and to detachment from the consolations which are at other times allowed to it. It has thus an opportunity of humble adoration of the supreme dominion of God over His creatures, and of more perfect union with His absolute will and ineffable wisdom.

Holy writers further assign certain reasons for this discipline of the soul of which we speak. In the first place, the exercise of passive mortification helps us very much in gaining the spirit of subjection to God. We are always inclined to imagine that we are our own masters, that we have a right to ease and repose and enjoyment, to a present reward for any labour that we have done. Our Lord seems to touch this propensity when He speaks of the lord who, after his servant has been ploughing or feeding cattle, does not bid him at once go and sit down to meat, but rather first to make ready his master's supper and gird himself, and serve him, and then afterwards take his own meal. 'Doth he thank that servant for doing the things which he commanded him? I think not. So you also,' He says, 'when you shall have done all these things that are commanded you, say, we are unprofitable servants, we have done that which we ought to do.'[12] Our condition here is of necessity one of toil and labour, of one enterprize for God after another, and the time for consolation and rest is not yet. Again, the experience of the mortifications of which we are now speaking has a great value as a means of humiliation. Even St. Paul was subjected to this discipline, as he tells us, and, 'lest the greatness of the revelations should exalt him,

[11] 2 Cor. vii. 5.   [12] St. Luke xvii. 7—10.

there was given him a sting of his flesh, an angel of Satan to buffet him.'[13]

Again, although consolation and interior sweetness very often help the soul on wonderfully in the path of virtue, there is still some danger lest it become too much attached to them for their own sake, as is the case with persons who are immoderately grieved when they are withdrawn, and so show that it has not been simply for the sake of God that they have loved them. On the other hand, the discipline of suffering advances the soul which bears it with patience even more rapidly, and at the same time more securely. There is no other way by which we can arrive at perfection so swiftly as this. And again, another reason for the use of this method on the part of God, lies in the great resemblance to our Blessed Lord which is thus formed in the soul. For we have already said that the suffering which came from without was the kind of suffering which God especially chose for His Incarnate Son, as also for His Immaculate Mother. Our Lord was seized and bound and scourged and crowned with thorns by others than Himself, they tore His garments off Him, and laid the Cross on His shoulders, and fastened Him thereto, they insulted Him and mocked Him and pierced His side with a lance. What comes to us in this way, comes more directly from the hand of our Father than any mortifications which we can inflict upon ourselves with our own hands, which, after all, do not wound us severely and, if they are not gentle in their blows, are at least guided by our own will. Thus the mortications from others and from the Providence of God —such as bodily ailments, sickness, and the like, have the immense advantage of giving us the opportunity of direct and actual union with His adorable will, and

[13] 2 Cor. xii. 7.

of resignation to the decrees of our Father concerning us, which is not so directly afforded us by inflictions of the other kind.

It is, of course, true that this discipline of involuntary mortification is used by God for many others besides the souls who are so especially dear to Him. It is the way in which He frequently awakens the sinner to a sense of his condition, or preserves from the dangers which would otherwise beset them, souls which are too weak to resist the temptations of worldly prosperity and a life of enjoyment. He uses this discipline to weak souls also, who would have no courage to take up the Cross of themselves, if it were not laid upon them by Him. But in whatever aspect we regard the use which God makes of this discipline, it cannot fail to witness to the truth of which we are speaking—the truth that mortification of some sort is an essential foundation for the saintly and even the Christian character. And the many miseries of the world, the sorrows of human life, the sufferings especially, which seem so often to fall on those who deserve them the least, or at the times when they are the least deserved, have a halo of heavenly light shed upon them, when they are looked on as the chastisements which the most loving and merciful of Fathers sees good to make the lot of His children, in order that they may not miss the ineffable blessings which the laws of His government attach to the virtue of mortification.

CHAPTER III.

Fasting.

St. Matt. vi. 16—18 ; *Vita Vitæ Nostræ*, § 33.

ENOUGH has now been said as to the general law of mortification, and its necessity for the regaining—with all that increase of blessings which may be expected from the ineffable bountifulness of God, Who is the Author of the dispensation in which it is made possible for us to regain it—of that state of order and tranquillity which was lost by the fall of man. We may now pass on to the particular point at which our Lord touches this general law in His Sermon on the Mount. Fasting, as has been said, is the direct correction and punishment of that appetite, the undue indulgence of which brought about the Fall. It stands in the spiritual and ascetic system for the whole range of the many kinds of external penance and self-chastisement. Catholic theologians tell us that the obligation of fasting rests upon the natural law, in so far as the mortification of the passions, which is the fruit of fasting, is in general necessary for salvation in our present condition. The time, manner, and degree of fasting are matters which it belongs to the Church to determine. Thus, if the Church had not fixed the times and modes of this holy exercise, we should still be obliged to practise mortification of this kind, in order to gain the ends for which it is the natural and appointed means. These ends are beautifully expressed by the Church, in the Preface which is used in the Mass during the sacred penitential season of Lent, in which she addresses herself to God, *Qui corporali jejunio vitia comprimis, mentem elevas, virtutem largiris et præmia.* We find the same classification in one of the sermons known under the name of St. Augustine, wherein fasting is said to purify the soul, to elevate the mind, to make the flesh subject to the spirit, the heart contrite and humble, to scatter the mists of concupiscence, extinguish the fires of lust, and kindle the fair light of chastity.

The threefold fruits which are mentioned by the Church in her Preface seem to be arranged with reference to the three states or ways in the spiritual life, the way or state of purgation, that of illumination, and that of union or perfection. St. Bernardine, whom we have before so often followed, draws out, in his usual manner, the fruits of fasting under these three divisions, allotting four fruits to each. It is well to dwell on these from time to time in meditation, especially in days like our own, when, from many various causes, there is so much inclination to excuse ourselves from the ancient discipline of the Church, sanctioned by the authority of so many saints of all ages. We have already seen the theological ground, as may be said, for the necessity of mortification, and it is well to add to this the consideration of the immense benefits which holy writers connect with the slight penance of which we are speaking. What is to be desired is, not that fasting and other bodily mortifications should be rated more highly than they deserve, as weapons in the spiritual warfare, or that the practice of them should be forced on persons whose state of health and physical strength does not make it expedient or safe, but that no one should consider the exemption from them as a matter of congratulation, or be indifferent to the duty of compensating to the soul in some other way, as far as may be possible, for the loss which it may sustain by their abandonment, and this quite apart from all question as to the obedience due to the law of the Church and the example of our Lord. For in this, as in other similar cases, those who do not observe the law because they cannot, and who would observe it if they could, are in a very different state, as to the gaining of the benefits which its observance conveys, from those who account it a great boon to be freed from its observance. The latter class of persons are not at all likely to think of endeavouring to gain, in any other way, the benefits which fasting ordinarily secures to those who practise it in the true spirit of penance. They will need very much to be freed from the false notions with which the world at large regards this holy observance—notions which are grounded upon an erroneous theology and a false view of the condition of man in his present stage of existence. For such persons the truths which set before them the immense blessings which the soul may receive or forfeit by the observance or non-observance of this holy discipline may be of great advantage. The same truths will spur on the courage of the true children of the Church in these practices of penance, and enlighten those whose strength is not equal to these practices, as to the objects at which they should aim in whatever exercises they may adopt as a substitute for them. It is well then to know that if fasting were not enjoined upon us, as it is, by the Church, it would still be the favourite exercise of all those who truly understood the needs of their souls, the dangers of their present condition, and the great advantages which flow from this simple observance. And this can hardly be learnt better, than by studying the thoughts of such a writer as St. Bernardine in the sermon to which we refer.[1]

The Saint tells us, in the first place, that fasting restrains the body and its unlawful appetites, and thus performs the great object of the way of purgation, because it sets the superior part of man to rule the lower, and to treat all its seductive promptings with austerity. The acts of mortification are severe, and their exercise fosters manliness and virtue, it subdues all softness and laziness, as St. Paul speaks of chastising his body and bringing it under subjection. He refers to the direct reason for this of which we have spoken —that by the disobedience of gluttony the flesh first rebelled against the soul, and by the obedience of abstinence the flesh is again brought into subjection to the soul. He adds that it is ridiculous to speak of not being able to tame the passions of the flesh, when this can certainly be done by fasting. There is no castle so strong that it cannot be reduced by famine, and no fire so violent but that it can be extinguished by want of fuel. In the second place, fasting has a natural and just power of making satisfaction for sin, which consists in unlawful indulgence, and so may be compensated for by restriction upon what is lawful in the way of pleasure. The third fruit of fasting under this head is, that it prevents evil, by afflicting the body, and so weakening the concupiscences which are the seed of sin. And, in the fourth place, it appeases and turns away the anger of God, for He sees the flesh reduced to subjection, the soul humbled in fasting, as David says, and future faults guarded against in the same way, and thus His mercy is turned towards us, and He even forgives us the chastisements which He had prepared to inflict. The great Scriptural examples

[1] St. Bernardine, Quadr. *De Christianâ Religione*, Sermon v.

Fasting. 39

of this treatment on the part of God, are the wicked King Achab,[2] and the heathen Ninevites, of whom it is written that 'they believed in God and proclaimed a fast, and put on sackcloth, from the greatest to the least,' their King ordering it, and saying, 'Who can tell if God will turn and forgive, and will turn away from His fierce anger, and we shall not perish?'[3]

The Saint then goes on to speak of the fruits of fasting which belong to the illuminative way. These again are four. First, he places the enlightenment of the mind, both as to matters of conduct and matters of speculation, then the nourishment of the spiritual faculties, then the healing of mental infirmities—sometimes even of bodily ailments—and, in the last place, the strengthening of the mind and the will. As regards the fruit of enlightenment, he quotes the words of Isaias—'Whom shall He teach knowledge, and whom shall He make to understand the hearing? Them that are weaned from the milk, that are drawn away from the breasts.'[4] Thus Moses received the law on Mount Sinai after his long fast, while the people at the foot of the mountain were led by intemperance into idolatry. The exercises of prayer and contemplation, in which a clear insight into heavenly things is acquired, reading, preaching, and all others of the same kind, are greatly helped by abstinence. Daniel, Elias, and St. John, are instances in Scripture of saints who have received revelations after fasting, and we have in the Church many examples like that which St. Bernardine quotes of St. Francis, who wrote his Rule and saw the vision in which he received the stigmata after a long fast. As to the second fruit, our Lord in the desert, after His long fast, when angels came and ministered to Him, is the type and pattern of those who are

---

[2] 3 Kings xxi. 27.
[3] Jonas iii. 5—10.   [4] Isaias xxviii. 9.

nourished by God, spiritually or even corporally, after such abstinence. The next two fruits do not need much explanation. The spiritual diseases which are healed by abstinence are many, and it happens not unfrequently that the ailments of the body yield to the same discipline. In the last place, abstinence strengthens our courage, makes us ready for perseverance, enables us to suffer with patience, to labour with constancy, and press on manfully and fearlessly along the road of perfection.

The fruits of fasting which relate to the unitive way are also four. St. Bernardine calls them the eradication of self-love, the sacrificing of the body, the triumphing over our enemies, and the opening of the gates of glory. For the root of self-love is in our sensuality, coarse or refined, and by means of fasting sensuality is destroyed. Fasting is the beginning and the principle of that sacrifice of the body of which St. Paul speaks when he says, 'I beseech you, brethren, by the mercy of God, that you present your bodies a living sacrifice, holy, pleasing to God, your reasonable service.'[5] The body was intended to be the perfectly docile and willing instrument of the soul in the service of God, which consists in the practice of virtue, and in our present condition it has to be brought back to this state of happy obedience by the discipline of mortification, of which fasting is the beginning. And then, when the root of self-love has been torn up, and the body subdued to be a holocaust in the worship of God, it is not much to add that our external enemies are conquered by the same holy means. Our external enemies are, in the first place, the devils, who reign and make their abode in souls pampered with luxury, indulgence, and pride, and whom our Lord overcame in the person of their chief in His own fasting. In the second place, our enemies are

[5] Romans xii. 1.

external trials and sufferings, and in the third place, difficulties and great achievements for the service of God, which are overcome and carried out by means of fasting. Elias is here again the great Scripture instance which is referred to by the saints. 'When fasting,' says St. Ambrose,[6] 'he shut up the heavens, brought down the rain, called fire from heaven, was caught up into Paradise, and obtained admission to the presence of God. The more he fasted, the more he merited.' And, as to the fourth of these points, it is but natural that the gates of glory should be thrown open to men by abstinence and mortification, as they were of old closed against us in consequence of self-indulgence.

Such, then, are some of the fruits which the saints promise to us as the reward of a faithful obedience to the laws and the spirit of the Church in the matter of bodily self-denial. They deserve special attention in days like our own, when, from various causes, the Church has felt it right to go to the extreme of indulgence in her prescriptions in this matter, and when too many of her children are inclined to seek for still further relaxation of the ancient discipline. It cannot be denied that there are probably many more in times like ours who are physically unable to observe the old rules, or even the modifications which are now commonly allowed. This may be the result of the increased care taken of sickly children or of invalids of any age, who would otherwise sink into the grave sooner than they do. It is probably, also, the fruit of the great strain and hurry and excitement of modern life, which wears out human vigour sooner than it need be worn out. Nothing need be said of those who are for so many various causes exempted from the obligation of the full observance of

[6] *De Jejunio.*

the law, except that they should endeavour to find means for repairing to their own souls the loss which they may incur, though without blame, by their weakness. For there are many kinds of self-denial beside those which affect the strength of the body, and these should be used by such persons with a wise prudence, lest they should be put to shame by the children of this world, who will always make up for necessary losses by industry which is within their reach. But it is to be feared that the growing eagerness for exemptions from the wholesome discipline of the Church has other causes besides those which have been named. The age is one of great softness, while the false doctrines which practically deny the fall of man and the other truths on which, as we have seen, the system of mortification is rested by the Church, are extremely rife, and affect many who are still nominally believers in revelation. To fast and practise other mortifications of the kind which seem so degrading to human pride is to protest against these pernicious falsehoods. The Church may be considered to have warned her children against them in her own way, by the definition of the Immaculate Conception of our Blessed Lady —a doctrine which is unintelligible if the doctrine of the universality of original sin and all its consequences be not alike true and most momentous. And it is curious to remark on the inconsistency of those who exclaim against this definition, and at the same time practically deny the doctrine of the fall of man. Almost in the same breath they tell us that the Immaculate Conception of the Mother of God involves the falsehood that our Lord did not take on Him a nature which was ours, and that the dignity of our nature is too great for us to need the physical discipline of fasting and other mortifications. But, on the other hand, the more, as children of the Church, we rejoice in the prerogative, by virtue of which

Fasting.

Mary was preserved from the common lot of the descendants of Eve, the more, surely, ought we to humble ourselves in the thought of the miserable condition which that common lot entailed upon all others but her. Nor can there be any more practical way of asserting this truth in the face of an unbelieving and scoffing world, than that of the highest possible esteem for those holy exercises which that lot, as inherited by ourselves, has made so necessary for us. It would not be a result out of keeping with the analogy of the history of the Church, if the age, which has witnessed the solemn assertion of the truth of our Blessed Lady's immunity from the sin of Adam, should also be marked by a great revival of the ancient and most wise discipline of the Church in the matter of mortification.

CHAPTER IV.

Our Father in secret.

St. Matt. vi. 15—18; *Vita Vitæ Nostræ*, § 33.

WE may now pass on to the injunction which our Lord here gives as to the secrecy which is to be observed by Christians when they are practising mortification. It seems at first sight to go rather further than the precepts before given as to the avoidance of human applause. We are told not only not to do our mortifications before men, or to hide them, as far as may be, from our own thoughts—as when we are commanded not to let our left hand know what our right hand doeth—but also to anoint our head and wash our face, that we may not appear to men to be fasting. It is not certain whether our Lord's words imply more than that we are to wear the ordinary appearance of men who are neither afflicting themselves nor regaling themselves in any unusual manner, or whether they mean that we are to assume the semblance of those who are feasting and rejoicing on some special occasion. In the first case, we are told to preserve our usual appearance; in the second, to put on an appearance which is directly at variance with our true state, and which is not usual with us.

To do the last, would be to impose upon others for the sake of not being thought virtuous or observant in any extraordinary degree. There have not been wanting beautiful instances among the saints of God of men who have done this. They have deliberately sought to give the impression that they were different from what they were. They have hidden their humility under a semblance of arrogance, they have seemed to be impatient or angry or disobedient, or at least simple and foolish, when they have been all the time really practising the virtues contrary to the failings of which they have made themselves suspected. The foundation of this taste, if we may so call it, in them has been their clear insight into the truth of the extreme value of human contempt for the advancement of perfection, and into other kindred truths, such as the worthlessness of the opinions of men, and the immense blessing of that near resemblance to our Lord, in the treatment which He met with at their hands, which cannot be attained in any way so perfectly as in this. Thus we find that a saint so perfectly moderate as St. Ignatius, who was always guided by reason and divine prudence, would yet have wished to expose himself to public ridicule in the streets of Rome, if there had not been other reasons against his so doing. In the case of the saints who have actually been examples of the conduct of which we are speaking, those other reasons are overruled by an inspiration of the Holy Ghost, Who breatheth where He listeth, and occasionally chooses ways for the sanctification of the servants of God which are not His common ways. Nor is this anything so new as to be peculiar to the Gospel Kingdom. There are certainly many actions in the Scriptural accounts of the ancient saints of God which have this grotesque character. In the Christian ages we have such examples as are found in the lives of St. Symeon Salos and others —actions which are not so much to be imitated as to be admired, but which it would nevertheless be very foolish to reprobate as inconsistent with true and high sanctity. But, as has been said, an extraordinary impulse of the

Holy Ghost is needed to justify the following of such examples, as in the case of other extraordinary actions of the saints which might otherwise have been culpable, such as the self-mutilation, or even suicide, of Christian women when they had no other way of saving their purity.

With these examples in the lives and actions of the saints before us, it will not seem strange, if so it were, that our Lord had recommended His followers to put on an appearance of joy and festivity at the time when they were practising secret mortifications. The case falls far short of those of which we have spoken, in which the servants of God have actually affected to be like the children of the world in matters far more serious than an appearance of innocent gaiety. It may be added, also, that the practice of austerity, even when it is very severe, has a direct tendency to fill the heart with joy, which often overflows upon the countenance and whole demeanour. The bright cheerfulness which characterizes the members of some of the most austere orders in the Church is proverbial, and when we call to mind the fruits which the saints assign to the observance of fasting only, there is nothing to surprise us in it. God is very abundant in the rewards which, even here and now, He lavishes on those who give up much for His sake. No labourers in the Church are more frequently overwhelmed with spiritual joy than those who devote themselves to missionary dangers among the heathen. None are so perfectly happy as those who abandon themselves entirely to His Providence: none so uniformly joyful as those who treat themselves with the greatest severity.

It may, however, be thought most probable that our Lord is not here enjoining any positive deception, by the affectation of a special and unusual state of rejoicing, but rather that He is recommending that we should simply show no outward signs of self-affliction. The injunction may mean nothing more than that the ordinary signs of cheerfulness are not to be omitted when we fast, but that we are to let our outward garb and demeanour be as usual. The object which is to be gained is that which is mentioned, 'that you appear not fasting unto men.' And this precept is given in direct contrast to the practice of the hypocrites, who not only fasted, but 'disfigured their faces,' that is, as it seems, adopted some unusual show of grief and suffering at such times. Our Lord, therefore, would have us keep to ourselves and to God whatever we do in the way of mortification, and take care that it does not meet the eyes of men. The same principle, of course, may be applied to special devotions or religious practices of any kind, which are all to be between ourselves and our Father, while it may also regulate our manner of practising the virtue of religion in common with others. We are thus brought to the thought of that beautiful kind of hidden sanctity which consists in appearing to be like other people, while we are in truth exercising ourselves in the highest virtue. For there are many great saints of God who have not seemed to do anything extraordinary at all. They have lived with and like others, they have had no special practices of devotion or austerity not common to the companions with whom they have dwelt. They have eaten and drunk and slept and studied and laboured and conversed like other people, and yet they have all the time been doing these common things in a way of their own; and, by the attention, devotion, and pure intention with which they have done them, by the intensity and fervour of their interior affections, the carefulness and prudence and heroic charity and supernatural motives which have characterized their conduct in the sight of God, they have raised their actions to the very highest level of sanctity. Such must have been, in great measure, the sanctity practised by our Lord and our Blessed Lady and St. Joseph at Nazareth. It would seem that such pure and lofty holiness was not so very difficult, inasmuch as it requires no departure from the common path of Christian duties. But it is in truth far more difficult than it seems. For even virtuous men are not always superior to the temptation of practising most readily the virtues which strike the eyes of men, and there is much temptation to invert the order in which God would have us carry out the exercises of a holy life, according to which the precepts come first, the counsels next, then the things for which we have special inspirations, and last of all, those to which we are prompted by our own particular devotions or tastes. But any departure from the common practice or order in these matters involves a certain amount of singularity, and this is just what is inconsistent with the kind of action of which we are speaking. The love of singularity sometimes fastens on the most trivial points, matters of opinion on some open question, the manner of performing some ordinary exercise or duty, even on such things as gestures and pronunciation, as to all of which there is a subtle satisfaction and pride in having ways and methods of our own.

It is easy to see how the practice of this kind of virtue, as of every interior exercise of the spiritual life, is aided by the consideration of God, of Whom our Lord speaks in this part of the sermon, as our Father Who is and Who seeth in secret. We have already noted this change in the language of our Lord. In the earlier passages of the sermon He speaks of our Father in Heaven, and it is by that title He bids us address God in His own prayer. When He comes to the three great works of which we have been speaking, He introduces the title of our Father Who is in secret. The introduction of this title seems to be occasioned by the mention of the hypocrites against the imitation of whom He is warning us, for they address themselves to men, who see the outside only. But our Lord continues to use this title throughout this part of His instructions, and seems thus to encourage us to make ourselves familiar with the thought of our Father, Whose special attribute in Sacred Scripture it is more than once said to be that He knows the heart. Thus we are taught not simply to conceal our true life from the eyes of men, but to open it altogether to God, Whose eye, indeed, we cannot escape, but Whose presence and close inspection of all our thoughts we may remember or forget. Our Lord would have us not forget it, but rather use it as a spur to exertion, a motive of purity of intention and of perfection in the actions which are thus directed to God, an occasion of acts of filial love in offering them to Him, and exercises of faith and hope as well as of charity.

Here is the simple principle, which will not only make the foregoing precepts easily practicable, but which will further make it seem the merest childishness to address ourselves to the eyes of men. Men, in truth, can know little of us here and now. Hereafter we shall know one another in the true light of God's presence. But now we all live in our own hearts and thoughts far more truly and deeply and incessantly than in the presence or company even of those who are dearest to us, and whom we try in vain to make our most intimate friends. Let friendship and affection do their utmost, there is still a wall between us which we cannot pierce, and which perhaps, in the miserable weakness and pettiness of which we are conscious, we can hardly wish away. Our life is truly a lonely life, if we are to have no nearer intimacy than such as we can give and receive from others like ourselves. Friends and intimates come and go. It is seldom that we keep them during all our lifetime. A thousand circumstances may separate us, even if our hearts are always unchanged, and if no cloud comes between us; and the uncertainties of outward condition are not so sure to part us as the certainty of death, which takes away one after another, and leaves us, when we are most fit for sympathy and most in need of it, in the solitude of bereavement. When we speak of Heaven as our home, the words are not only true, inasmuch as it is the place of our Father's abode, where we are to be ever blessed in His presence, but also because it is the only place where we are to enjoy to the full that brotherly love and intercourse with one another and with the angels and saints, which is enough to satisfy the cravings and the capacities of our hearts for the companionship of others like ourselves. As far as such union can be had now, it is the greatest earthly happiness of which we are capable, and yet the very intensity of that happiness is in truth but a witness to the still more perfect blessings of the same kind which await us hereafter. For we cannot but be conscious that here we can only be present to and know one another imperfectly, and that there is much in us which if it were known, could not be a ground of love.

God alone knows us thoroughly, and His patient love alone can bear with us as we are. Our life is not more perpetually our own secret than it is the possession of God. His eye pierces every corner of our heart. Every fibre of our being, intellectual, spiritual, and moral, quivers in the intense light of His presence. He is our Lord, our Master, our Creator; He supports our existence as He has originally called it into being; He is the efficient Helper in all that we do, so that without Him we do not live, or move, or exist; He is our Judge, to

Whom we are accountable for the use which we make by our will of every particle of being and moment of time, of thought and speech and desire and imagination and action. But yet our Lord does not call Him Master or Creator or Helper or Judge, but our Father Who seeth in secret, as if without the consideration of His Fathership we could not bear the truth of His all-penetrating insight. This our relation to God as His children is, moreover, the special work and gift to us of our Lord in His Incarnation, it is the relationship in which we are most closely and perfectly one with our Lord Himself. It is the relationship also in which it is better that we should honour Him than in any other, it is that which makes our service to Him most surely a service of love, it is that which involves the truth of the certainty of His assistance to the efforts we make to serve Him, and to live in His presence, and which encourages in us the hope of the great reward which our Lord promises us from our Father if we live for Him. For all these reasons it is well that in our practice of the presence of God we should aim especially at remembering Him as our Father.

The thought of the presence of God, which is thus suggested by our Lord, involves the other thought of the choice which God has made to be not only present in His universe, and especially in the human heart, but also to be present by a manner of presence which is so hidden. He is our Father in secret. In no other way, indeed it may be said, could He leave us enough in the possession of our liberty; and yet we know that in Heaven itself it was not impossible for the rebel angels to use their free will to offend Him. But God has so completely hidden Himself in His creation that it is possible to forget Him altogether, as if He chose to make Himself an object of search, and delighted in the exercise of faith and love, which will not be baffled or satisfied without forcing their way to the retreat in which He abides. These virtues would not be so precious if He were not so hidden. Most marvellous is it that He is at once so hidden, and yet that the whole creation speaks of Him, and that the lineaments of His character and attributes are stamped on everything that He has made, and on the whole universe in which He has placed them. For not only does each creature of His reflect Him in some degree, but the order and harmony and mutual dependence in which He has willed that they should combine, as in one great whole, witness in another way to His eternal goodness and wisdom and power. And yet it is possible to study the universe as a whole, or its parts one by one, and to let the beauty and ease and might with which the whole moves on, according to the laws which He has given, stand as a screen between us and God. It is the same with His manifestation of Himself in Providence and history. In each of these He is present with all the brightness of the sunlight to those who watch for Him, and yet so hidden that thousands fail to discern Him. In His own especial kingdom of grace, also, He uses secondary means to produce the effects which are yet in a peculiar manner His own acts, as in the sacraments, and though He is always working on our souls, He still hides Himself, and places the chosen things and persons, through whom or which He operates the marvels of His interior grace, between us and Himself. All this points to a concealment of Himself on the part of God, which is still transparent to the eye of faith and to the loving heart of children. It points to a manifestation of Himself in some respects like that of our Lord after the Resurrection, not to all the people, but to chosen witnesses. St. Paul speaks of God's retirement, as it were, from the gaze of the world, as having had for its purpose that men 'should seek God, if haply they may feel after Him and find Him, although He be not far from every one of us;'[1] and as it was the misery of the pagan world that so few men actually did thus feel after God and find Him, so is it the misery of Christians that so few, even with the true faith in their hearts, and the whole system of the Church all around them, live habitually inside the veil which floats between the all-present God and the eyes of the children of the world.

Thus it is that the precious exercise of the presence of God, which would naturally have been the constant and easy occupation of all reasonable men, and especially of those who have the gift of Christian faith, is one of the rare possessions of the most favoured servants of God. It is not possible to know anything rightly about Him without understanding that He must be present to all His creatures, in the threefold manner of which spiritual writers make mention, that is, by essence and presence and power. To remind ourselves of this truth by an act of reason or of faith, is to exercise His presence in the sense in which we are speaking, and to live in the habitual consciousness of this truth is to live in the presence of God. It is possible to go further, and to exercise the imagination by representing Him to ourselves in some actual form or picture, as when we imagine our Lord as a child, or on the Cross, or as reigning in Heaven, and yet present to us, or when we use some imaginary representation to set before us the three Divine Persons of the Ever Blessed Trinity. This, however, though it is sometimes recommended and practised, may fatigue the head by the strain on the imagination. On this account we are told that it is

[1] Acts xvii. 27.

better to make our consciousness of the presence of God the fruit of the exercise of faith, a faculty which can never break down or weaken under exercise, and we are recommended to choose the truth of God's presence in our heart as in a temple or shrine, a heaven in which He particularly delights, as the foundation of our exercise.

In this way we practise recollection, as well as the presence of God. We withdraw into our own hearts and remind ourselves of the truth on which St. Paul insists so earnestly, that we are the temples of God.[2] We think of Him as present within us, guiding, protecting, and ruling us, and there, far from the tumult and noise of outward things, we sit, as Magdalene sat at Bethany, at His feet, and listen to Him or address Him and converse with Him, and lay before Him our thoughts and designs and cares and troubles and all that is of interest to us, as children with their father or as a bride with her spouse. This sort of converse with God is spoken of by St. Paul to the Ephesians, where he bids them be 'filled with the Holy Ghost, speaking to themselves in psalms and hymns and spiritual canticles, singing and making melody in their hearts to the Lord.'[3] Here we have what we may consider as a sort of revelation by St. Paul of the exercises of the presence of God, with which he was familiar. He recommends to others what we may well suppose to have been the interior life of his own fervent heart. The main characteristic of this interior converse is evidently joy. It is praise, adoration, petition, thanksgiving, all that variety of affections and acts which are to be found in the psalms and hymns of the Church. There is here a whole world of interior activity, for each single word that St. Paul uses corresponds to some single class of affections, which may include many

[2] 1 Cor. iii. 16.   [3] Ephes. v. 18, 19.

varieties within itself. The passage in this respect reminds us of another in St. Paul,[4] where he enumerates in passing, as it were, the different kinds of prayer which can be made in the Church—supplications, prayers, intercessions, and thanksgivings, each of which heads is distinct in itself. We may also gather from the passage to the Ephesians that we may find the greatest advantage from the use of the words of Scripture, especially the psalms, as furnishing us with thoughts and expressions to be used in our converse with God, and that short ejaculatory affections, taken from such sources, will aid us much.

As has been already said, it might have been thought that this holy exercise would have presented no great difficulty to Christians, at least to such as are in earnest in their service of God. It is but the practical use of a truth, which no one, not even a philosopher with right notions about God, could question, a truth which is at once of immense importance and of infinite consolation to us. The wonderful fruits which are promised to the practice of the presence of God, both in Scripture and in the writings of the saints, are so necessarily connected with its nature and the truth on which it rests, that they cannot be treated as exaggerations by any one who considers the subject even by the light of reason. We have the express command of God, we can see how the true nobility of man must consist in conversation with Him, and, if nothing else, at least the natural gratitude which we owe to the Giver to us of a gift so incalculably beyond our deserts as the capacity to hold intercourse with Him, would bind us to its constant exercise. This might be said, even if that exercise were not fraught with so many blessings. It is clear that nothing can be more powerful as a preservative

[4] 1 Timothy ii. 1.

from sin, as an aid against temptation, as a remedy against sloth, as a support against human respect, as a shield against the influences of the world and the devil, that nothing will help us better to eradicate vices, to get rid of the penalty due to past faults by interior affections, to moderate the passions, to advance in all good, to make our works holy and perfect, to raise ourselves above the dissipation of idle and unprofitable thoughts to the pure, calm, tranquil, and happy atmosphere which is around the throne on high, the atmosphere of love and wisdom and unshaken peace, than a practice such as this. Why is it difficult? Its difficulty is one of those facts in our present condition which witness most forcibly to the extreme weakness of our nature and the depth of the wounds which it has incurred in its fall. We are so turned to lower and visible things as to find little taste or inclination for lofty objects of thought. As a child prefers his toys to his studies, so do we raise ourselves with reluctance to the thought of God from the vanities of the world of sense. Our imagination is full of visible pictures and finds spiritual realities too great a strain. We do not use our faculty of imagination well. For years perhaps it has been fed upon trifles, if not upon garbage, things of sense and objects of pleasure, and it is haunted, as it were, with the phantoms of the guests which it has received so willingly, till there is no room left in it for the pure majesty of God. And in many cases our life has been spent among the delights of Egypt, and so the soul has no taste for the Bread of Heaven, for holy thoughts and affections, which may remain without shame in the presence of the Lord of Angels.

Anything that increases in us the love of God, any continual exercise of interior humility, as well as the attentive practice of the exercise of which we are speaking, all prayer specially addressed to the gaining of this grace, will help us to overcome the difficulty which at first besets us. It may be said in conclusion that the very words of our Lord, in which He bids us look to God Who is and Who sees in secret, seem to point to the thought of God's presence within ourselves as the foundation on which we are to raise the sanctuary in which we are to dwell with Him, as St. Catherine of Siena made an interior cell for herself in her thoughts, when she was prevented by her family from living in actual solitude, and forced to occupy herself in the most distracting employments. And it need hardly be added that the best and most profitable way of this exercise is that which does not so much rest in the simple contemplation of God, but which passes on either to converse naturally with Him about the objects of thought or care which come across us as the moments flow on, or to offer to Him one after another the actions, interior or exterior, on which we are occupied. In this way the things which might otherwise be the sources of our distractions are made the steps of the ladder by which we rise to God. In this way we work in His presence, and so, as we may hope, with a more certainly pure intention and with a more powerful impulse of His grace. With this help from the creatures and circumstances around us, and with that other which is suggested by the words of St. Paul as to the psalms and hymns and spiritual canticles with which we are to sing and make melody in our hearts to the Lord, it ought not to be so difficult to us to lift our thoughts habitually to Him, Who is so near to us and indeed within us. This is indeed the true life of continual prayer of which the Apostle speaks, and, though it cannot be reconciled with dissipation and worldly excitement, curiosity about the gossip of the day, and inquisitiveness into the doings and concerns of others, it will certainly be found, by those who have the courage to practise it, as great a source of unfailing spiritual strength and joy, as it is also a shield against the temptations of the life of sense and passion.

CHAPTER V.

Treasure in Heaven.

St. Matt. vi. 18—19; *Vita Vitæ Nostræ*, § 33.

AFTER our Lord's instructions as to the three great works of almsdeeds, prayer, and fasting, the Sermon on the Mount proceeds to a number of heads of doctrine, of which it is not in all cases easy to discern the connection. It does not, however, follow that there is no connection or order in this latter part of this Divine discourse. We have already said that we may have our Lord's words reported to us in a concise form, and that He may, at the time of the delivery of the Sermon, have amplified the heads which are set down, without of necessity adding any topics which are entirely omitted. If that were the case, we cannot be surprised if the connecting links between one passage and another are just the items which are wanting to us. But we cannot doubt that there is a steady and beautiful onward march from one point of perfection to another, even though each step be not marked in a way that is beyond mistake. We cannot suppose that there is anything left to accident in the arrangement of these precepts and counsels, and we must be content to do our best to trace the connection, even though we cannot have perfect confidence in our own power to discern it without the chance of mistake.

At the point which has now been reached our Lord passes from His instructions about the manner of fasting and of performing other works of the virtue of mortification, to the precept against laying up treasure upon earth. He here begins a series of instructions which rise, as it were, one above the other, until He reaches the climax at the precept against being solicitous even for the morrow. This precept is in strong contrast to that against laying up treasure, but at the same time it relates to the same subject-matter. The contrast is therefore one between the practice of a counsel in its lowest form and that of the practice of the same counsel in its most perfect and sublime development. Persons who are not solicitous even for the morrow are not likely to be foolish enough to lay up treasure upon earth, while the most natural form in which the tendency to store up can be indulged is that in which provision is made for the morrow. We have, therefore, every reason for considering both precepts as belonging to the same chain, and for looking on the intermediate instructions as connected with both. This will become more evident as we proceed in the explanation of each. But we must first see whether there is any link of connection between the precepts which have last been considered — those about fasting — and this new chain, on the consideration of which we are about to enter. At first sight it would seem difficult to connect the doctrine about doing all our works of self-denial with the purest respect to God alone with that which now follows. And yet it must be clear that the same soul which looks to God alone as the witness and judge of its mortifications, will be very ready to receive our Lord's doctrine as to the disregard of earthly goods and the estimation of heavenly treasures which is now to be considered.

When it is remembered that our Lord has ended each head of the instruction which has preceded with a reference not simply to God as the witness of our secret almsgivings, or prayers, or mortifications, but by speaking of the payment which these actions will receive at the hands of the Father Who is and Who sees in secret, it is more easy to understand the connection which we are seeking. Our Lord does not vary His language in the three cases; He says in each 'He will repay thee.' This language is in strict accordance with what He says about the hypocrites, who receive their reward in each case from the esteem of men. But it conveys a distinct reference to an accumulation of merit, and, as it were, to a debt of reward which is owing to us by God. Thus it naturally suggests some further instruction on points connected with this. When we turn from our Lord's language to the things themselves of which he speaks, we find still more reason for this connection of ideas. For the Christian doctrine with respect to almsdeeds, prayer, and fasting, and the whole multitude of good works which are embraced under the same heads, regards them as meritorious of rewards in heaven—as the coin by which the glories of heaven are purchased, and, consequently, as forming in the truest and highest sense, the treasure or store of the children of God. It is to some such story that St. Paul refers when he writes to St. Timothy, 'I know Whom I have trusted, and I am certain that He is able to keep that which I have committed to Him against that day.'[1] That which those who lead a good life, and serve God faithfully, commit to Him against the day when all are to be judged according to their deeds, consists of good works done for Him, not for any earthly motive of honour or esteem, and left, as it were, in the charge of His most

[1] 2 Tim. i. 12.

faithful remembrance against the moment of trial on which eternity depends. Thus the thought of the Christian's treasure in Heaven, and of the care and diligence with which it should be accumulated and multiplied, follows very naturally upon that of the reward which is due to good works, done in secret, for the eye of our Father alone.

Moreover, as long as there is danger of the applause of men being sought by those who work good works, who fast, or pray, or give alms, or practise any other virtue which can be appreciated by men, it is of no use to urge the frequentation of such works. No treasure can be laid up in Heaven by them. Thus the precept about laying up treasure in Heaven requires that about neglecting the esteem of men as its natural safeguard, and as the condition of its usefulness. On the other hand, when Christians have been sufficiently grounded in faith and esteem of the approval of their Father Who is in secret, as the one reward to which it is worth while to look, they may then be exhorted to multiply their good works, and to endeavour to make them as precious as possible in the sight of God, by all the holy industries which have been suggested by the saints for that purpose. For the only danger that could hinder their gaining the full reward due to such works has been already removed. Thus our Lord, after speaking of the repayment which the three great works of justice would receive at the hands of His Father, lets, as it were, His Sacred Heart loose in the precept which follows, and insists on the heaping up of that reward to the highest possible extent under the natural image of the treasure in Heaven. Thus also does our Lord begin a new head of teaching with reference to the good things of this world, as to which He wishes to lead us to perfect detachment. He begins by forbidding us to store them and hoard them, but He ends, as we shall see, by raising us above even that natural care concerning them, when most necessary, which is shown by providing for the morrow.

The precept of which we are now to speak is couched by our Lord in that rhythmical and antithetical form in which the Jews delighted. 'Lay not up for yourselves treasures on earth, where the rust and moth consume and where thieves break through and steal; but lay up for yourselves treasures in Heaven, where neither the rust nor moth doth consume, and where thieves do not break through nor steal; for where thy treasure is, there is thy heart also.' The images used by our Lord seem to be chosen for the purpose of exhausting the various ways in which earthly goods may perish to the owner. They may decay of themselves, as the metals that are consumed by rust; or they may be destroyed by external agents, as the materials on which the moth feeds; or they may be stolen, and so be lost to the owner, as the treasures of any kind which thieves may take away. But heavenly treasures are in themselves imperishable, and can be affected by no mischief. They are stored in the Heart of God our Father, and no one can deprive us of them. The same images, more or less, can be traced in Sacred Scripture before our Lord's use of them, and we find them reproduced in the language of His Apostles after Him. Thus Tobias says to his son, not rising quite so high in thought as the treasure in Heaven, 'If thou have much, give abundantly; if thou have little, take care even so to bestow willingly a little. For thus thou storest up to thyself a good reward for the day of necessity.'[2] St. Raphael carries on the teaching, using the contrast which our Lord draws out—'Prayer is good with fasting and alms, more than to lay up treasures of gold; for

[2] Tobias iv. 9, 10.

alms delivereth from death, and the same is that which purgeth away sins, and maketh to find mercy and life everlasting.'[3] And the precept of our Lord is echoed by St. Paul, in words which recall the passage before us: 'Charge the rich of this world not to be high-minded, nor to trust in the uncertainty of riches'—here we seem to trace the image of the moth and rust in the mind of the Apostle—'but in the living God, Who giveth us abundantly all things to enjoy'—here is a tacit reference to the doctrine of the care which God takes even of the fowls of the air and the lilies of the field—'to do good, to be rich in good works, to give easily, to communicate to others'—here we have a practical explanation of the precept of laying up treasure in Heaven—'to lay up in store'—or treasure—'for themselves a good foundation against the time to come, that they may lay hold on the true life.'[4] And St. James, whose words are always full of reminiscences of our Lord's imagery, threatens the rich of the world in a strain like that of one of the old prophets: 'Go to now, ye rich men, weep and howl in your miseries, which shall come upon you. Your riches are corrupted, and your garments are moth-eaten. Your gold and silver is cankered, and the rust of them shall be for a testimony against you, and shall eat your flesh like fire. You have stored up to yourselves wrath against the last days.'[5] Thus there is hardly any feature in our Lord's language which is not repeated by this Apostle of the Circumcision, though our Lord leaves the more terrible side of the picture to be drawn by the Apostle, and speaks Himself most directly of the blessedness of the treasure that is laid up in Heaven.

We may add to these considerations that of the marked way in which our Lord Himself has expanded and ex-

---

[3] Tobias xii. 8, 9.
[4] 1 Tim. vi. 17—19.   [5] St. James v. 1—3.

plained the doctrine which He here sketches, as it were, in outline. Many of His parables, and of the exhortations given at the same time without any figure, refer to this head of His teaching. Such are the parables of the talents and pounds, and such also is that of the wicked steward. These, taken together with the other direct teaching on the same subject, make up a considerable part of our Lord's instructions to His disciples. The burthen of the whole is the truth that we are here as men who have received a certain capital with which to traffic for our master, and that it is our duty, not simply to preserve what we have received, but to multiply it and make it very fruitful. We are labourers for eternity, and time is short; but we have a capital confided to us which is capable of immense increase, and our life is arranged by the providence of God in such a way that we have the most wonderful opportunities for heaping up riches, by the right use of time. This view of human life is over and over again urged upon us by our Lord, as if it were very easy for us to forget it, or not to understand it, and as if the losses to which we are liable, in consequence of neglect or folly, were such as we are as yet incapable of appreciating. Thus He does not scruple to set before us the example of the wicked steward, bidding us imitate him, not in his wickedness, but in his resolute use of the means which were still in his power after his master had given him warning that an account was to be exacted of him. We may almost say that the truths on which our Lord most frequently insisted were this of the necessity of working and using the opportunities afforded us, and the other kindred truth of the need of vigilance, that we may not be found unprepared by Him when He comes to us at death. Both these truths need a very lively and practical faith, penetrating the importance of daily and common life, and of the immense issues which depend on the use which we make of it, as well as the danger in which all, even the servants of God, are involved, of forgetting the things of the soul and of eternity under the present pressure of those of time and sense. All experience shows the truth of our Lord's saying, that the children of this world are wiser in their generation than the children of light, and the lessons are many indeed which the eager worldlings of the day may read to the children of the Church for their use of the heavenly treasures which their Master has confided to them. We may draw out in a few words the main truths which belong to this prominent part of our Blessed Lord's instructions to us.

We may notice, in the first place, that our Lord's precept may be understood literally, as to the use which is to be made of whatever treasures, in the common sense of the word, we may possess, and also as extending very far beyond the use of visible and tangible treasure to that of the moral and spiritual goods which may be represented thereby. As to this first sense, we can hardly help thinking of the Blessed Martyr St. Lawrence, the Deacon and Treasurer of the Roman Church. Through the whole of the beautiful Office which is used on his feast, the part of his history which relates to the right use of earthly treasure is continually commemorated. The persecutor, as St. Leo tells us in the Lesson for the feast, was gloating over the thought of the rich prey which he would acquire by the plunder of the treasure committed to the care of St. Lawrence, who showed him a great crowd of poor persons, to feed and clothe whom the treasure had been spent—treasures which, as St. Leo adds, were so much more perfectly secure and safe, as they were proved to have been spent in a more holy manner. St. Lawrence is made to recur to this again and again in the Office. 'Leave me not, holy Father,' he says to the Pope St. Xystus, 'for I have already spent the treasure which thou didst intrust to me.' 'The treasures of the Church he gave to the poor.' 'Thy treasures I have already spent.' 'O Hippolytus, if thou wilt believe in the Lord Jesus Christ, I will show thee the treasures, and I promise thee eternal life.' 'The property of the Church, which thou seekest, the hands of the poor have already carried into the treasuries of Heaven.' This then, according to our means and opportunities, is the true way of storing up wealth, property, whatever is precious and valuable among earthly and visible things — to give them to the poor, like Zacchaeus, or Barnabas, or to spend them in the service and worship of God, like the blessed Magdalene. But as these material riches are here used as the images and symbols of goods of a far higher order than themselves, it is enough to have mentioned this first sense of our Lord's words before passing further.

It cannot be a difficult thing, in the time and country in which we live, to understand the details of the image which our Lord here uses. There have been times and places in which the simple members of great societies have lived on, from generation to generation, in the enjoyment of abundance of all things necessary to life, in the largest sense of necessity, and have had but little thought as to the advantage or supposed duty of growing rich and heaping up treasures for the future. But such times are not ours, and, in the pressure and strain in which the struggling populations of modern Europe live, there are but few who are exempt from the cares of money-getting and money-hoarding. This condition of things makes it, at all events, easy to understand what must be done in order to carry out our Lord's precept as to laying up treasure in Heaven. The accumulation of wealth implies three things. It implies, in the first place, capital, which is the essential material with which the work must be undertaken. Capital is invested in merchandise, wares, stock, or property of various kinds, and then it must be taken to the most profitable markets, and sold or exchanged in such a way as to produce the largest return. If we apply our spiritual capital in the best way, if we dispose of it to the best advantage, in the most profitable works, and without wasting it or allowing it to lie idle, then we shall have fulfilled to the utmost of our power the injunction to lay up treasure in Heaven. It is not difficult to see how this must be translated into the language of practical life, in order to apply to the profitable traffic of which our Lord speaks elsewhere. Our capital is the grace of God. Grace is the only coin which has value for the Kingdom of Heaven, and can procure us treasure that will last throughout all eternity, where there are neither rust nor moth to destroy nor thieves to break in and steal. The market in which we are to use our capital is the time which God gives us to labour in. The night cometh—how swiftly and noiselessly it steals on!—and in the night no man can work. The wares, the merchandise, the investments in which our grace is to be employed are good works of every kind—though here, as the wise merchant chooses his investments with the greatest possible care, and shows his forethought and skill chiefly in their selection, so does the wise dealer in the wares of eternity prove his prudence in the careful choice of his state of life, or of his occupations day by day, so as to waste none of his time nor labour at anything in vain.

Some holy writers have gone into great detail in following out the thoughts here suggested, but it may be enough in this place to leave them in outline. The three principal thoughts on which our meditations should insist are the value of grace, the value of time, and the importance of using both with prudence as well as the greatest possible fervour. For the first two objects it is well to renew over and over again, from time to time, the considerations which have struck us on such subjects at times of retirement with God, and the teachings of the saints with which we may have met. For the third it is well to make ourselves masters of the practice on which St. Ignatius so much insists, of election and forethought in the choice of the works on which we are to be occupied, the virtues at the attainment of which we are to aim, and the like. The words of St. John about our Lord, when he is speaking of the miracle of the multiplication of the loaves in the desert, 'He Himself knew what He would do,'[6] are sometimes applied in the sense of this deliberate forecasting which is recommended to us in our employment of our time, in which nothing, if possible, should be left to chance, everything arranged beforehand with discretion and choice, the blessing on which is not forfeited, even if it often happen that what we have designed to do is defeated, and either obedience or necessity compels us to turn to something altogether different from our intended occupation. Nor again, as we shall presently see, is this forecasting of our employments at all contrary to the precept which our Lord, in this same part of the Sermon on the Mount, gives us against 'solicitude' for the morrow.

As to the value of grace, we may well suppose that our Lord, when He spoke to His disciples about treasure in Heaven, would turn in thought to that heavenly gift, the choicest of all that God has given unto His creatures, a more beautiful and wonderful boon than any that fall within the range of natural powers or excellencies of any kind, a boon which raises them to whom it is given to a new state and dignity in His Kingdom, which makes them near and dear to Him, with a dearness and a near-

[6] St. John vi. 6.

ness which are without parallel even therein, and of which an Apostle has not feared to say that they make us partakers of the nature of God Himself.[7] Grace is the dwelling of the Holy Ghost, the third Person of the ever Blessed Trinity, in the souls of those to whom it is given, imparting to them His own sanctity and goodness, enriching them with the dower of His own precious gifts, clothing them with the splendour of supernatural virtues, theological and moral, beginning with the glorious gift of charity, which binds them to God in supernatural union, making them the adopted sons of God, with the rights of children and heirs, giving them the power to work and act with operations so precious, that they are meritorious of eternal rewards, of the beatitude of Heaven and the clear sight of God in which that beatitude consists. There is in a sense no limit,[8] St. John says, to the gift of grace, and it opens to us all the treasures of God, to take of them as we will. His whole Kingdom is ours by virtue of this gift—the immense condescension of the Incarnation, the ineffable privilege of feeding on the Body and Blood of the Incarnate Son, are boons which become, as it were, natural in the case of those to whom He has first given Himself in the gift of grace. It is a little thing, after this, to be the fellow-citizens of the angels, to have the whole of the family of God for our helpers and defenders, to be able to satisfy for our sins with the same good works which are meritorious of eternal glory.

As for the value of time, our Lord has often spoken of it, and His Apostles have repeated His teaching. It is

---

[7] 2 St. Peter i. 4.
[8] St. John iii. 34. What is meant by saying that grace is in a certain sense infinite, is explained by the author from whom many of the thoughts in this chapter are taken, Father Eusebius Nieremberg, in his work, *Del Aprecio y Estima de la Divina Gracia*, l. i. c. xiii. He quotes and applies to grace what St. Thomas says of charity, 2a. 2æ. art. 24, art. 7.

sometimes useful to meditate on this truth by way of taking the judgment, as it were, of Heaven and Purgatory, and Hell itself, as to the inestimable treasures that may be lost or won in a single moment of that time which we are so glad to get rid of, as it were, at any price. A moment of time for the use of grace might empty Hell. If the angels and saints could envy us anything, that thing would be the time which we have and which they have not, time in which they might raise themselves still higher and nearer to God than they are, in which they might do what they cannot do, that is, suffer something for Him, and thus add something to the glory which their service renders to Him. But perhaps the warning as to time which may strike us the most may be that which comes to us from the wistful and longing souls who are detained in Purgatory, and who would give so much for a particle of the hours or years which they may have let go by with the same carelessness which we show in their use. No starving child of misery and want gazes in through an open window on the plentifully furnished board at which a party of revellers are seated, hardly touching or thinking of the abundance of the provisions which are spread out before them, with a yearning half as intense for but a few of the crumbs which fall from that lavish banquet, as that with which the poor sufferers in Purgatory long for some share of the rich treasures of grace and time which are neglected by us. The Blessed in Heaven know the value of time by the fruits which they enjoy from having used it well. The suffering souls know it from the pains which they endure from having failed to use it, and the lost souls know it for the same reason, and also because if they had but one moment of it more they might change their state for ever thereby. We alone are blind. Our life is short; a great part of it, perhaps has been already wasted; of the years which remain we cannot reckon on the whole, so much has to be spent in sleep or weakness or sickness, and this treasure, which can never be recovered when it is once lost, is streaming away at every moment. We need a great light from the other world to make us see the danger in which our neglect of these eternal truths is continually plunging us.

There are some general recommendations given by holy writers as to the careful use of grace which may be cited here, while we leave for another place the various more detailed rules as to what some writers call 'heavenly negotiation' which may be of practical use. The first of these general rules relates to the sacraments and their use. The sacraments are the fountains and channels of grace, by means of which the merits of the precious Blood of our Lord are communicated to us. The grace which we thus receive is not purchased by any merits of our own, and yet we may receive more or less grace in these blessed gifts according to our disposition. We are therefore not to content ourselves with receiving them worthily, that is, in a state of grace, but we must endeavour to receive them with dispositions as perfect as possible, as if the fruits of our Lord's Passion and the treasures of heavenly grace were to depend as to their amount on ourselves. Hence comes the immense importance of attending with an especial care to our reception of the sacraments. Thus it has been the habit of some saints to offer up all their actions as preparation for the sacraments, and to make one Communion the preparation for another. The acts of virtue which are done in this intention have a double value, in themselves and on account of the character of preparation which is thus given to them. In the same way, actions that are done by way of satisfaction as imposed in the Sacrament of Penance have a fresh power of expiation on that account. For the Church puts into the mouth of her priests words the extent of which is very large, 'what soever good thou shalt do, or whatsover ill thou shalt suffer, be unto thee for the remission of sins, increase of grace, and reward of eternal life'—and these words are understood as adding to the works specified a kind of quasi-sacramental efficacy for the purpose mentioned. Again, it is the doctrine of theologians, that a good work is more or less meritorious according to the degree of grace in which the person is who works it, as our Lord said that to him that hath, more shall be given. Here then is another way of adding to our treasure in Heaven, by endeavouring to increase very much in grace, and thus gain the power of increasing more and more.[9]

It may be observed that these recommendations rest ultimately upon considerations of doctrine which no Catholic can gainsay. They are not merely the devices of a devotional spirit unsupported by certain truth. On this account it is not well to slight them. The same may be said of other recommendation of the same character, which we find in the same authors. Such is that which urges us to think very much indeed of the efficacy of the adorable Sacrifice of the Mass, and to remember that as it is always offered for all the faithful, we have a special interest and part in every single Mass which is offered at any time and in any part of the world. But it cannot be doubted that the profit which we receive from this blessed Sacrifice is greater or less in proportion to our actual devotion or our want of it, and we are thus led to the thought that we should as far as possible multiply

---

[9] Many of the thoughts here suggested will be found in another work of the author named above, his *Codicia santa de gracia y mercieminlos*.

the Masses from which we derive special benefit, by forming the intention of assisting in spirit, with as much devotion as possible, at all the Masses which are being offered up all day and all night in the various parts of the world, as the morning breaks on one region of the earth after another.

Another industry of the same sort is that which reminds us that the actions which are in themselves meritorious are comparatively few, whereas we perform a large number of acts during the day which are in themselves merely natural, necessary, and indifferent. But we have the blessed life of our Lord on the earth to help us as to these, for He lived among men as one like the rest, sin only excepted, and thus we have the whole of the actions of His daily life, not only to furnish us with an example how to please God in all, but also to make everything that we do meritorious by virtue of union with His actions. In order to this they must be offered in union with His perfect service of His Father, even in the most outwardly indifferent actions of His life. In the same way, our good works, which, if we are in a state of grace, have a meritorious character in themselves, may be made far more so by virtue of actual union with the merits of our Blessed Lord. Again, all good works may be made still more pleasing to God, if they are carefully performed with the distinct motive of His love to turn them, as it were, to gold, if we do them with the special intention of pleasing Him thereby. Again, we may derive benefit even from the good works of others, with whom we are united in the blessed Communion of Saints, by rejoicing in them, by desiring to share in them, and by thanking God for them, when we hear them spoken of or when we read about them. St. Mechtildis is said to have asked our Lord how much merit He gave to those who rejoiced in the grace which He granted to others. And He is said to have replied that He gave to such as much merit and glory as to those who received the grace in which the others rejoiced. Again, there is a merit to be gained even by desire, which, as St. Gregory of Nazianzus has said, is a coin by which glory can be purchased, and therefore there is foundation for the holy industry of those who tell us to desire great things for the glory of God every morning, as that all the grains of sand on the sea shore, and all the particles in the air, might be so many hierarchies of angels occupied in loving God and Him alone. The same is to be said of the frequent use of ejaculatory prayers, especially acts of love, of the habit of making very often during the day spiritual communions, or of receiving spiritually other sacraments, or again of the great care which some pious persons take to gain all the indulgences of the Church with the utmost devotion and contrition, and of other similar practices.

But the field on which we have thus shortly entered is very large, and it would be easy to lose ourselves in it. Two more such devotions may be enough for the present. The first relates to our prayers. These are of course always addressed to God through our Lord, but we do not perhaps always dwell in thought on the full meaning of our own words, and it is recommended that we should gain the habit of presenting the merits of our Lord with a very lively faith to the Eternal Father every time that we make our prayer, reminding Him specially and earnestly of the obedience of His Divine Son, in Whose name we ask. And all our prayers will gain another special beauty in the sight of God if they are always accompanied by a direct internal act of perfect resignation to His Divine will as to the matter which we ask. The other devotion which may be mentioned, is that we should insist very much on making full use, according to the intention of God, of the intercession of the saints and angels in Heaven, and of the gratitude of the holy souls in Purgatory. There are here mines of treasures of inestimable worth, which we may be inclined to pass over and fail to use to the utmost. We are sometimes content with defending the Catholic doctrine on such matters, as indeed we are bound to defend it, whereas we may lose very large portions of the grace in this world and the glory in the next, which God has put within our reach, because we are not as hearty and as constant and as large in the practice of this devotion which we nevertheless defend. The Christian is like a child with an almost boundless inheritance, or like a king whose realm is too immense for him to be able to develope all its riches without very great exertion and industry. Persons in such positions are often content with leaving many fertile sources of revenue unworked, which would be of infinite value if care and labour were applied to them. It may matter but little to a wealthy nobleman, whether all the mineral treasures on his distant estates are left for his successors to utilize, and the king of a vast country may go to his grave in peace, without finding the need of the territories which he has neglected. But the Christian has a commission to labour for God, and it is his condemnation not to have used any means of grace and merit which he had within his reach. And yet to how many are these great resources, of which we have just spoken, hardly more than names! As we read over the names of the saints in the Litanies, or in the Canon of the Mass, or in the Martyrology, they are to us a set of words which convey, perhaps, some superficial remembrance of men or women who have lived and died in the service of God, and perhaps we know just the slightest details of their martyrdom or of their witness to the faith. But to God these few syllables recall in each case the whole of His own loving providence towards a soul which has been wonderfully dear to Him, on which He has conferred even exceptional graces, a long life, perhaps, of merits known to Himself alone, of beautiful acts of virtue, of heroic sacrifices, of glorious sufferings, of victories over temptation, of defeats of the evil one, of correspondence to the example of our Lord, which has led up, by a natural process of causation in the spiritual order, to the crowning triumph of faith which has overcome the world in the sight of the world itself. How is it possible but that such souls should be immensely dear to God? When we consider our Lord's teaching about the rewards of the faithful servants, how uniformly He makes it consist in power as well as in enjoyment, how His whole Kingdom is one of prayer, and what great promises He has made to induce us to believe that prayer is almost omnipotent with Him, how is it possible to doubt that the saints who reign with Him have a power in this respect, which is one of the great ordinary agents in the government of the world and in the distribution of His choicest graces of every kind? We do not need to prove this as against those who deny it. And yet we may find in the end, that, much as we may have used the power and the charity of the saints, and of the Queen of saints, and of the angels, in some special needs, still this great resource, as God has intended it to be, has been in great measure laid up in a napkin in our daily life, and the daily honour which, as children of the Church, we pay to God for some one or more of His saints, has not brought us the daily treasure of boons through their intercession, which His mercy had prepared for us, because we have not been diligent enough in the hearty veneration which we were bound to pay them. In this, then, as in other matters we may be in danger of treating the opportunities of laying up treasure which God has given us in the manner of the unprofitable servant, who was so severely punished for not using what he had received.

It is remarkable that the words with which our Lord concludes this head of His instruction, seem to change the motive which He had before adduced for not laying up treasure on earth. It is not only, or even chiefly, that our labour is wasted in so doing—that we can accumulate no permanent or secure wealth, nothing that will truly avail us in the world to which we are going. That is bad enough, but there is a worse consequence, which He now adds: 'For where thy treasure is, there also will thy heart be.' It is a natural consequence, that what we labour for and provide for and make the end of all that we do, should be the object of the love of our hearts. And it is indeed a calamity that souls which are created by God for Himself, should really spend themselves upon the worthless goods of this world. On the other hand, we are safe indeed if we are labouring for Heaven. We may not feel that sensible devotion which is granted to some favoured souls, which makes it impossible for them to doubt that they love God, and helps them on along the path of perfection as if it had no difficulties. This is a great boon, though it may sometimes be mistaken for substantial devotion. But a life that is spent in laying up the treasure of good works in Heaven, however laboriously and painfully, cannot be a misdirected or an unfruitful life. God sees the heart, and He knows that the heart follows the store. Here is a test which cannot fail. Our Lord's words imply, that if our heart be truly fixed on God and on Heaven, all must be right with us. It cannot be that He will let a heart that is devoted to Him go astray. Rather, as it is the heart above all things that He looks to and asks for, it is quite certain that His tenderest love and His highest rewards will be for the hearts that truly love Him. But how are we to be certain about our own hearts? The love of God is something so different from what we call love, when it is directed to anything sensible and like ourselves, it is so independent of feeling and softness and emotion, while on the other hand it is so easy to mistake mere feeling and sensibility for the sterling devotion of the will in which this love consists, that we may often fear that we have it not while we have it, and we may often think that we have it while we have it not. In this difficulty, the words of our Lord enlighten, calm, and reassure us. 'If you love Me, keep My commandments.' Actions are the true fruit and the true proof of love. And if our life is spent in increasing our store in Heaven of what is pleasing to Him here, and of what He will crown to His own glory hereafter, we may take to ourselves this blessed promise, that our hearts also will be in Heaven.

It may also be remarked, that our Lord here seems to show the use of that knowledge of mankind on which St. John remarks, when He tells us that 'Jesus did not commit Himself to men because He knew what was in them.'[10] The proverbial words into which He has thrown His teaching, embody a great truth which men are always ready to evade if they can. They are always saying that they may labour for the world and not be of it, that they can spend their time and thoughts on temporal matters, and make them the great end of their daily life, and all the time have their hearts detached from them. It is possible, no doubt, to be occupied with temporal matters for the love of God, and to be in truth serving Him in the midst of the distractions of a life which lies altogether along the beaten path of the

[10] St. John ii. 25.

world. But then He is the great object of affection, and all that is done in the handling of secular business is done with a pure intention for His glory, and is laying up treasure in Heaven rather than upon earth. Persons who lead this kind of life do so out of obedience to duty, like the royal saints whose feasts are celebrated by the Church, or the holy men who have had to leave or to refrain from the cloister for the public service. But with the ordinary run of men whose life is spent in amassing wealth, or in the pursuits of ambition of various kinds, the saying of our Lord holds true with a force which is confirmed by all experience, 'where their treasure is, there also their hearts will be.'

CHAPTER VI.

The Eye of the Soul.

St. Matt. vi. 22, 23; *Vita Vitæ Nostræ,* § 33.

THE last words of our Lord, on which we have commented, seem to imply a truth which may be considered as the foundation of the doctrine which He places next in order. When He says, 'Where thy treasure is, there also will thy heart be,' He seems to take it for granted that every one has a treasure somewhere. Man is here in a state of trial, and everything that he does, all the acts of his heart, all the words of his tongue, all the deeds of his will, are noted down, and form the store which is to be opened for him in the next world on his entrance into which he is to be judged, according to that store which he has laid up for himself. The same idea is seen in the words of St. Paul to the Romans, where he says, 'According to thy hardness and impenitent heart thou treasurest up to thyself wrath against the day of wrath and revelation of the just judgment of God, Who will render to every man according to his works.'[1] Whether we will it or not, we are treasuring up for ourselves, day after day, for the Day of Judgment and the long years of eternity. The difference between the good and the bad is not that the one treasure up and the other do not, but only in the quality of the treasure which they lay by. The most thoughtless butterfly in the most frivolous circle of the gay world, as well as the most grave and serious of philosophers, or the most vigilant of the servants of God, is day by day adding to this treasure. Every moment it is increasing, whether for good or for evil. It draws after it silently the heart, and the affections are where that treasure is. For, in truth, if we refer to some other sayings of our Lord, it is, as we shall find Him say, the heart itself which, in the first instance, determines of what kind the materials are of which our store in the next world is made up. He told the Jews, who were finding fault with Him, and carrying their opposition so far as to be in danger of the great sin of blasphemy against the Holy Ghost, 'How can you speak good things, whereas you are evil? For out of the abundance of the heart the mouth speaketh. A good man out of a good treasure bringeth forth good things, and an evil man out of an evil treasure bringeth forth evil things.' Thus we have, as it were, two stores or treasures. The first is in our own heart, out of which are the issues of life,[2] as the Scripture says, and accordingly as our heart is good or evil, so are the things which proceed from it good or evil. A good heart is a fountain of living water, rising up in the sight of God moment after moment, and filling the air all around

---

[1] Romans ii. 5, 6.   [2] Prov. iv. 23.

with the fresh spray of virtue and grace, while an evil heart is a source of the foulest corruption, welling forth in filth and poison and pestilence on all around. And the second store which we have is that of which we have been speaking, the treasure which we are piling up in the next world, which is evil or good according to the wickedness or goodness of our hearts. It is not wonderful, then, that these two should be connected; that the evil heart should heap up for itself an evil treasure, or that the evil treasure should draw after it the evil heart. If we wish to know of what kind is our treasure, our heart will reveal the answer, and if we ask of what sort is our heart, our treasure in the next world will tell us.

There is yet a further truth in connection with this subject, to which our Lord now seems to proceed. The treasure depends on the heart, and the heart follows the treasure; but what is it that make the heart good or bad? The will is a blind power, guided by the mind. It reaches forward to that which is set before it by the intelligence as good. Here then, it might seem, is a safeguard against evil-heartedness, because the intelligence is not free, and cannot close its eyes to the light of reason. Alas! here is the very subtlest and most fatal danger of all, the danger of a perverted mind, a false conscience, a traitorous guide ruling in the name of truth, and directing the heart in the pursuit of evil. This may explain, in brief, the connection of the passage before us. Our Lord seems to be engaged in suggesting a series of reasons and motives for detachment from worldly cares, and for the perfect and even heroic reliance on the providence of God, which is so extremely important in the spiritual life. He has begun, as has been said, with the negative precept against laying up treasure upon earth, which is the foundation on which

He intends to rear the far more entire detachment which He has in His mind. The first motive which He adduces for not storing up on earth, is the uselessness of such care, inasmuch as we can lay up nothing here which we can be sure of retaining. He adds, in the second place, the danger to the soul of engrossment in earthly gains, which are certain to attach the heart to themselves. The last words on which we commented, 'Where your treasure is, there also will your heart be,' seem to call to His mind the influences which rule man, and to suggest to Him the still further danger which is pointed out in those which now follow. The heart is the seat of the affections, and the organ of the will, and it is a great misery when the heart is set on worldly things, on interests which fade, on goods which cannot satisfy. And yet there is a still further danger, the denouncing of which appears to be the object of this next head of our Lord's teaching. The heart may sometimes pervert the head and distort the mind, and then reason itself, which is the natural corrective of the errors of the will, becomes their slave, and the mind itself comes to take evil for good and good for evil. Then the whole man may be bent on a perverse object, conscience may no longer resist, or, instead of resisting, may actually dictate what is wrong, and thus all scruples may be silenced, and the chances of recovery immensely diminished. The best state of a man is when his mind's eye is enlightened by faith and reason, and so he is able to pursue, with all his might, the good and high and holy end which God would have him follow, without any interior conflict or hesitation. A perfect, pure, and simple intention directs all his energies, and his whole life is full of light. The worst state of a man is when this is practically reversed, when evil is deliberately pursued, being proposed to the will as good by the perversion of the mind. Then the light that is in us is darkness, and, as our Lord says, 'How great that darkness must be!"

'The light of thy body is thy eye. If thy eye be single, thy whole body shall be lightsome. But if thy eye be evil, thy whole body shall be darksome. If then the light that is in thee be darkness, the darkness itself, how great shall it be!' The image which our Lord uses is easily understood. The eye is not in itself light, but it is the organ of light. By means of the eye the light that is all around us becomes available to us for the purposes of life, and without the eye that light might be shed around us in vain. In this sense the eye is the light of the body. It opens to the body the world which light places within our reach. The hands and feet and other members of the body can perform their functions, the whole man can move about, and use his limbs and faculties, under the guidance of the eye, which puts him in relation to the universe around him far and near. As long as the eye is sound and healthy, all will go well; but let the eye be false, let it represent things not as they are, in colours not their own, in wrong position and distance, let it exaggerate their relative size or proportion, or let it be so weak as not to reach them when distant, or not to see them clearly when near, then all will be wrong, and the whole body will blunder, stumble, or fall. The hands will seek to grasp what is not within their reach, one thing will be mistaken for another, and the man will be worse than if he had no eye to guide him at all. He will think he has light when he has really darkness. Such is the image which our Lord here puts before us.

If we turn now to the truths which are represented by this image, we find them to be something of this kind. What light is to the eye, and to the whole body which is guided by the eye, that truth is to the soul. The part of the soul which is the organ of truth, the recipient, like the eye, of light, is the intelligence. It is not light itself, but it is the faculty by which truth is received, and through which the whole man is guided in accordance with truth. This is what our Lord calls 'doing truth.'[3] The intelligence acts upon the will, which is the ruler in man, both as to body and as to soul; and the will, guided by the intelligence, makes all the practical choices, in the series of which our moral existence consists. The will really chooses nothing which is not in some way represented to it as good by the intelligence, nor does it refuse and reject anything but what the intelligence puts before it as bad and to be avoided. What a perfectly sound and healthy eye is to the body, that an intelligence which drinks in all the rays of truth which falls upon it, and conveys them without fault or defect to the will for its guidance, is to the soul. But the intelligence may be out of order as well as the eye of man, and, what is worse, the diseases of the eye are involuntary, but the diseases of the intelligence are frequently wilful in a high degree. There may be distortion, or lack of perception, or false colouring, or error in the proportions and relations in which one thing may stand to another, bad perspective, or inability to reach the things which are far off, as things of faith and eternal truths usually are, or a tendency to see dimly the things which are closest to us, as are the true interests of the soul. And in all these cases it may be the evil will which has produced the disease, wholly or in part. In such cases there is terrible mischief to the moral life, mischief like that to the body when the eye is altogether diseased—not simple darkness, but darkness taken for light.

[3] St. John iii. 21.

It may seem at first sight not very easy to decide what it exactly is which our Lord here speaks of as the eye of the soul. In truth, the soul receives through the intelligence light of more kinds than one, and for more purposes than one. For it may be enlightened as to things which are to be known in various ways, either for the purpose of grasping necessary truth, or for the purpose of guiding itself as to matters of conduct. Reason and faith may illuminate it, and the illumination may issue in the dictates of conscience or in the formation of intention. In all these cases we have need of light, in all these cases light, that is, truth, is the guide of life, as well as its joy and peace. We may, therefore, safely take our Lord's words in their full and large sense, and consider that He is speaking in the first place of truth in all these several manifestations, and insisting on the danger of that corruption of the light which is in us, which may happen in all.

It may perhaps help us here to call to mind the magnificent account which is given in the Book of Ecclesiasticus of the light which God originally gave to man, which he still retains, even in his unregenerate state, as far as it was natural, while that portion of it which was lost by the Fall, as being beyond nature, is restored in a certain degree and to a certain extent by the gift of regeneration which all Christians receive in their baptism. It is worthy of note how large a part of the gifts of God to man here spoken of belong to the intelligence. 'God created man out of the earth, and made him after His own image. And he turned him unto it again, and clothed him with strength according to himself. He gave him the number of his days and time, and gave him power over all things that are upon the earth. He put the fear of him upon all flesh, and he had dominion over beasts and fowls. He created of him a helpmate like to himself. He gave them counsel, and a tongue, and eyes and ears, and a heart to devise, and He filled them with the knowledge of understanding. He created in them the science of the spirit, He filled their heart with wisdom, and showed them both good and evil. He set His eye upon their hearts to show them the greatness of His works, that they might praise the Name which He had sanctified, and glory in His wondrous acts, that they might declare the glorious things of His works. Moreover, He gave them instructions, and the law of life for an inheritance. He made an everlasting covenant with them, and He showed them His justice and judgment. And their eyes saw the majesty of His glory, and their ears heard His glorious voice: and He said to them, Beware of all iniquity, and He gave to every one of them commandment concerning his neighbour.'[4] It will not be necessary here to analyze the statements in this great passage theologically, or to attempt to draw out the whole system of truth which it contains. But it bears witness to the truth of the law of God written in the hearts of men, to which St. Paul appeals in the Epistle to the Romans, to the natural illumination of reason, to the instructions and law of life given as 'an inheritance,'—in which we see a distinct allusion to declarations as to the will of God and the rule of life which were to be handed on from generation and generation, thus forming what we may call a primitive revelation intrusted to tradition for its continual preservation and communication. Here there would seem to be three several illuminations, which, of course, are not independent of each other in their subject-matter, as the natural law must be reasonable, and the teachings of tradition would confirm both reason and the law of nature. There are also certain far

[4] Ecclus. xvii. 1-12.

higher gifts spoken of in this passage, for Adam was wonderfully filled with preternatural and supernatural endowments. But for our present purpose it may not be necessary to consider these in detail.

We have already had occasion to mention that it is commonly taught in the Church that even some of the precepts of the natural law may become obscured in the hearts of men. There may be ignorance as to at least the deductions from the first principles of that law, as in the case of the law which enacts purity and the sanctity and unity of marriage. Many nations of antiquity did not consider this law to be violated by offences against purity short of adultery. It is probably the same now over great portions of the globe which are not Christian. The ignorance of the law against polygamy is well known. There have been very curious perversions, and even, so to speak, reversals of the natural law in this subject-matter in many nations, of which we need not speak here, in which cases it has been thought good and meritorious to do what is in itself sinful. Much the same may be said as to the natural law of justice or that which forbids murder, and we see the same substitution of darkness for light in the diabolical invention of human sacrifices, in which the deliberate murder of their brethren was made to be an act by which men could please God and win His favour. The law of revenge, again, is an instance in which what is distinctly forbidden is turned into a duty. These are but a few instances in which the light of the natural law has been turned into darkness by the action of the perverse will, bent on the indulgence of evil passions, and aided, it cannot be doubted, by the suggestions and illusions of the spiritual enemies of God and man, who rejoice especially in that degradation of the human race which consists in the obliteration of the natural law. In such cases, the voice of conscience itself, which is the practical application to action of the conception of the intelligence as to right and wrong, is made to speak against the law of God. Nor, as we shall see, are these the only cases in which this miserable darkness is put in the place of light.

We may go on to consider the light of reason, which is the guide of human actions and judgments, assisted, of course, by the ordinary helps of grace, which are denied to none. This ordinary light, for which we so often forget to thank God, is sometimes met with in the course of His providence as entirely distorted and turned into darkness. This is the case of insanity, a fearful scourge, which makes a man equal to the lower animals, and takes away from him the responsibility of his actions. But there are degrees of mental disease which fall short of this worst form, and in many men it is possible that the will has so perverted the reason that, on points as to which self-interest or passion are concerned, the light may have been practically turned into darkness, and a man who is perfectly sensible and judicious on all other points, may persuade himself that this or that is reasonable which is in truth the height of folly. The reign of reason in the upright soul, its rule over the passions and appetites, its guidance of the will in the choices which have to be made as to conduct, is a beautiful creation of God, the exercise of which does Him honour and fills the life of His creature with light and joy. And so, on the other hand, there are few ruins more lamentable, few defeats of God's designs in creation —if we may ever speak of His designs being defeated— that are sadder to witness, and that lead to more misery, than when reason is either partially or entirely dethroned, and much more when the perversion can be traced in any way to the obliquity of the will.

Another guide of the soul, higher in its nature than the light of reason, is faith. It is by faith that we receive all the many rays of light which God imparts to us as from Himself by means of those who speak in His name, and which we therefore receive as coming from Him, the Infallible Truth. By means of faith, the eye of the mind reaches to truths which are in themselves too high for reason to grasp, and receives a stronger, clearer, and more certain apprehension of other truths which are not beyond the range of man's natural powers. In the glow of this light man can march with certainty and confidence along the path of his eternal destiny, and deal without faltering or fear of failure with the realities of the unseen world, like a mariner with an unerring compass to guide him across the waves of a pathless ocean. God, the soul, the end of his being, the law of his life, the standard of duty and conduct, the divine truths of faith, containing so many things concerning God Himself which are entirely above reason, the difference between the temporal and the eternal, the value of time and grace, the responsibility of the will, the issues of the choices which he is making day after day and hour after hour, all these things are clearer and more substantial to him in this marvellous illumination than the things of sense in the light of the sun. And so he is able to act on them with a certainty and a courage which would be absolute folly if the light by which he is guided were dim or treacherous. At every step he risks the best treasures and hopes of this life for the promises of faith. These enable him to form high designs and undertake great enterprises and conceive noble aims, to risk life itself, and to confront death without fear. He can endure, because, as St. Paul says, 'He sees Him that is invisible.'[4] There is nothing

[4] Heb. xi. 27.

so beautiful or so glorious to God in the moral world as the life of faith, not only as it is exhibited in the great saints and special friends of God, but as it is led over the whole Church by thousands upon thousands of Christians in common vocations, by young and old, by the ignorant, as this world reckons them, as well as by the learned, by men and women of every character and every capacity, high as well as low, laymen as well as ecclesiastics. The life of a Christian penetrated by faith is supernatural in its aims and motives and actions from morning to night; it is a conversation in Heaven, a service like that rendered to God by those who see His face; yet a service paid to Him on the part of those who are still in the prison of the corruptible flesh, still in exile and in the misery and danger of the battle-field, in which our enemies are not flesh and blood like ourselves, but 'principalities and powers, the rulers of the world of this darkness, the spirit of wickedness in the high places.'[5]

The knowledge which we possess of truth on the authority of another is a participated knowledge, and is in character like that of the witness himself on whose word we believe. The faith of which we are speaking rests on the word of God, by whatever instrument or testimony that word may be conveyed to us, and the knowledge which it imparts to us has something of the clearness and firmness and strength which belong to the Divine mind. It is not wonderful that such knowledge should give a power and energy to actions and lives founded upon it which are beyond the ordinary range of human capacity. The life is indeed full of light which is illuminated and penetrated by faith. It is not wonderful that our Lord should have made to faith promises so magnificent as to seem to confer upon it almost Divine

[5] Ephes. vi. 12.

power. He tells us that whatever we ask in prayer, believing, we shall receive. He tells us that if we have faith like a grain of mustard seed, we shall be able to move mountains. These prerogatives appear natural enough when we consider what is the light with which faith enlightens us. The life of faith is in truth a Divine life. Every corner and particle of such an existence is steeped in what St. Paul calls 'the power of an indissoluble life.'[6] But the full dignity and stature to which faith can raise the soul are seen only when the Divine gift is perfectly possessed, and when no other, or rather no false light, crosses that which streams from the witness of God. Our Lord says that the eye must be single, it must be without any admixture of foreign and adverse elements, it must receive as in a vessel into which nothing else finds its way, the heavenly illumination of faith. There is no portion or particle of the faith that can be lost without injury to the perfection with which the rest is held. Thus it is easy to see how in this case also light may be turned into darkness. The truths of our faith are beautiful and sublime, but they impose restraints on the mind and will against which nature is fain to rebel. When this happens, then begins the reign of darkness for light, and the misery to which that reign gives birth. Even what seem to be the most abstract propositions in the Christian Creed cannot be laid aside without mischief to the whole. The loss of the single doctrine of unity, which is carried into the region of practice by the commission of the sin of schism, paralyzes the fruitfulness of the truths which remain when that truth is denied. In such a case the light that seems to be in the persons or the community lying under the guilt of separation from the Christian unity becomes a kind of darkness, because

[6] Heb. vii. 16.

charity dies out, and with it all true spiritual life. Much more is this evidently true when the doctrines of the faith which have been forfeited are such as relate directly to the means by which the spiritual life is maintained in the Christian Church, as the sacraments, or the sacrifice of the altar, or the priesthood, or the ever-abiding and infallible doctorate of the See of St. Peter.

But the moral misery is perhaps still more pernicious when, instead of the true teaching of the Catholic Church, men have false guides and lights which lead them into positive errors on the same subject-matter as that of the doctrines which they have rejected. These falsehoods have as distinct and definite a power to generate darkness, even in the moral order, as the Christian truths to produce light and life. The Calvinistic doctrine of predestination is a clear teaching of what is insulting to God in the highest degree, and it has a perfectly plain and evident tendency to make men disregard the moral law. The same may be said on other grounds of the Lutheran doctrine of justification by faith. There is hardly any moral turpitude which may not be traced to some such false teaching under the name of truth.

If this is true even of perversions of Christian doctrines which have been taught by men who have yet professed the religion of our Lord, how much more clear is the darkening tendency of the false religions which have had so much hold upon the world, many of which still survive by the side of the Christian Church! In all these we see darkness instead of light —darkness put in the place of light—asserting itself as the guide of life and the rule of conduct, the law of men's actions here and the foundation of their hopes hereafter. It is indeed terrible to think of the lies as to God, as to His character and His laws, as to the duties of man and the conditions of salvation, which have been imposed upon so many millions of souls for whom our Lord has died, and which have been accepted by them as the true light according to which their life was to be ruled. But it is not in the false religions of the heathen world outside the Christian pale alone that this deadly imposture is to be found. Whatever a man believes or holds as true with regard to his condition here, its prospects and laws and issues, is to him in the place of the faith which God has intended to be the common light of all men. There is a creed of modern science, falsely so called, a creed as to the origin of man, or the existence of spirits, or the freedom of the will, or the immortality of the individual soul, or the obligation of the moral law, or the responsibility of man to a higher Lord than himself, which denies in all these matters the teaching of our Lord and of His Church. This deadly creed is as light to thousands of men in the most civilized countries of the world, the countries which owe the most to the long labours and achievements of the Christian centuries. It is darkness in the place of light, taking away man's faith in God, in the obligation of morality, in the future account to be given of his actions, in the life of the soul after death, as well as in the resurrection of the body, in the merit of virtue, and the reward promised to good works. This is a creed as debasing and degrading to all that is high and noble in humanity as the fetish worship of the most superstitious savages in the world. It leads, like the old paganism of Greece or Rome, to sensuality and cruelty, to materialism and brutality, and so by no circuitous path to the extinction of all intellectual life and cultivation. The light that is in such men is darkness, and darkness great indeed. Men have only to act resolutely and without faltering on the principles of this mock philosophy, and there is nothing to hinder them from reaching the same extremes of barbarism which have been attained under the influence of the creed of the false prophet, or under the blood-stained superstitions of the Aztecs or the Hindus.

The lights of reason and of faith deal with general truths, although practice and action are founded upon them. They may be said to combine with the natural law which is written in letters of light in the heart of every child of Adam, to inspire the conscience, which is the representative of the voice of God, directing or warning him as to matters of conduct, which are naturally and necessarily particular and individual. For when conscience is analyzed it is found to be simply the intelligence pronouncing, according to the light by which it is illuminated, as to what is right and what wrong to do or not to do.[7] We need not point out either the obligation of obedience to a certain conscience, or the immense joy and light which are shed through the soul by a consistent and faithful use of this

---

[7] Suarez, *De Legibus*, lib. ii. cap. v. § 15, thus distinguishes 'conscience' from the 'natural law.' He says, 'It is sometimes said to be the same, as we have quoted above from St. Basil and St. John Damascene, because conscience is nothing else than a decree (*dictamen*) about things to be done. Nevertheless, in rigour these two things are different, for a law signifies a rule generally laid down concerning things to be done, while the conscience signifies a practical decree in something particular, so that it is rather the application of a law to a particular work. Hence the conscience has a wider range than the natural law, because it applies not to that law only, but any other also, whether divine or human, and not only a true law, but a supposed law. For there may be sometimes an erroneous conscience, there cannot be an erroneous law, for such a law would be no law, and this is especially true of the natural law, of which God is the author. Again, a law properly refers to what is to be done, but conscience is concerned also with what has already been done, and therefore it is said not only to bind, but also to accuse, to bear witness, and to defend, as may be seen in St. Thomas i. p. q. 70, and i. 2æ q. 19, art. 6, in which places the subject of conscience is discussed.'

The Eye of the Soul. 95

Divine gift, the characteristic of which is that it speaks with an authority which can be derived from a source no lower than the supreme Master and Lord of human nature and life, and implies an appeal to His tribunal as the ratification of its decrees. As conscience is given us as the appointed guide of our conduct, it is our duty never to go against it, and thus it may sometimes happen that although in itself erroneous, it still rules us, and must be obeyed. The perfect use of this gift secures our happiness, for we can never be punished by God for following our conscience, unless in the case of a voluntary and culpable ignorance of the law, and a deliberate refusal to inform ourselves as to some obligation which we desire not to submit to. In every case but that we may say, in the words of St. John, 'If our heart do not reprehend us, we have confidence towards God.'[8] Extreme care, such as St. Paul tells us that he practised, in keeping our conscience 'free from offence both towards God and towards man'[9] will be rewarded by a great light, an intense delicacy, a wonderful and sensitive quickness in detecting the approach of evil, or in discerning the choice most entirely in accordance with the designs of God, and other perfections of which this faculty is capable, and of which we see examples in the saints; while, on the other hand, anything like laxity, or any subtle violence that we may put upon it, perversity in turning away from its behests, inattention in enlightening it as to the duties of our state, or of any position in which we may unexpectedly find ourselves, and other faults of the same character, will be punished by a sluggishness and dulness of conscience which may lead us into great falls and dangers. But there are cases in which this most precious faculty is perverted and hardened in a manner that St. Paul speaks of when he

[8] 1 St. John iii. 21.   [9] Acts xxiv. 16.

says that the heretics of the latter days shall be men 'whose consciences are seared.'[10] In some men this light is indeed turned into darkness, and darkness rules the soul as if it were light.

It is possible in matters of ordinary conduct and of plain morality for a deliberate and obstinate will to force the conscience until evil is put in the place of good and good in the place of evil. But such perversion is far more possible, and unfortunately far more common, in the case of which the Apostle speaks, that of the leaders and teachers of sects, heresies, and schisms in the Church. Such men are usually consumed with pride, which blinds them to truths which all but themselves see, and overspreads their souls with darkness like that of Egypt, darkness which can be felt. They put themselves, their own judgments and interpretations of Scripture or the Fathers, in the place of the Divine authority of the Church, and thus become the slaves of their own fictitious infallibility. St. Paul tells his disciple Titus not even to attempt to convert them. 'A man that is a heretic, after the first and second admonition, avoid, knowing that he that is such a one is subverted and sinneth, being condemned by his own judgment.'[11] This is the most fearful case of men in whom the light that is in them is darkness, the very guide which God has given them to lead them to Him is so perverted that it seems to lead them away from Him in His own name. Over such men reason and argument have no power. Their position forces on them the terrible necessity of doing the work of the adversary of God in keeping others away from the Church, and in doing this they often act with an assumption of personal authority which implies practically a claim to individual inspiration or an extraordinary

[10] 1 Tim. iv. 2. [11] Titus iii. 10, 11.

mission from God. They have been known not to shrink from insisting on the exclusion of Catholic priests from the deathbeds of persons who have no hope of salvation except in submission to the Church, and from taking upon themselves to answer at the judgment-seat of God for the safety of those who have no faith whatever in their ministrations. These are, indeed, some of the most fearful illustrations of the meaning of our Lord's words as to the greatness of the darkness of the soul when darkness is in the place of light.

These considerations naturally conduct us on to another, though not an entirely different, sense in which our Lord's words are taken by some of the Fathers, the statement of which is necessary in order to give to the passage before us the fulness of meaning of which it is capable. In this sense, the light which is in us, and which makes the whole body lightsome if it be what it ought to be, and darksome if it be what it ought not, is the intention which gives their formal character to all our actions. The intention is an act of the will directing the action to a certain end, but this end is represented to the will by the intelligence as good, or at least as an object of desire. In this sense the light which has shone upon the mind, from whatever source, natural or supernatural, it may have come, is, as it were, sphered in a guiding star to which we look as we go forth to action. The intention by which we direct our life and each particular act is in this sense the light of our whole life. It is seen by God alone, and furnishes the measure by which He estimates everything that we do, and, more than that, all that we mean and desire to do. Thus a good intention may confer a high merit even upon actions which in themselves are indifferent, while carelessness in the formation of intention may make the actions which are best in themselves mere matters of routine, and so unworthy of a great reward. Good actions, again, may be spoilt by a perverse intention, as in the cases which our Lord has already mentioned in this Sermon, when almsdeeds or prayers or fasts have been performed for the sake of the applause of men. We are thus introduced to the consideration of the whole doctrine concerning intention, on which so much has been said by spiritual writers.

Every intention, whether good or bad, is founded upon the representation of the intelligence, as has been already said. It therefore belongs to this head of our Lord's teaching, which is concerned with the light within us, which is the practical guide of our footsteps. It is not necessary to dwell on the truth of the duty of avoiding an evil intention. It is more important to remind ourselves of the waste, as it may be called, of possible intentions, which may produce a great barrenness in the soul which is unwatchful of its opportunities, and so issue in the loss of a thousand occasions of laying up treasure in Heaven. The good intention which gives a merit of a supernatural and heavenly character to our actions, may be either actual, virtual, or habitual. An actual intention is one which is present to the mind and will at the time at which the action is performed, and this is the intention which, as far as is possible, it is desirable that we should have, in order to give our actions their highest price in the courts of Heaven. But it is not always possible to retain the recollection which is required for this constant direction of our actions to God, and a virtual intention, which is an intention once made and unretracted, is enough to give them the character which is requisite in order to their high merit. And, moreover, there are many actions which are in themselves so engrossing, in the occupation of the mind which they require, that their substantial perfection might suffer if the mind were diverted from them, by the necessity of forming the intention at every stage. Thus a virtual intention is sufficient. An habitual intention is the remaining and abiding direction of the soul, in consequence, not so much of a particular intention formed at any one moment, as of the ordinary and continual bent of the will in the same direction. In all these cases a real and true influence is exercised on the action; for in the case of the reversal of the intention once formed, which happens when men allow themselves to be under the influence of some vicious motive after having intended to perform their actions virtuously, the motive which has last obtained the mastery rules the actions which follow, and the virtual good intention no longer exists.

It is here that the chief practical danger is to be found. A man may have begun well, but his own taste or pleasure may creep in during the course of the action, which thus becomes spoilt, and loses its supernatural value. Or again, self-interest, or the subtle love of human praise, against which our Lord has so carefully put us on our guard, may come in in like manner and ruin what has been well begun. It is enough for the enemy of our souls to spoil the action anywhere, whether it be at its birth, or in mid course, or at its close. Certain tests may be used which may enable us to discover whether the work has been done for God or for ourselves. If there has been disturbance or passion in its undertaking, it is probable that human motives have insinuated themselves, as the place of God is in peace. If there has been carelessness and negligence in the manner of performing it, it has probably been done out of routine, or because it is the rule to do it, and not directly for God. If there is anxiety as to the way in which it is received by others after it has been accomplished, self-love has probably not been a stranger to it. If we are put out by the ingratitude or want of correspondence to our work on the part of those for whom it has been done, then also self-love rather than the pure desire to serve God has been partly its motive.

Another head of doctrine on this subject is that which relates to the several kinds of good intention with which our works may be directed to God. One writer who has often been followed in this work speaks of various kinds of good intention.[12] The first and the lowest of these is the intention of those who do what is good and virtuous out of fear. Our Lord Himself constantly appeals to this motive, as when He tells the Apostles and disciples not to fear those who can kill the body, and after that can do no more, but to fear Him Who can destroy both soul and body in Hell.[13] The eternal punishments of God, His marvellous and inscrutable judgments, whether in this world or in the next, are the motives of this intention, which is good, but not the highest which men can form. The second kind of intention is that of those who serve God and direct their actions to His service out of the hope, which His great promises and well-known faithfulness and magnificence awaken in their hearts, of a wonderful reward in the next world and of great protection in this. If the first kind of intention be that of servants, this intention is that of labourers for hire, and we have only to call to mind the number of our Lord's parables which speak of us under that image, to remember how often He uses this motive also. But the third intention is higher than these, the intention of those who serve God as His

[12] See Alvarez de Paz, *De Inquisitione Pacis* (the third part of his great work), lib. iii. p. 1. c. 8.
[13] St. Matt. x. 28.

children in order to give Him pleasure by their service. This intention is of gold, in comparison with that of the labourers for hire, which may be said to be of silver, that of servants being of brass. It imitates God, and in that respect also belongs to His children—for He has conferred on us all that we have received from Him out of love, and not for any gain that can accrue to Him from us. This is the motive which influences friends in their service one to the other, and it has a nobility and greatness of its own which raises it far above the others, however good in themselves.

This kind of intention is again divided by the author whom we are here following into three, which He calls right, simple, and godlike, *deiformis*. It belongs to a perfectly right intention, not only to avoid all that can in any way displease God, but also to direct to Him the otherwise indifferent actions of life, which are done in order that He may be pleased by us. This consideration brings back to the mind the immense number of actions, capable of being thus directed, and so made meritorious of an eternal reward, but which are continually wasted, even by those who would rather suffer anything than offend Him deliberately. Thus St. Paul bids us, 'Whether we eat, or drink, or whatever else we do, to do all things to the glory of God.'[14] We find the Apostle's words explained by the great Basil for his monks[15] in a way which illustrates this doctrine. He says that a man eats to the glory of God, when he calls to mind the benefits which God has bestowed upon him, and shows by his manner of feeding that he does not forget the presence of God, nor eat as a slave of his appetite, for the sake of the pleasure which he may derive from that action, but as one who has to labour for God, and requires strength to support him in the

---

[14] 1 Cor. x. 31.   [15] *Reg. Brev.* 196.

exertions which the commandments of his Master impose upon him. He adds also that our actions are made more meritorious by the addition of more motives of virtue than one. For as a man may commit a great many acts of sin by one and the same action—as for instance, if he steals in order to have the means of tempting another to sin with him, and desires in that other sin to take away his neighbour's reputation, or to avenge himself for some wrong which he has received—so the same virtuous action may be done for a number of good motives, as if a man were to fast in order that he might imitate our Lord, and please God by an act of mortification, or to offer the act as thanksgiving to God for His benefits, or to satisfy for sins, or to win from Him some virtue, or to gain pardon for the faults of others, living or dead, or to overcome the passion of gluttony, or to gain strength against the temptations with which the evil one may assail the virtue of purity, or to practise obedience to the precept of the Church, or to acquire greater glory in Heaven for hunger and thirst after justice, or to have something to give to the poor by means of self-denial. No one of these ends excludes the rest, and it is certain that the same work, done with a direct intention for them all and each singly, will have greater value in the sight of God than if it were done for one or two only. We have here a wonderful device for that increase of the merit of our good actions which came under our consideration in the preceding chapter, for it cannot be doubted that our treasure in Heaven may be immensely added to it in this manner. Thus even indifferent actions are made to glow with a celestial light, and everything that we do in this way becomes an exercise of the love of God, by means of which our growth in grace is wonderfully advanced.

After this form of intention, which he calls right, the

author goes on to speak of the other two which have been named above. He makes simplicity of intention consist in something more than that doing everything for God which we have just now described. For it is something beyond that, to do everything in such a way and with such an intention as to make it a means of union with God in heart and mind. This is the one necessary thing of which our Lord spoke to St. Martha, when everything that is done is reduced to unity by the consciousness of God's presence and the loving desire to show Him affection in all that we do. For God so loves each soul as to care for it as if there were no other in the world to care for, and it is but right that a soul that loves Him should, in return, think of nothing but Him, and perform its actions so entirely for Him as to do them as they would be done if there were no one else in the world to witness them. He is the end of all. If mortifications are practised, it is that the soul may be purer in His sight; if virtues are exercised, it is that He may see in us more spiritual beauty; if we labour for our neighbour, it is that He may see that we are not barren of good works. If the needs of the body are provided for, it is that we may not lack strength to serve Him. The last kind of intention, which is called deiform, is that of those who forget themselves altogether, their own comfort or happiness or advantage or honour, in order to think singly of what conduces to the glory of God. This is hinted at at the end of the passage on which we are occupied, where our Lord bids us seek first the Kingdom of God and His justice, and then everything else shall be added to us. For, if we think of nothing but what is of the interest of God, He is bound to take care of us, and thus all our own interests are safely lodged, as it were, in the hands of One Whose power is as unlimited as His love and wisdom.

It is obvious that these several kinds of intention rise one above the other in a beautiful gradation, and that, while none of them are unworthy of Christian souls, the later in the scale are higher and more perfect than those which precede them. They are all summed up and placed in their right proportion in a few words of St. Ignatius, in one of the great rules which he has laid down for his religious children. He bids them in the first place strive to have a right intention, not only in their state of life, but also in all particular things, seeking therein to please and serve the Divine Goodness for its own sake, and for the singular benefits wherewith He has prevented us, rather than from fear of punishments or hope of rewards, though, as he says, we ought to draw help to ourselves from these also. Here we have the doctrine not to be content with a general or virtual intention. In the second place, we have the various motives which can influence our intention arranged in order, first the love of God for His own intrinsic goodness, then the love of Him for the blessings which He has bestowed on us, in which love there is some slight admixture of our own interest, then we have the hope of rewards and the fear of punishments, which are not so much to be made directly the ends for which we serve God, as motives by which in case of need we can help ourselves to serve Him more perseveringly and courageously. And it seems as if the Saint had not only taught us in this passage what is the highest kind of intention, but had also pointed out the way by which that intention may be made easy. For he goes on to say, that we are to lay aside as far as possible the love of all creatures, in order to place all our affection on their Creator, that is, as far as our frailty will allow, we are to love no creatures for themselves, but God alone with all our affection, loving Him in all, as he goes on to say, and all in Him, according to His own most holy will. Creatures, then, are to be loved by us in such a way as may make us love Him, and what we love in them must be good, and He must be the end of all the love we give to them. Then St. Ignatius adds the rule by which all the exercises of this love are to be regulated, as to the time and place and manner and degree, the more or the less, and all that relates to the love of creatures in God and God in them—all is to be governed by the most holy will of Him Whom we thus love. Thus, the way to form in ourselves this purest and highest kind of intention is the practice of the love of God, and the particulars, so to speak, of this practice are to be ruled by the will of God, ascertained, as far as may be, in the manner that is open to us, by His law, or the precepts of His Church, or the obligations of our state, or the rules of our Order, or the injunctions of those who are in the place of God to us, or by the choice of what is most to His glory in matters in which we are left to our own guidance.

Those who are familiar with the Exercises of the Saint whom we have been quoting, will not be at a loss as to the manner in which St. Ignatius would have us learn the love of God. We need not here dwell upon the famous meditation which he has placed at the close of the Book of the Exercises, the several points of which are so many steps in the perfect love of God. It is enough to remind ourselves that the foundation of love must be knowledge, and that in the Exercise just mentioned, as in all others designed for the same purpose, the consideration of certain truths concerning God's dealings with us in the way of love, is made the ground on which our practice of love to Him is based. We thus find the same general conclusion applicable in the case of intention as that of the other forms of light of which we have been speaking—whether we consider the light that is in us to be the light of reason, or the light of faith, or the judgment of conscience, or the deliberately formed intention by which our actions are to be guided, we find in all these cases that the intelligence which is given to man as the guide of his will in the choices which it has to be continually making, may be almost to an indefinite extent perverted or warped by the predominance of any passion in the soul. The light of reason is clear and beautiful, the light of faith is glorious with the radiance of Heaven, conscience speaks with a power that implies authority, intention has the gift of turning all our actions into reflections of the incomparably precious service which the Incarnate Son of God rendered to His Father when He dwelt amongst us. And so great is the power of a malicious will, even as to what seems to be truth, that reason may be made to prompt to injustice and wrong, cruelty to man and dishonour to God may seem to have the sanction of faith, conscience may be made to speak the behests of ambition or avarice or lust, and even the holiest of works and callings may be turned against God by a perverse intention. Our Lord elsewhere insists again on this same truth in different words,[16] where He seems to unite the thought of this passage with that of another which precedes it in the Sermon on the Mount, about the intention of any one who lights a candle to place it where it may give light. It would seem as if He were there speaking of the light of conscience, which God has given to men to be their guide, and He adds, that they are to take heed that the light that is in them be not darkness—as if there were real and great danger

[16] St. Luke xi. 34.

that so it might be. And, as has been said, the connection of the passage before us may be explained in this way —that our Lord has before His mind the power of the love of earthly treasure to pervert the conscience so as to make it prompt to evil.

CHAPTER VII.

Single Service.

St. Matt. vi. 24; *Vita Vitæ Nostræ*, § 33.

IN the passage before us, our Lord seems to call before His mind one great truth after another, in order to draw from each a conclusion or argument for the main purpose of the teaching on which He is occupied. He has already spoken of the store in Heaven which we all have the opportunity of laying up, day after day, and of the manner in which men commonly use their opportunities in this respect. The heaps of bad or good treasure seem to grow under His eyes, and then He turns to the truth which points out the reason why the store in the one case is good and in the other evil—namely, the power of the will in perverting the mind, and so making the light which is given to us to guide our choices the very cause of the folly and wickedness with which those choices are sometimes made. And our Lord could see, as no one else could, the difference between these several issues—the perfect and fruitful beauty which He describes under the image of a body entirely 'lightsome,' the defacement of that beauty in the case of those in whom light and darkness alternate in their mastery, and the full hideousness resulting from the entire triumph of evil, where darkness is put in the place of light.

Another and most momentous truth seems now to occupy Him. Man is not really labouring in this world for himself, but for a Lord to Whom he belongs by as perfect a right of property as any slave to his master or any inanimate object to its possessor. He is not his own, and he is therefore not risking his own interests merely when he labours and stores up for evil, nor is he free to labour or not, nor is he to seek his own advantage only in all that he does. Another part of the same truth is this—that man cannot emancipate himself from this law of his condition by throwing off, as his free will allows him partially to do, the blessed service which he owes to his Father and Lord. He must serve some one, and if he will not be the servant of God, he must become the slave of the devil, so that his choice is not whether he shall or shall not serve, but only which master of the two he shall make his lord. The service of the one is incompatible with the service of the other. There can be no possible alliance or compromise between them. Moreover, the two services differ, not only in their legitimacy and unlawfulness, but in the happiness or misery which they entail on those who adopt them respectively. Again, the simple truth that we are the servants of God, while it imposes on us the duty of making the service to which we are bound the one single object of our cares, also secures us against all possible danger to our own interests in attending to it. Such is the character of our Master, such the beneficence which He shows even to the least and most insignificant of the creatures whom He has made to have a place in His Kingdom, that no one can serve Him or belong to Him without having the full security of His infinite power and wisdom for the provision of every possible want and for the protection which may be required against any possible danger. Thus the argument for laying aside all anxiety and care for earthly things, and temporal riches, which is first rested on the dominion and sovereignty of God, is grounded at last on His most tender and thoughtful care for those who belong to Him. We are bound to serve Him, even if we lose all that is needful in this world for the sake of His service. This is the sort of service which the kings and great ones of the world exact of those over whom they rule. But when we do give ourselves to His service as to the one single object of our thoughts, then we find that He cares for us with a diligence such as He might use if we were really of vital importance to Him, and, more than that, He requires it of us as a part of our service, and as a proof that we belong to Him, that we leave to Him the care of all our interests as if they were His and not ours. He does not even tell us to pray for these temporal needs, and then leave them to the providence of our Father. He bids us, on the contrary, abandon the care of them altogether, in order to devote ourselves and all our energies to the interests of His Kingdom.

It is, as it were, a point of honour with God never to let those who work for Him want for anything. Thus even when there are great interests at stake in the cause of truth, as when the Apostles had to stand before kings and princes to give an account of the doctrine which they taught, they are forbidden by our Lord to premeditate what they shall say,[1] God reserving to Himself to put into their mouths the answers which no one would be able to gainsay or to resist. If this is the case with regard to the defence of the truth in argument, how much more may God be expected to provide with all abundance for the mere temporal needs of those who give up all other cares in order to devote themselves entirely to His service! Such is a general outline of

[1] St. Matt. x. 19, 20.

the passage of the Sermon on the Mount now before us. We may devote the present chapter to the consideration of the first great truth which it contains—that of the dominion of God, of the extent to which we belong to Him, especially if we have any special commission to labour for His glory, and of the impossibility of any compromise between His service and that of the world.

There is a kind of beautiful gentleness and delicacy, if we may so speak, about the way in which our Lord introduces the first of the series of truths on which we are now to comment. He does not simply say, Remember, after all, that you are not here to work or hoard for yourselves, but for your Master. That is a peremptory decision of all difficulty about the question as to which He is now speaking, the question as to storing up in this world or in the next. But He says, Remember you cannot do what is impossible—you cannot serve two masters. A Master you have already, Whom you are bound to serve, and you cannot have another. It is not only that nothing that you can lay up here will escape decay or pillage, it is not only that the only treasures which abide are those which are stored in Heaven, it is not only that if you heap up riches here, here your heart will be, and that there is the very greatest danger that your love for earthly goods and gains will so distort your judgment and blind your conscience as to make you fall into sin for the purpose of acquiring more or retaining what you have. This is not all. You are not free. You are not your own. You belong to God, and for Him alone you are bound to labour. And I tell you further that, some master or other you must serve, and you have only to make your choice between the service to which you are bound, and another service, which will be imposed upon you if you seek the good things of this world. Combine the two services you cannot. They cannot be combined, because they are hostile in character, and the feelings which they call forth in their servants are incompatible. You cannot love both at once, or cling to both at once; if you love the one, you must hate the other; if you cleave to the one, you must neglect and despise the other. It is against your duty and allegiance and loyalty to endeavour to serve both; but if it were not so, you could not succeed if you tried.

This truth of the sovereign dominion of God is the main burthen of many of our Lord's parables, especially those which come latest in the course of His teaching, and it is constantly referred to by the Apostles. St. Paul uses it in the Epistle to the Romans to silence the difficulty about the reprobation of the Jews and the call of the Gentiles. But we may here confine ourselves to its importance in the personal teaching of our Lord. It seems to be almost the one dominant idea which runs through His teaching of the Holy Week in the Temple and on the Mount of Olives. It introduces an altogether new motive into the consideration of the matter more immediately before us now. That motive is no longer our own interest or profit, the prudence as regards ourselves of treasuring in Heaven, and the like. It brings in the notion of obedience and duty, of a law upon us which we are bound to obey without question. Our Lord was fond, as we shall find, of the thought of the command laid upon Him by His Father, and chose, as we may say, to die for our sins when and as He did, out of obedience. He impressed on the Apostles that they too were servants and labourers with a certain definite work to do. Thus the 'servant' or 'slave of Jesus Christ' is the title in which they seem to delight in above all others, and they use it as a sort of official designation at the beginning of their Epistles. On the same principle we are to account for the immense importance attached to obedience in the spiritual life, and to the rule of obedience as the foundation of all perfection and fruitfulness in religious orders in the Church, and indeed in her whole system. We find the Saints afraid to undertake anything without obedience, and, when a thing has been decided on, desiring that the merit of obedience should be added to it, by the positive command of a lawful Superior. The addition of the notion of the service of a master changes altogether the ground on which the question of solicitude about earthly things has hitherto been treated in this passage. For a new relation is introduced—the relation between a Superior who has the right to command and the servant whose business it is to obey. But, as we see in the course of the next few verses, this relation is double—it binds the master to the servant as well as the servant to the master, and it is from this feature in the relationship that our Lord draws a whole chain of arguments for that abandonment of temporal cares to which He is here leading on His Apostles.

The first conclusion, which follows from our relation to God as our Master, is that we can serve no one else. That is, we can serve no one else who stands to God in any position but that of a subordinate who represents Him to us, and whose power depends on and is derived from Him. We can serve God and the Church, God and our parents, God and the State, when there is no usurpation on the part of the State of power which does not belong to it—because in all these cases we serve God in the Church, in our parents, in the State. It would be enough to rest the incompatibility of a double service upon the simple idea of what service in the abstract requires. But there is something more in our Lord's mind. He has before Him, not an abstract case of any two possible masters, but the reality of the rival claims on the heart of man of God and our great enemy the devil. This is the true alternative in the question before us now, and so our Lord characterizes the issues of the two alternatives in words which are precisely adapted to the contrast which lies before us. The true Master is God; the usurper, who endeavours to put himself in the place of God, is the devil. When he tempted our Lord in the desert, he arrogantly and falsely claimed for himself the kingdom of the world and all its wealth and power, whereas in truth he is only permitted to use these things as the means of temptation to us. On this account our Lord here speaks of him, or alludes to him, as the master whom all the servants of earthly interests and riches must in truth serve. We have here, then, more than one head of consideration on which we may ground our meditations on the truths before us.

The first and most direct reason for the statement which our Lord makes as to the impossibility of serving two masters lies, as has been said, in the nature of the service, as it is drawn out for us in the Sacred Scriptures. The service of which the Scriptures are full is that entire devotion of a person to His Lord, which goes far beyond the modern ideas of the relation between servants and masters. The word commonly used by our Lord and the Apostles is the word which is more properly rendered 'slave.' Nothing short of this can in truth satisfy the entire sovereignty of God over His rational creatures, and, indeed, no earthly ownership can come up to the fulness of the rights of a Creator over the work of His hands. The service of a slave to his master is one of right, not of compact, and if the slave labours all his days for the master to whom he belongs, he does not do more than his duty. We have already quoted the words of our Lord, in which He seems to remind us of this truth. The master, in the second place, is not limited in his rights to a particular kind of service, or to a particular time. He is bound by the common laws of right and wrong, but there are no specified limits within those laws which fetter the arbitrariness of his commands. He may set one servant to one service and another to another service, and change them about as he chooses. Again, a master may use the services of his slave without paying him wages, the relation between them is not one of contract. Again, the slave has no right, after a certain time of service, to his liberty, which he can only acquire by the free consent of his master. In all these respects, the blessed service of God corresponds to what we call slavery. Over and over again does the thought rise to the minds of the children of Adam that they have made no contract with God, and that therefore they are not obliged to serve Him. They complain in their hearts that they have not been asked whether they would come or not into the world in which their probation is cast, whether they would agree to run the risk of incurring the eternity of Hell as the price of their having the chance of gaining Heaven. No, they have not been asked, because they are not their own. They belong entirely to Him Who has made them. It is for Him to fix the conditions of their probation and the risks of its issues, and the only law which He can observe is the law of His own ineffable holiness, justice, and goodness. But it is obvious that this kind of absolute property and dominion cannot be shared, nor can it exist except in the hands of One, that is, of God. It is the essential right of a Creator.

Moreover, the service which God requires of us is so complete and engrossing, that we come to the same conclusion on this ground also. Looking through the parables and sayings of our Lord which bear on this point, we find that the servants of whom He speaks are expected to be active and industrious in His service; they have money and goods committed to them which they are not only to preserve unhurt against the time when they are to be demanded of them, but which they are expected to multiply; and if they do not do this, they are to be severely punished. Such is the lesson of the parable of the Talents. Again, the servants of God are to be employed by Him in the work of His Kingdom, as when they are sent out, in the parable of the Marriage Supper, to compel people to come in. Again, they are sent on dangerous embassies, such as may cost them their life, as in the parable of the Wicked Husbandmen. Again, they are the executioners of the justice of their Master, as in the same parable, where the servants of the King are sent to chastise the rebellious tenants. If they are to be so highly rewarded for their faithfulness, goodness, watchfulness, and other like qualities, they are also chastised for simple uselessness, without any other crime, and chastised also according to a strict rule, those who knew their Master's will and do not hold themselves ready, with many stripes, and those who did not know their Master's will with few stripes. This is the teaching of our Lord in St. Luke.[2] When they have done all that is commanded them, they are to expect nothing as of right, but to say that they are unprofitable servants.[3] And, on the other hand, great fidelity and loyalty are expected of them. Our Lord cannot forget, nor wish us to forget, that at the same time that we are the servants of God we are also His children. Thus the servants of the householder, in the parable of the Cockle, are represented as having a keen interest in the fruitfulness of the harvest field, and in the parable of the Unmerciful Servant, they are set before us as resenting the hard

[2] St. Luke xii.   [3] St. Luke xvii. 10.

treatment of one of themselves by his brother-servant. They are to imitate their Master in His mercifulness, and it is to be their highest honour to be as their Master, as our Lord tells the Apostles in His great charge to them before He sends them forth to preach,[4] thus opening out the whole doctrine of the Cross which they are to undergo for His sake, especially as His followers in the work of the salvation of souls.

If there is anything that seems hard and severe about these conditions of the service of God, which show us how entirely engrossing that service must be, all such impressions vanish at once when we remember, as is indeed hinted by our Lord, that the character of our Master becomes more and more known to us in proportion as we give ourselves entirely to His service. Our Lord does not speak of two services, but of the two masters. The work itself, indeed, in which the service of God engages us is the noblest as well as the happiest in the world. It consists in the highest actions of which our nature is capable, it brings us across the loftiest objects of knowledge and contemplation, it reveals to us the magnificence and glory of the creation of which we are a part, and of the conditions under which our lot is cast. But in all that we have to do as servants of God, and especially if we are called to His service in any special manner or degree, we learn Who it is that we serve in the reasonableness and easiness of the yoke which He puts upon us, in the liberality with which He supplies us with all that is wanted for the execution of our commission, in the manner in which He takes the intention for the deed, and considers in all that we do the desire of the heart as the same as its accomplishment, in the greatness of His promises to encourage our faithfulness, and in the over-abundant munificence of the rewards which He bestows upon us. Some, indeed, will

[4] St. Matt. x.

be inclined to carry this thought further, and consider the whole life and teaching and example of our Blessed Lord as one great revelation of the character of our Master, made, among other things, for the especial purpose of drawing our hearts to Him, and making His service a delight and an ambition to us for its own sake, because it is His.

Our Lord uses four remarkable words to express the contrast between the service of God and the service of His enemy, as to the impression which the knowledge of each will produce on the heart. He says that no man can serve two masters, and, as we have seen, He had in his mind God and Satan as the two possible masters between whom the choice has to be made. No man can serve the two, 'for he will either hate the one and love the other, or he will sustain and endure the one and despise the other.' The alternatives before us, therefore, are these, either to hate the devil and love God, or to put up with and endure the devil and despise God. We are brought to choose the service of God by hating the devil and loving God, and we are led to choose the service of Satan and the world by making up our mind to sustain and endure the yoke of the world, and to make light of and despise God. When our Lord speaks of hating the one and loving the other, He seems to put Satan before God in the order of thought. For the service of God begins with us by the detestation of sin. We find out, like the Prodigal Son, the miseries of our condition, the height from which we have fallen, the hardships to which we have made ourselves subject, and, above all, the cruelty and meanness of the 'citizen of the far country,' to whom we have made ourselves slaves. Then there comes in the thought of our Father and our Father's house, the happiness and care which reign there, because He is so good. And so we hate the tyrant under whom we have placed ourselves, and a fresh spring of love towards the Father Whom we have left bursts forth in our heart, a fountain of living water, as our Lord says, always fresh, never drying up, feeding and fertilizing our whole life with the charity that never fails. This is the service of the true Master, the Father Whose children we are, even after we have made ourselves unworthy of the name, and fit only to serve Him as hired servants. We may very well take the case of the Prodigal as a full illustration of this passage. After his return to his home and his welcome by his Father, we may be sure that his one great motive for faithfulness and devotion in his duties would have been the love of his Father, and that, at the same time, if any overtures could have reached him from the cruel master from whose slavery he had escaped, he would have turned from them with intense repugnance and with a great loathing for the character of him from whom they proceeded. But those who serve God have not only to meet with the overtures from the devil which may be addressed to themselves—they find him in their way on every side, spoiling everything that is good, working through all instruments, often through good men more than through bad men, defiling, debasing, hindering, perverting, stamping out the seeds of good before they begin to germinate, and blighting the fair prospect and promise of fruit when it was almost ripe. The knowledge which the servants of God acquire of the character and policy of Satan is certainly of a kind to make them hate him with all the intensity of which their hearts are capable as the enemy of God and man.

On the other hand, the service of Satan may very well be illustrated, in reference to our Lord's words, by that earlier stage in the history of the Prodigal Son which intervened between his departure from and his return to his Father's house. It was, in the first place, a hard servitude, without joy, without freedom, without indulgence, without mitigation—something that human nature can perhaps tolerate and make up its mind to when it is inevitable, but which it can never love. Love is a word that can never be applied to the relations between Satan and his servants. But as man must serve some master, he may endure and sustain the hard service of Satan, even though he have nothing better to feed upon than the husks of the swine. But what is the attitude of the servants of Satan towards God? He is their lawful Master, their true Father, and every item of the work which they do for the tyrant under whom they have placed themselves is work against their Father's interests, and against the allegiance which they owe to their Master and King. They cannot forget God, or live as if He were not. Their conscience still remains, not entirely dead, and all their reason and all their recollections of better things are in revolt against the constrained and unnatural service which they have taken up. Even the evil which they do they are obliged to veil to themselves under the name of good, and they are forced to endeavour to persuade themselves either that God is indifferent or that He will overlook what they are doing, or perhaps they buoy themselves up on the hope that bye-and-bye they will repent. In each one of these mental processes there is contained something of a contempt of God or a neglect of His inspirations, an indifference to His warnings, a perversion of His laws, or the turning of His goodness against Himself, sinning in the hope of future pardon. And the harder the heart gets on its downward course, the more does it begin to share the contempt of God, if we may use such words, which is the habitual state of the fallen angels, who are too proud to accept of God's mercy, even if it were offered to them.

CHAPTER VIII.

Confidence in God.

St. Matt. vi. 24—34; *Vita Vitæ Nostræ*, § 34.

WE seem now to have reached almost the highest point in the gradually advancing teaching of the Sermon on the Mount. We look upon these marvellous precepts or counsels from the earthly side, and we are naturally more inclined to dwell on the failures of correspondence to their invitations or promises of which human life is so full, than on the fewer but most beautiful instances in which our Lord's Sacred Heart has had the consolation of seeing that the seed which He has so lovingly and so profusely sown has fallen on good ground and brought forth fruit a hundred-fold. So it is, that in contemplating the last verses on which we have commented, we are more inclined to dwell on the amount of time which is spent in laying up treasure where it can be spoiled by moth and rust, and on the many cases in which the light of the soul is in truth darkness, than on those in which the eye has been single and the whole body full of light. With our Lord we may suppose that it was different—that He allowed Himself to dwell on the brighter side of the picture, and that He saw all the glories and beauties of the kingdom of His Father upon earth as they were intended to be, and as they would have been but for the faint and unfaithful hearts of the children of the Kingdom. As has been said, if His children were really to give themselves heart and soul to the amassing treasure in Heaven, and if the purity of intention, the faithfulness to light, and the energy and activity of the will devoted to God which are described in the last verses of which we have spoken, had become the rule and not the exception among His servants, there would have remained no heights of sanctity too high for them to scale, no great enterprizes and achievements in His honour which they might not have accomplished. Our Lord must have foreseen all this, not as a general and indefinite possibility, but in the full details of the beautiful and entrancing picture. It is not therefore wonderful that we should find Him during a great part of the remainder of His Sermon giving precepts or counsels—in some cases the one, in other cases the other—which appear to be most directly addressed to those who are already entirely devoted to His service, and who have no other object in life than that of advancing His Kingdom. It is obvious, also, that some of these counsels are not to be taken in their fulness as imperative on those whose vocation is less high and less single. Hence we sometimes meet with difficulties, as if our Lord had been exaggerating when He enjoined on all Christians not to be solicitous for the morrow, or to think about food and raiment for themselves or their families. The truth is, that it is impossible to imagine in our Lord anything that approaches to an exaggeration, and that these counsels embody the highest and most important principles for those to whom they are directly addressed, while to others the same principles are applicable, though in a less direct degree, or only at certain times.

It must be remembered that, by a wonderful and most beautiful arrangement of God's providence over the works and actions of His Incarnate Son, our Lord's discourses and arguments—certainly those which have been handed down to us in the Gospels—were adapted in the first instance with the most perfect delicacy of adjustment, so to speak, to those to whom they were at the time and directly addressed, while at the same time they were so framed as to suit the needs and characters of the communities for whose direct benefit they were put on record by the several Evangelists, as well as those of the whole Church in subsequent ages, for whose use the Gospels have been preserved. The consideration, therefore, of the audience to which was addressed this part of the Sermon on the Mount on which we are now engaged, will help us very much to understand its drift, and we shall find that this consideration throws much additional light on the comparison which will hereafter come before us between the Sermon on the Mount, of which we are now speaking, and the Sermon on the Plain, of which we shall have to speak in a subsequent part of this work. The mass of the multitude to whom the Sermon on the Mount was delivered, was composed of persons who were already far advanced in the school of our Lord. The measure of their advance is that of the distance between the beginning of the teaching of St. John Baptist and our Lord on the one hand, which may be summed up in the words, 'Repent and do penance, for the Kingdom of Heaven is at hand,' and the Beatitudes on the other hand. Out of this great multitude our Lord had not yet selected the Twelve Apostles, but it is clear that there was already some kind of incipient organization among them, which, perhaps, but for the opposition against our Lord on the part of the authorities which became very pronounced soon after this time, might have ripened into something like that community of life which sprang up, as if by the necessity of a natural law, as soon as the Church was founded in Jerusalem on the Day of Pentecost. At all events, it may be assumed that there were large numbers among those to whom the precepts or counsels of which we are now about to speak were addressed, who were really called to spend their lives in the direct service and advancement of the Kingdom of Heaven and in the perfect practice of evangelical sanctity—or in the latter, when external circumstances or the will of God in their regard, did not permit of the former. They were to embrace directly and absolutely the service of the One Master—as directly and absolutely, to speak with perfect plainness, as those whose vocation is to the religious life, whether in its contemplative or active form, or in a form in which activity and contemplation are, as far as is possible, united, as in that close following of our Lord which is set before His disciples by St. Ignatius in the famous meditation of the 'Two Standards,' which, as we shall presently see, furnishes so marvellous a commentary on this passage of our Lord's Sermon.

Such persons are called, in the first instance, and as to the first step from which all others are to follow, to perfect evangelical poverty, at least in spirit, and if possible in act. The doctrine which is drawn out by St. Ignatius in the meditation to which we refer explains the reason on which this principle rests. The Saint shows how Lucifer, on the one hand, instructs his emissaries to endeavour to attach men to property, wealth, and worldly goods, in order to lead them on to the love of honour and the esteem of the world, and so to great pride, the certain and fruitful parent of iniquity of every kind. He shows also how our Lord, on the other hand, teaches those whom He sends to help men to their salvation to make them love poverty, in order to lead them to love contempt and worldly dishonour, and so to found themselves in true humility, from which the whole beautiful family of the Christian virtues will spring up. The attachment to wealth and property with which Satan desires to begin his work with men, is not that attachment which is in itself sinful, as when the goods which are desired and cherished are loved with an inordinate and engrossing love, or are to be acquired by injustice or fraud. In the same way, the love of poverty which it is the object of our Lord to instil is the love of the state and condition as such, and not merely detachment from possessions which cannot be held without sin. It is clear enough to any one who has the slightest practical acquaintance with the book of which we are speaking, that it would be simply absurd, at the stage of the Exercises at which this meditation is placed, to ask any one who is passing through them to make a choice between serving God and serving Satan—between keeping and breaking the law of God. The person who makes the meditation of the 'Two Standards' has made up his mind from the very beginning to serve God as the Master of his being, and also to follow our Lord's example; but he has to be instructed in the way in which our Lord and Satan respectively act, in leading men to good or to ill. Now it is obvious that a great number of the hearers of the Sermon on the Mount were just in the position which is supposed by St. Ignatius in those to whom the Exercise of the 'Two Standards' is proposed. They had already gone so far in the following of our Lord as to have left their homes, at least for a time, and thus to have abandoned their ordinary means of living; they were also united into some kind of organization, which would imply a common rule of life and a common fare. When we come to the Sermon on the Plain, which was delivered some months later than this time, we find our Lord speaking to His disciples as already poor, not only in spirit, and as exposed to hunger and thirst, and derision, and persecution. It would seem, then, that the lessons here given had taken effect upon a certain number of hearts—and surely, nothing can have been more fitting to nerve them to that abandonment of human cares and resources which is required for the adoption of such a manner of life than the considerations which are here crowded together in a few verses by our Lord, and on which we must endeavour to dwell shortly one by one.

Our Lord begins by connecting the counsels on which He is about to insist with the doctrine which has immediately preceded it, about the impossibility of double service. He had at first spoken simply of two masters in the abstract: He now specifies the two, the simultaneous service of which is impossible—that is, God and Mammon. He does not say Satan, or the Evil One, but Mammon, because, as it seems, the point on which He is insisting is the necessity of freedom from all care as to the common necessaries of life, which are provided for by money, and not simply the necessity of abstinence from sin. It is, then, the service of money, the care of the means of sustenance for our daily life, which He declares to be incompatible, in the case of those to whom He is speaking, with that single and perfect service of God to which He invites them, and which, a few verses later, He describes as the seeking the Kingdom of God—the entire devotion of the intelligence and the will and all the energies to the advancement of God's glory in every way in our power. This kind of service cannot be combined with even the ordinary natural attention to earthly cares which is not in itself blameworthy, and to which in a certain measure ordinary Christians are obliged. That this kind of service of Mammon is more directly meant by our Lord, is clear from the examples which He gives o being solicitous for food and raiment. The more absolute and entire service to Mammon which is paid by those who make the accumulation of wealth the great object of their existence, to the neglect of the eternal interests of their souls, of their duty to God, of justice and religion, is too far removed from the condition of those to whom this Sermon is addressed to need any special denunciation on our Lord's part. His argument is drawn from the simple principle of the incompatibility of the two services. Because you cannot serve God and Mammon, 'Therefore I say unto you, be not solicitous for your life, what you shall eat, nor for your body, what you shall put on.' To be so solicitous, then, is to seek to endeavour to serve God and Mammon at the same time, which He has declared to be impossible.

The same conclusion as to our Lord's meaning follows from the words with which this argument is confirmed. 'Is not the life more than the meat, and the body more than the raiment?' This can only mean, as it seems, something like this: You are the servants and the children of God, and therefore you must not be solicitous for lesser matters when He has already given you greater, in the gift of which, moreover, the promise of all that is necessary for the maintenance of what is so given is included. God cannot have given you your life, which is a very great gift, and yet dependent, according to the law of its nature, upon numberless and continual supplies, day after day, of external necessaries which are by no means in your own power, without, by this very arrangement, which makes you so dependent, implicitly promising you that you shall not lack what you so much want in this respect. The life is more than the meat, and therefore you may surely trust that the meat will follow the life. The body is more than the raiment, and therefore raiment will not be lacking to the body. Your life and your body you have once for all given you, although their sustentation is a gift continually new. Food and raiment are necessities to you which must be supplied, not by nature, but by Providence, the Providence of Him from Whom the other greater gifts have already proceeded. Here, again, as has been pointed out, it is not anything superfluous or ornamental, such as great wealth or splendid robes, or anything that may be dispensed with, for which we are urged to be entirely dependent on our Father, but simple food and raiment, without which our life cannot be maintained, nor our body sheltered from heat or cold.

The argument which is contained in these words of our Lord rests upon the character of God, Who must be too good and too wise to create us with so many needs and in a state of dependence so entire, unless He was also prepared to supply our needs as they occur, and to prevent us from suffering on account of our inability to furnish ourselves with what we require. If God, then, calls us to a work, or a condition of life in which we are shut out from taking even the ordinary precautions as to these matters, it is clear that He thereby pledges Himself that we shall not be left destitute because we have followed His call. Our Lord goes on to argue from the knowledge of God which we are all meant naturally to acquire from the creation around us, and which forbids us to think that it can be consistent with His character to allow us to want. 'Behold,' He says, 'the birds of the air, for they neither sow nor do they reap, nor gather into barns, and your Heavenly Father feedeth them. Are you not of much more value than they?' This is the true wonder of the visible universe, especially of the animated part of

God's works—the marvellous providence by which the daily needs of all the countless orders of living creatures are supplied. It is a marvel ever increasing, as our knowledge increases of their numbers, their wants, their habits, their relations to the climates under which they thrive, the parts of the world in which they are placed, and the manner in which their mutual relations and juxtaposition are arranged for them by the system of nature. Our Lord's words imply that an honest study of animated nature in this respect leads, of necessity and easily, to an intelligence of the immense care and forethought with which God has provided, as the Psalmist says, 'food for all flesh,' and thus opens to the Christian naturalist a path of study which he may pursue with the certainty of rich rewards both in the knowledge of what we call nature and in that of the goodness of God. And then, after this short reference to a line of study open to all, and which, as He implies, ought to be familiar to all, He urges an argument similar in force to that which He has already used about food and raiment. First He had said, God has given you life and body, will He not provide the lesser gifts of food and raiment? Now, He says, God cares for the birds of the air, and for all His creatures who have life, and are not you of much more value than they? He that feeds the young ravens, will He not take care to feed you?

Our Lord's next argument is one, the meaning of which is not so clear at first sight. It implies that the solicitude and anxiety against which He is warning those who belong to Him, and are engaged in His service and in the advancement of His Kingdom, are unadvisable on other grounds, that is, on the ground of their uselessness. 'And which of you,' He says, 'by taking thought, can add to his stature one cubit?' That is, there are certain things which are altogether beyond your means of provision, and which you cannot achieve however much solicitude you may use. Such is the stature to which your bodies grow—you cannot add to it, whatever you do. In another passage, much later in His Public Life, where the same image as well as a great part of this same context is repeated,[1] our Lord has been speaking of the foolishness of providing for many years of life, after the example of the Rich Man in the Parable, when death may be at hand at any moment, to defeat all our arrangements. This, then, is another thing which is altogether beyond our reach—to add a day to the life which God has allotted to us. The argument against solicitude for food and raiment which is drawn from such truths as these, seems to rest on the fact that there are so many elements in our daily life and its continuance which are altogether beyond our own power, that we should be most miserable, and, indeed, altogether unprovided for, if we had not our Father in Heaven to watch over us, and that therefore, when we are devoted to His service, it is only reasonable and natural that we should leave to Him the entire care of ourselves. And, if we remember that these words are primarily addressed, in the passage in St. Luke as well as in this place, to those who are called to occupy themselves simply in the advancement of God's Kingdom, or to incur the risk of temporal losses for its sake, we may understand them as signifying that the care of all material and temporal matters relating to such service of God is so entirely taken by Him into His own hands, that any human anxiety and solicitude on such heads will fail and turn out as useless as if a man were to sit down and spend hours in considering how he might make himself taller or shorter. That is, there are certain

[1] St. Luke xii. 22, seq.

things as to which care and solicitude are profitable, and certain other things as to which they are useless. In the case of ordinary men, it is of some use to provide for food and raiment, it is of no use at all to be solicitous about making themselves taller or shorter. In the first case, God blesses the care and forethought, for they are means which He desires men to use in such cases, when they are not prevented by higher duties. It is right to use such means, simply because He has so appointed. But with you, our Lord seems to say to His disciples, even this care is taken out of your hands, and therefore any solicitude which you may expend upon it will be as utterly useless as that which might be foolishly wasted upon endeavours to alter your stature. And indeed it is frequently found in enterprizes for God, in the founding of new works for His glory, in missionary undertakings, and the like, that He absolutely rejects, by some providential stroke, any provision of human resources which may have been made, as David would not have the armour of Saul when he was to go forth and do battle against Goliath in the name of the Lord of hosts.

Our Lord now goes on to argue against the solicitude for raiment in the same way as against anxiety as to food. 'For raiment why are you solicitous? Consider the lilies of the field, how they grow; they labour not, neither do they spin, but I say unto you that not even Solomon in all his glory was arrayed as one of these.' For there is a beauty about flowers and other such works of God which no loom on earth can rival, just as all the mechanical skill in the world is surpassed by the wisdom and power which are shown in the birds, fishes, or insects. 'And if the grass of the field, which is to-day, and to-morrow is cast into the oven, God doth so clothe, how much more you, O ye of little faith!' The argument is exactly the same as that which has been already adduced as to food, from the care which God takes of the birds of the air. It implies that those who are called to live entirely for the work of God's Kingdom are under a special Providence, beyond that which takes care of mankind in general. They are exempted even from the ordinary solicitudes of human life, and what would be in others idleness and a neglect of labouring, according to the common lot of mankind, for their daily bread, is in them a duty imposed upon them, by their obligation of attending to the one end to which they are devoted, and also by the obligation of relying entirely on God for these material things. The more entirely does a man give himself to the advancement of God's glory in some apostolical vocation, or to communion with God in contemplation, like the early Fathers of the desert, or the contemplative Orders which inherit their position and work in the Church, the more is he bound absolutely to trust himself to the care of his Father in Heaven for all secondary matters.

In the next words, our Lord repeats His precept, in order to enforce it the more urgently. 'Be not therefore solicitous, saying, what shall we eat, or what shall we drink, or wherewith shall we be clothed?' And He adds two more reasons for this freedom from solicitude to which He attaches so much importance as one of the chief foundations of perfection in His service. The first of these reasons is that such solicitude is the natural badge of heathenism. 'For after all these things do the heathens seek.' Whatever may be the form of false religion under which men live, it is a matter of certainty that it will teach them that they must rely on themselves and not on God for the needs of their daily life. It is the characteristic of all false religions, as also of all imperfect forms of Christianity, to represent God as less loving and fatherly than He is. Heathens may be generally described in the words of St. Paul, as having no hope and being without God in the world. It is not wonderful that under such a belief as to God, the heathen should be anxious as to food and raiment, and the ordinary necessaries of life. But as Christians live in the light of truth, and especially of the truths which relate to God as our Creator, our Provider, our Redeemer, it is incumbent on them to show by their practical confidence in God the difference between their religion and their hope and the religion and the hope of the heathen. And lastly, our Lord argues from the truth that God, Who knows all things, and watches with a most tender care over all His creatures, so that not a sparrow falls to the ground without Him,[2] knows that His children have need of all these things. 'For your Father knoweth that you have need of all these things.' It is enough that He knows it—for nothing more is required to move His Fatherly Heart, as our Blessed Lady was content to bring the needs of the bridegroom and bride at Cana before our Lord, saying simply, 'they have no wine,' and Martha and Mary thought it enough, instead of any formal request, to send to our Lord the message that 'he whom Thou lovest is sick.' In the case before us, our Lord does not even bid us make known our wants, in the way in which they are made known to God in prayer. He speaks as if even prayer, such as that of our Lady and of the sisters of Lazarus, were superfluous. Not that He would forbid us to pray, but that He wishes so much to insist on the truth that God has charged Himself with the care of all these things.

Our Lord's next words seem to express an inference drawn from the whole chain of arguments which He has adduced, but chiefly from God's knowledge of our

[2] St. Matt. x. 29.

needs, which was last spoken of. 'Seek ye therefore first the Kingdom of God and His justice, and all these things shall be added unto you.' The Kingdom of God is in general the glory of God in His Church, and thus under this head we may include all the work of the vocations of those who are His ministers or servants in any special way, whether as teachers, or preachers, or priests, or as having any share in the various branches of the Apostolic office, or the doctorate, as missionaries to the heathen, or administrators of the Church's organization, or founders, rulers, or members of religious orders, and the like, or to those silent but mighty workers for the common good who are withdrawn altogether from contact with the world in order to commune with Him in prayer and contemplation. All such vocations are specially devoted to the preservation, working, or advancement of the Kingdom of God, in its most literal and technical sense. There is, of course, a wider and larger sense, such as that in which all spiritual good in ourselves and others comes under the name of God's Kingdom, and thus we glide insensibly into the other thought, which our Lord subjoins, when He adds, 'and His justice'—that is, the practice of virtue of every kind, all which is so much service done to God. Thus He addresses His hearers as having this one special commission received for their one Master, this one single all-engrossing service to pay to Him—the advancement of His Kingdom and His Justice. And of these He requires that their whole thoughts and cares and time are to be given up to this. As the merchant wakes up, day after day, to occupy himself and all his energies on the one object of multiplying his store, investing his funds with profit, using every opportunity which may occur, and contriving every possible scheme for turning his money to account; or as the ambitious man neglects the care of his home, or of his estate, or the attractions of society and pleasure, in order to work simply for his own political advancement and aggrandizement—so our Lord would have those who have the vócation of which we are speaking neglect everything else, in order to give their whole minds and hearts and energies to the furtherance of God's Kingdom. And then He promises them that if they do this, all the temporal means which they require for the support of their daily life will be added to them—that is, God will provide them.

Lastly, as if to point this instruction in the most practical way, and to show how extreme and rigorous He desires our diligence to be, not to attend to any but the one business before us, He adds His famous words about to-morrow, which contain the closing argument which He adduces on this head: 'Be not therefore solicitous for to-morrow'—not even for the immediately urgent needs which are all but present are we to divert our attention from the work of to-day,—'for the morrow will be solicitous for itself.' It will have its own cares, and you will have, when the time comes, the grace to cope with those cares which is not given to you now. 'Sufficient for the day is the evil thereof.' You have enough in the evil with which you have to contend to-day to engage all your strength; you must, as it were, take your enemies in hand one after another, as they come to meet you, without any doubt that the strength required for each day will be supplied you by your Father.

We may return in the next chapter to some of the thoughts which are suggested by the particular arguments here adduced by our Blessed Lord. For the present it is enough to dwell on the general beauty of the whole of the passage. If we are to measure the importance in our Lord's mind of a precept or command by the pains to which He seems to put Himself to urge it upon our attention, we must see in this counsel of absolute confidence in God on the part of those who are engaged in work for His glory, one of the heads of teaching which must have been most dear to Him. We seldom find Him using so many reasons for the same conclusion. It may be that this was, at the time, the most difficult step onward in the path of His service which was to be taken by those who had already advanced far, and of whom He was about to ask still more. It may be that, looking on beyond these through the Christian centuries, He saw how many of the spiritual glories of His Church required this confidence and detachment, issuing in the renunciation of earthly goods and the practice of evangelical poverty enforced by vow, as their necessary foundation. It may be that He saw how much of the failure of the work which He desired to see carried out in the world would have to be traced to pusillanimity and cowardice in this respect, tying the hands of God by the pettiness of human and worldly considerations, and ruining the prospects of His greater glory. It may be that in His tender condescension for our weakness in this matter, He lavished reason after reason to convince us, and poured Himself forth about the lovingness and bountifulness of His Father's providence, a subject on which His Heart always dwelt with immense gratitude—all the more as mankind in general, who are endowed with intelligence concerning God's marvels in His Creation and Providence, in order, among other reasons, that they may praise Him for them in the name of all the universe, were to be so niggardly in their thankfulness to Him. For whatever reason, it is clear that He considers this precept of confidence as most essential to the foundation of the great work for which

He looked to His Church and to the most chosen and favoured among His children.

It is also certain that, great as is the importance in the spiritual order of absolute detachment from worldly cares, and of the practice, as well as the spirit, of poverty, which, among other things, so certainly generates that joyous childlike confidence in God which is the condition of the greatest achievements for His glory, still the precept which we are now considering extends beyond the actual words of our Lord to many other subjects which are included in them in principle. Solicitude for food and raiment is the simplest and most natural result of our sense of our own extreme dependence on external things and indigence of them. But this precept is addressed to all who have any great work to do for God in any way. All such works begin from a small seed, generally with much opposition and difficulty, and require, above all things, faith and confidence in God, like that for the want of which our Lord here upbraids His disciples, as He afterwards upbraided them when they woke Him up in fear when the ship was covered by the waves, and as, on another occasion, on the same Lake of Galilee, He reproached St. Peter when he began to fear and so to sink in his attempt to walk on the waters. The works which have to be done for God in His Church are marvellous and multitudinous in their variety—works of zeal, works of charity, corporal and spiritual, the housing of orphans, the founding of schools or colleges for the ignorant, the building of churches or hospitals, or convents and monasteries to be the homes of contemplative souls, the founding or reforming of orders, the conversion of heathen nations, and the furnishing fresh supplies of missionaries. No doubt the rich and great of this world are moved by God to assist in such works, and many of them have often been the fruit of the beneficence of Popes or prelates, employing for the service of God the revenues of the Church herself. But in general these are but the secondary instruments whom God employs, and the originators of these mighty works, which require resources far beyond the food and raiment of which our Lord directly speaks, have been the poorest of the poor, or rather men and women who begin by making themselves altogether poor before such undertakings are committed to them. All such persons must begin by an absolute confidence in God for the supply of the means which are necessary for the accomplishment of their several enterprizes. They must look to Him for the men, and the learning, and the influence, and the opportunities, and the sanction of authority, as well as for the material means, of which they begin by being entirely destitute. Their life is consequently a continual exercise of this heroic confidence; time after time they have to see their hopes fail, their resources dry up, their friends abandon them, their schemes opposed and laughed at, their characters assailed, their persons ill-treated, and time after time deliverance and succour, and new friends and companions and protectors in their work, spring up at their side, just as their hopes have seemed most sorely disappointed. It would be difficult to find, in all the variety of great works for God, of which the histories of the saints are the chronicles, any considerable number that have been begun except in indigence, and that have not had to make their way against opposition from good persons.

This may suffice for the present as to the extent of the precept which is here given to those who have any special work for God committed to them. It must, however, be remarked, that the principle which is here urged by our Lord upon such persons in particular cannot be without its application to others also, to whom our Lord's words may not be so directly addressed, but whose case falls under them when it is considered in the light of other precepts also, which will be seen to modify or explain this. Thus, although it cannot be said that all Christians, of whatever vocation and position, are bound by these words to take no more thought for food and raiment, and other things necessary for themselves and their families, than the birds of the air or the flowers of the field, so neither can it be said that any class of Christians are exempt from the law which forbids overanxiety as to these things, and which enjoins the most absolute confidence in God as our Father.

In the first place, it is clear that our Lord cannot mean to condemn labour or ordinary care for the support of life in those whose vocation does not exact of them the entire devotion of their lives to spiritual things. It is certain that St. Paul laboured with his own hands for his support, and for that of his companions, on his Apostolic journeys, and that it is one of the great glories of the Church to have made labour and industry of every kind honourable instead of disgraceful, as was the case under the corrupt civilization of the Roman Empire. St. Paul did this, as he explains, in his First Epistle to the Corinthians, not so much from necessity, or because he had not a right, like the other Apostles, to 'live by the Gospel,' but as a matter of principle and perfection, that he might, as it were, give something of his own to God, beyond that which was enjoined upon him by his Apostolical office. Our Lord has not repealed the original sentence passed on Adam after the Fall, by which he was to eat his bread in toil and in the sweat of his brow. Solomon bids the sluggard go and study the industry of the ant,[3] just as our Lord here bids us study

[3] Prov. vi. 6.

the confidence of the birds. There have been heretics in the history of the Church who have taken these words as literally obligatory on all, and the Fathers have written against them.[4] St. Paul had frequently to contend with the spirit of idleness among his heathen converts, and he says to the Thessalonians, 'If any man will not work, neither let him eat.'[5] It is the vocation of the greater part of mankind to labour for their own sustenance and that of their own families, and even the comparatively small class in all communities who have superabundant wealth and possessions are not therefore exempted from the law of labour in their own way, for the administration of large estates, and the management of property, involves work, and it is on such persons that in all healthy commonwealths the enormous burthen of the conduct of public affairs is imposed. All such men, like those whose career lies in the liberal professions, or in the pursuits of commerce, trade, and the like, are required to give a certain amount of care, attention, and diligence, which more or less occupies a great part of the time at their command, to the duties of their station or calling, and these duties cannot be well discharged without a thoughtful provision as to coming wants and the resources necessary to meet them. In this sense, therefore, our Lord, Who is the author and founder of society, cannot forbid such provision.

What our Lord does forbid, as unworthy of the children of our Heavenly Father and the servants of the one Master, is expressed by the word solicitude. That is, He forbids anxiety, and disturbance of mind, He forbids all diffidence and unfaithful doubting about the results of our exertions, when we have done what we can, as if God were not ready to prosper them, or as if,

---

[4] The Euchitæ. See S. Aug. *De Operibus Monachorum.*
[5] 2 Thess. iii. 10.

if it pleases Him that they should fail, there were not in His power other ways of providing for us. He forbids superfluous care and wearisome toil over what is, after all, a secondary matter, and that intense strain of anxiety about temporal affairs which engrosses all the thoughts and prevents the heart from rising to higher things. In the parable of the Sower, He puts as one of the great principal causes why His Divine Word is barren in the soul, that the cares of this world, and the deceitfulness of riches, choke the Word, and it becomes unfruitful. St. Paul bids the Philippians, 'Be nothing solicitous, but in everything, by prayer and supplication, with thanksgiving, let your petitions be made unto God'[6]—as if God would not hear our prayers unless they were made in a cheerful and hopeful spirit. All overstrained anxiety and doubt as to the issue of our work is also a result of diffidence in God as our Father, and implies disobedience to the precept, 'Cast thy care upon the Lord, and He shall sustain thee.'[7] The engrossing nature of earthly cares is described by St. Paul, when he says that, 'They that will become rich fall into temptation, and into the snares of the devil, and into many unprofitable and hurtful desires, which drown men into destruction and perdition.'[8] When the necessary attention which we pay to earthly affairs leads on to the greed for money, for having a great provision laid up beforehand, when it takes away the mind's peace, and prevents our turning easily to devotion or to recreation when the time for toil is over, it is certainly excessive and mischievous, hostile to our spiritual good, and likely to make us servants of the world rather than servants of God.

In truth, no where in a Christian country ought we to have far to go in order to find persons whose life is one of daily toil, who do not lay by much in store, who

[6] Philipp. iv. 6.   [7] Psalm liv. 23.   [8] 1 Tim. vi. 9.

have never very much in hand beyond what is required for their immediate needs, and who are yet free from anxiety, cheerful, hopeful, confident in Providence. Such is the state of many thousands of poor in Christian countries, who live from week to week, or month to month, perhaps with some little fund to fall back on in a savings bank, but certainly without all that provision for the very possible contingencies of bad times, short work, sickness, old age, or unforeseen calamities, which is thought necessary in higher classes of society. They marry when they have a fair prospect of work, but their settlements are not very substantial, they have large and flourishing families of beautiful and healthy children, for whose clothing and good schooling they trust to Providence without being disappointed. They help one another with a readiness and largeness of charity, in comparison with their means, which put to shame even pious persons of higher classes. The possibilities of the future may be black, but they do not cause them much anxiety. In such populations we see a practical comment on these words of our Lord forbidding overdue solicitude—they bear witness to this golden precept of confidence in God, in a manner not altogether unlike that in which the countless children of St. Francis and other religious founders bear witness to the same. On the other hand, when the picture is changed, when the practical heathenism of over-anxiety about temporal matters—to the uncertainty of which the experience of every human being witnesses—pervades all classes and destroys their trust in their Father, any Christian thinker will see abundance of reason for mourning over his fellow-men, and for recognizing the ineffable wisdom and tenderness for our happiness which are shown in this precept of our Lord. When the spirit of greed, of anxiety, of hoarding, descends from the higher classes to the lower, then indeed a Christian country has a plague ravaging its people, which may be as fatal as the Black Death itself. Piety dies out with confidence in God, the bright sunny joyousness which is the charm of peasant life is withered up. The underground agitator against society and religion finds his converts ready to his hands. Vice runs riot among the unmarried, who are afraid of the expense of marriage, or it ruins, in a still more loathsome form, the fruitfulness of marriage itself. These are but specimens, in the political and social order, of a whole multitude of miserable results which illustrate but too faithfully the maxim of the Apostle, that the love of money is the root of all evil. Alas! it is sometimes not the peasant only, but the pastor of the peasant, who is infected by the plague of over-anxiety for worldly means. The priest is tempted to save, and he leaves behind him a store of hoarded wealth which entails upon his next of kin a heritage of misery. Or, as sometimes happens, the work of God is hindered because the ministers of the altar are fearful that their means of support may be interfered with. The evil of over-anxiety takes a thousand forms, and in all of them it works "to the lesser glory of God." There must not be too many churches, or too many schools, or too many convents, or too many Colleges—the advancement of religion must be sacrificed to selfish fears. Confidence in God's Providence is the very foundation of the temper of God's children, and when it is once lost, there is no misery into which they may not be led.

What has now been said enables us to sum up the teaching of our Lord in this great passage, and to explain certain common difficulties, already referred to, which may arise as to its right interpretation. The chief of these difficulties is, of course, that which concerns the character of the teaching here conveyed—

whether we are to consider it as conveying precepts, or counsels, as it is called, of perfection? In answer to this, it is obvious to reply, in the first place, that there are certain injunctions in this passage which no one can suppose to be simply counsels, which we are at liberty to follow if we choose or not to follow. No one can be exempt from the command to serve only the one Master —no one can be at liberty to choose between the service of God and the service of mammon. In the same way, when our Lord goes on in the following verses to say that we are to seek first the Kingdom of God and His justice, it is impossible to suppose that He is giving a counsel and not a precept. The truth is, that the principle of the service which we owe to God as our one Master, which is founded on our relation to Him as His creatures, is the basis of the whole passage, and it is only when that service makes it our duty to care, to a certain extent, about earthly matters, such as food and raiment, that we are exempt from the precept which binds others, to abandon the care of all things to Him. What has been said in the few last paragraphs is enough to show, that even when we are in such a position, by the arrangements of His providence, as to have a geeat many obligations of a temporal kind laid upon us, we are still under the law which forbids all solicitude and anxiety, such as interfere with the service to Him and the confidence in Him which are of necessity in His true children. But after this has been considered, and the universal obligation of the principle here laid down has been secured, it is also clear that the strict precept about taking no care about temporal matters, is in some cases a precept, and in others a counsel, or rather a precept the principle of which but not the letter is obligatory. It is a precept on all those who are called to the special Apostolical vocation, or to the entire service of God in prayer and communion with Him which is the essence of the contemplative life, and the precept applies to all those to whom God commits any great work in His Church, as to which the very fact of His so committing it to them is a kind of assurance that He takes on Himself to find the means for what He has enjoined. Such persons are put by Him on the footing of children, who have a message to deliver or a special work to do, as to which He desires to charge His special providence, and nothing else.

But it would be a great mistake to think that such persons alone are under the obligation of this precept. The obligation may come home to any one in any vocation at certain times—for we are all God's children, we are all bound to serve the one Master, and we are all liable to be called on to brave any risk or apparent danger in His service. In a great kingdom, the actual burthen of risking their lives in military service falls on certain persons alone in ordinary times, but there may be seasons of danger when all citizens are bound to come forward, to leave their trades or their professions or their peaceful homes, and place themselves under arms for the safety of the common country. A call of this kind may come home to any one in the course of an ordinary life—and it is not wonderful if the service of the great King should at certain times be as pressing in its exactions as the interest or the safety of a country or a city. God has a right to the lives of us all—it would not be too much for Him to require that all Christians should be called on, in the course of their trial, to bear witness to their faith at the risk of all that is dear to them, or of life itself. He laid that burthen largely on the first generations of His Church in the Roman Empire—He has laid it largely on whole communities, from time to time, as in the case of the

Japanese Church. It is, therefore, quite possible that this precept about the disregard of all earthly matters, which is conveyed in principle in what is here said about food and raiment, may be brought home as of obligation to any Christian under some particular circumstances of his life. One very frequent case is that of persons whose earthly means of support are in some way or other connected with danger to their souls. It may seem hard for them to have to go forth and sacrifice everything for the safety of virtue, of purity, perhaps, or honesty, but then the command urges them, and God charges Himself with the care of all things that are necessary for them. In the same way persons may find that, if they are to abandon some course of sin, which involves some evil company or unlawful friendship, they may have to think what they shall eat or drink or wherewith they shall be clothed, but in spite of this, they must, at the risk of salvation, follow their conscience and break off all that endangers their soul. And again, a very common case is that of persons on whom the light of truth has dawned, showing them the falsehood of some pretended form of religion, of some sham Church or heretical communion, in which, it may be, they have spent the greater part of their lives, whose bread they are eating, and on their connection with which their whole social position, or even their livelihood, depends. In such cases the sacrifice which becomes of obligation is often very far more painful than that of money or means of sustenance —it is the separation from home and friends, from husband or children, from scenes of usefulness which God seems to have prospered, from all things around which the tenderest and noblest affections of which our nature is capable can entwine themselves. But in all such cases the duty of obeying the one Master, of seeking first the Kingdom of God and His justice, and of neglecting all earthly considerations, because peremptory and exclusive. Our Lord's words seem to lay the burthen on us as gently and as sweetly as the nature of the case permits. He knew what was in store for those whom He was inviting to a close following of Himself. He could not, as yet, speak to them of His Cross—and thus it seems to be that that great constraining argument is wanting in these exhortations to the utter singleness of service which He here requires. But He supplies the force which is thus absent by the truth on which His Sacred Heart so much loved to dwell—that of the ineffable tenderness and carefulness of His Father over all His creatures, and much more over such of His children as might be called on to expose themselves to any insecurity or danger for His sake. For those who have once learnt to trust themselves absolutely to the care of God, and to seek simply and singly what is for the service of His Kingdom, would be prepared, when the time of need came, not only to be without provision of food or raiment, but to brave the whole fury of the world and to undergo prisons and tortures and death itself in their witness to His truth.

CHAPTER VIII.

The day and its evil.

St. Matt. vi. 34; *Vita Vitæ Nostræ*, § 33.

THE last sentences of the passage on which we have been commenting may be considered separately, as urging on the disciples of our Lord, and on those who have the same great vocation with them, to whatever extent they may share it, as well as on those on whom may at any time fall the duty of a great sacrifice for God, certain great principles which, when unfolded in meditation, will be found very pregnant indeed with spiritual instruction. It is one thing not to be solicitous about food and raiment and such temporal matters, and another to seek with all our heart the kingdom and the justice of God. It is clear, however, that we are right in considering that our Lord means to point out that the solicitude against which He here warns us is a great impediment to the fulfilment of the precept which follows about advancing the Kingdom of God with all our might. And this is confirmed by the manner in which He returns to the negative precept against solicitude, after He has laid on us the positive precept about seeking the Kingdom of God. For He goes on to say that we are not even to think or be solicitous for the morrow. It has been pointed out earlier in this work, that this whole passage may be considered as furnishing a sort of tacit commentary on, and explanation of, the prayer which our Lord had taught His disciples. It is true that it begins with setting God before us as a Master rather than as a Father—but, as has already been explained, it is in that light that we are to regard God in all that relates to our service to Him, which is nothing more nor less than that laying up treasure in Heaven with which this passage begins. Soon enough does our Lord come to the idea of God as our Father —and we are thus taught that God is a Master Who is a Father, and a Father Who is a Master. But the absolute dominion and ownership of God is the principle on which the whole train of thought is founded. It is this principle and foundation, as St. Ignatius calls it, which has made so many saints and inspired so many wonderful efforts for the glory of God. That the saints are comparatively few, and that so many undertakings which concern so highly the glory of God remain unattempted or unaccomplished, can only be accounted for by the fact that there are few souls in which this Divine seed of truth becomes fruitful and multiplies itself a hundred-fold. Another great Saint has said, that with twelve truly detached men he could convert the world. And yet, after all, these words of our Lord about the Kingdom of God and His justice do but express the true and lawful direction in which all our aims and desires and projects and labours should be addressed. If He had not said what He has, the duty of our single devotion of ourselves to God's service in the utmost measure of which we are capable would arise from the relation itself in which we stand to God, and the truth that there is nothing else that is worth labouring for or thinking of is founded on the very constitution of our nature.

Thus, to return to the illustration of this passage from the order and substance of the petitions of the Lord's Prayer, it has often been noticed how the first things that we are told to ask belong entirely to the interests, so to speak, of God—to the sanctification of His name, to the coming of His Kingdom, to the perfect performance and accomplishment of His will. It is only after this that we are told to ask, not for all that we may ever want on earth, but simply for the supply of our needs for the present day. Here we have a very practical commentary on the words before us, in which we are exhorted not to be solicitous for food or raiment, or for the morrow. The next prayer which our Lord bids us make, is for the forgiveness of our trespasses, and this seems to be illustrated by the precept which immediately follows on that of which we are speaking—the precept not to judge others, which is enforced by the declaration that as we deal with others in this respect, so will God deal with us, and by the motive which is assigned—that we are not to judge, in order that we may not be judged. And the final petitions of the prayer, in which we are to beg that we may not be led into temptation, but delivered from the evil, seem to be referred to here in the warnings against solicitude as to temporal things, which, according to the doctrine of St. Ignatius, may easily lead us into all evil, and in the words of which we are now to speak, in which our Lord assigns as a reason against solicitude for the morrow, that sufficient unto the day is its own evil. It would seem as if our Lord meant us to understand that anything which is to us an object of great care and anxiety belongs to the category of evil—and we shall have to explain this truth when we come to speak more particularly of the 'evil of the day' of which our Lord speaks. It is clear that the point at which our Lord is, as it were, labouring throughout the whole passage is to induce us all, but more especially all those who have the high vocation to work directly in the advancement and the building up of His Kingdom or to suffer anything for it, to commit ourselves fully and unreservedly to our Father's care, while we are labouring simply and singly for His interests. His argument seems so perfectly reasonable as not to demand of us any extraordinary venture or boldness of faith, at least when the character of our Father is taken into consideration. A little further on, when our Lord is speaking of prayer, a duty so kindred to that of childlike confidence, He argues from the tenderness and bountifulness which might be expected in an earthly father of whom his children might ask bread. It would be unnatural for such a person to give them a stone instead of bread. So, He says, we may be sure that our Father will hear our prayers, for He surpasses all other fathers in the infinite measure of His goodness as also in that of His power. The same ground of reason, then, exists in the present case. If a son were set to work hard, or expose himself to danger or hardships, for some purpose in which the interests of an earthly father were engaged, it would be unnatural for the father not to supply him with all the necessaries of life and all that his well-being required. So, then, we must trust our Heavenly Father to look after all that we want, while we abandon the thought of everything else in order to labour unreservedly in His service.

When our Lord goes on to say that if we seek first the Kingdom of God and His justice, all these temporal things shall be added to us, He speaks in that impersonal way which He frequently uses when He is desirous of signifying the action of His Father in His providence. The words also seem to contain a reference to the many various ways in which that Providence works in the supplying of the needs of His creatures. Sometimes His action seems more immediate than in other cases. The work of nature is, in one sense, more directly the action of God than when He uses human means, or even when He works through the angels. The feeding of the birds of the air and the clothing of the flowers is the work of nature. And very beautiful indeed are the contrivances and arrangements of nature and her Maker for these purposes. The necessities of the servants and the children of God, whether for the maintenance of their lives or the supply of their homes and raiment and other manifold wants, from which they are not exempted in order that God may show His Fatherly care in providing them, are usually supplied by men like themselves, into whose hearts God has put it to serve Him in this way, and so to earn the blessing which He will give them in return. It is the same with the material means which His servants require in order to carry out the great works for His glory which they conceive under the guidance of the Holy Ghost, and again with the protection from many dangers which naturally confront them in their work. When human means fail, God can use His angels for the protection and defence of His servants, and He can supply their wants when He so wills in a miraculous manner. And the history of any great servant of His, or of any great work carried out for His service, is usually illuminated here and there, if not constantly, by the heavenly splendour of such interpositions. All this variety of action on the part of Providence, ordinary and extraordinary, the supplying of the needs of the saints from a thousand different sources, often those which seem to be most unlikely, seems to be denoted by the words chosen by our Lord, 'All these things shall be added to you.'

In the passage which immediately follows, 'Be not therefore solicitous for the morrow,' the doctrine of confidence in God is urged in a closer and more stringent way than before. We might be told in general to refrain from all solicitude, and yet it might seem that the needs of the morrow are so present that ordinary Christian prudence might require that they at least should be attended to. At the same time, these words suggest another great truth, of immense importance in the spiritual life. There are numberless matters, more momentous than food and raiment, which occupy our minds and make us anxious day after day, and our Lord seems now to include even these under the class of subjects to which His precept against solicitude is to extend. To-morrow is always an uncertain, yet imminent, future, for which we have to provide. And yet we are now warned not to be solicitous about it, and a strong reason is added why we must not be so. The morrow is to be solicitous about its own concerns, and the present day has enough for its cares in its own evil. A whole Christian philosophy of life is contained in these simple words, and we must now endeavour to draw out the chief truths on which that Divine philosophy rests.

The first truth to which these words direct our thoughts is this—that by the merciful arrangement of God's providence in the system of the universe in which we live, our life, short as it is, is not practically continuous and unbroken in its monotony. It is certain that we could not bear its strain if it were so. Neither our mental faculties nor our bodily forces could abide a life without a break for many days together. In His immense tenderness for our extreme weakness, God has divided our life into short spaces and intervals, by means of which day succeeds to night, rest follows on work, and the calm and inaction of sleep—in itself a sort of weakness and imperfection—relieve our hours of energy and activity. Our life itself is a continual growth or decay, season succeeds to season in the year, and the alternation of light and darkness is the law of the globe on which we have to spend our time of probation. This is not the rule of the whole universe. The heavenly bodies neither know nor require rest—their service to the law of their creation is as ceaseless as the homage of the glorious and mighty spirits before the throne of God, who know no rest day or night from worshipping Him and singing His praises, while at the same time they are for ever unweariedly carrying out His behests over the whole universe. Purgatory, Hell, and the great forces of the physical world, never sleep—day and night are the same to the eternal mountains, the wandering winds, the restless sea. But when we come to animal life on the earth, we find that the alternations of day and night, together with the rest which they seem to provide for, become necessities, on account of the incapacity of the higher creatures to dispense with them. And among all these creatures, no one shows his need of continual restoration and of constant supplies of sustaining power more than man. The life of the infant is almost a continual sleep, broken at intervals for the purpose of taking food. But at the best time of our lives, when we are most strong and vigorous, we can never bear the fatigue of many hours of continuous exertion, whether of body or mind, without rest, and our life itself breaks down if it is not supported by constant supplies of food. We are like plants that cannot rise, according to the instinct of our nature, towards Heaven, without something to lean upon and to cling to, or like children that cannot run many paces from their nurses' arms without falling.

God has provided for this utter feebleness of our nature, which extends to our intellectual energies as well as to our physical powers, by breaking up our life into days and nights, and laying upon us not more than the wear and tear of a few hours at a time. He intends us to get through and to bear and to achieve a great deal in the course of our lives, but we can only do this on the condition of taking but a little at a time of the work of brain and sinew, the energy of the mind, the strain of the will. Our life is broken up, so to speak, into a number of little lives. Nothing is so like to a new birth as the awakening which begins our day—it is the opening of a new page, on which as yet nothing has been written, and which it rests with us to make the record of the service of God and the faithful use of His grace, or that of neglected opportunities and violated obligations. We come as from another world to the new hours which lie before us. Nothing is so like death as the sleep which steals over us at night, wrapping us up in forgetfulness and weakness, protecting us by the cloak of darkness which is flung over the world, relaxing all the springs of our fitful activity, in order to refresh us and strengthen us for the trials and toils which are to meet us when we wake. Such is the sweet providence of God, hushing to rest after a few hours the bustle, the stir, the agitation, the strife and strain, of which human life is made up. The saints sometimes regret the necessity of submitting to this law of nature, which forces repose and inaction on the hearts which are burning with the love of God, and which would gladly never rest from thinking of Him and working for His glory. But they must obey in their way the common doom, and wait, for continued and unbroken activity in loving Him intelligently, for the eternal day of Heaven when night shall be no more. Alas! it is not only the service of the saints and the friends of God that is interrupted by night and the necessity of rest—if it were not for this providential break, it may well be thought that the world would become altogether intolerable in the eyes of its Maker, on account of the unceasing

The day and its evil. 155

offences against Him, the violences, the cruelties, the injustices, the miseries of every sort, moral and physical, which are at all events hindered and cut short by the close of day. As the sea and the mountains cut off the continuity of the land, and so provide many a home for liberty, for the exile and the oppressed, which would otherwise be denied them, so does night shield the weak from their persecutors and hamper the grinding tyranny of many cruel masters of mankind.

This intermittent life, to which man is made subject by the law of His Maker, is nevertheless continuous in a most true sense. We do not truly wake up to new scenes and a new phase of existence, morning after morning. We find ourselves where we were before we closed our eyes, with the same duties, the same dangers, the same temptations, the same sorrows and cares. But now we come to the next truth to which our Lord seems to wish to call our attention in the passage of which we are speaking. He says, 'Sufficient unto the day is the evil thereof.' Perhaps He had in His mind the complaint of the patriarch Jacob, 'that the days of his pilgrimage had been few and evil,'[1] and this is not the only passage in Sacred Scripture in which the days of life are spoken of as evil. The word which our Lord uses is not simply evil in the abstract or concrete, but the substantive word evil, evilness, or evilhood. That is, our life is full of what has the character of evil, or tends to evil, or comes from evil, or may be called evil, in some of the various senses of which the epithet is capable. It seems here to mean especially all that can be the subject of care and anxiety, of that solicitude against which this whole passage warns us. In this way it may be understood as signifying every kind of danger or trouble, from the darkest moral peril to the merely

[1] Genesis xlvii. 9.

physical causes of weariness and care. Our Lord does not hide from us this aspect of human life, though of course He would not have us forget, on the other hand, that life is full of good, and of opportunities, which the angels and saints might gladly welcome, for the joyous service of God and for the acquirement of merit, the heaping up of that treasure in Heaven of which He has been speaking. But here His direct subject is the carefulness and anxiety of which our life must ever be full as long as we are in our present state. It is full of moral 'evilness,' on account of our interior derangement, of the wiles of our enemies, and of the traitorousness of our own hearts, on account of the principles and dominant maxims of the world in which we live, of the power of bad habits, of the influence of evil examples, of our own cowardice and feebleness in good of every kind. We have a great many high duties to perform as Christians, for we have to worship God and to keep His law, to honour the saints and angels, to labour for the Church, at least in prayer, for the Holy Souls, for the conversion of sinners, for the perfection of the just, for the advancement of the boundaries of the earthly kingdom of our Lord. We have our consciences to watch over and to purify, our spiritual strength to renovate, our past sins to expiate, our coming death and future eternity to prepare for. We have the duties of our state to discharge, and to help our neighbour in charity and love according to our position and opportunities. We have to deal with enemies and opponents, both spiritual and human, we have to face troubles and losses and calamities, in ourselves and in others, and we have to do all this with feeble frames and distracted minds and hearts inclined to wander after follies, with energies spiritual, moral, and physical, which at the best are but poor. And then in the providence of God we have a great deal to suffer as well as a great deal about which we must toil and labour—interior sufferings, desolation, mental anguish, bodily weakness and infirmity, which often deepen into pain and disease, the forerunners of the final physical evil of all, which is to conquer us infallibly at last, the doom of death. It is difficult to draw out a catalogue of the evils of life which is not in many respects imperfect; but the few heads which we have enumerated may serve to represent the truth of the case sufficiently for our present purpose.

If all the evils of even a short life could be collected into one day, and set before us as to be dealt with at once, the prospect would indeed be intolerable. But our Lord reminds us now of the mercifulness with which this our task, of coping with a number of evils of various kinds, has been distributed for us over the whole area of our time of trial. We do not, indeed, meet evil by hazard, as it were, as if we were wanderers in a world which is full of it, and which is subject to no other power than itself. Everywhere we are children of our Father, and nowhere are we outside the limits of His Kingdom or beyond the protection of His loving providence. All this evil which we have to meet with is ordered by Him. In a certain true sense, He is the Author of it all, inasmuch as He permits it when it is moral and produces it when it is physical. 'I am the Lord,' He says by His Prophet, 'and there is none else; I form the light and create the darkness, I make peace and create evil;'[2] and in another place, 'Shall there be evil in a city, which the Lord hath not done?'[3] It is not only that all this, which as the Patriarch Jacob says, 'is against us,' is in the hands of God, but that He Who has arranged our life in its succession of stages and

[2] Isaias xlv. 7.   [3] Amos iii. 6.

intervals, has also allotted to each day and hour the particular task and toil which are to belong to it. And now we may complete the doctrine which relates to this subject by reminding ourselves of what is a principle in the Kingdom of our Father—that no trial or danger or temptation comes to us in His providence, but that it brings with it also the grace and assistance from Him which are required in order that we may meet it and deal with it successfully and triumphantly, if we do our part to use the aids which are at our command. But it is also true that these graces and helps from God are not given us before the time when they are needed. The evil comes in its appointed hour, and the grace comes in its appointed hour. And thus each day, in a certain sense, is complete in itself as a battle-field in which our loyalty and courage and strength are tried. The prayer of the day, and the grace of the day, and the faithfulness of the day, are set by God before Himself, as it were, and before the whole host of Heaven, to do battle with the evil and the danger and the temptations of the day. It has been noticed by a heathen poet, that God has of set purpose concealed from us the issues of the future—

> Prudens futuri temporis exitum
> Caliginosa nocte premit Deus—

and although the uncertainty of the future has sometimes prompted men to recklessness and an entire want of ordinary forethought and prudence, still it cannot be doubted that the intention of God in this arrangement of His government belongs partly to the counsel of mercy of which we are thinking in the present chapter. It is certain that our minds would often be oppressed by despair, and that we should be tempted to make ourselves altogether unfit for the service of our Master, if we could always foresee even the immediate future.

But in the face of the considerations on which we are dwelling, this concealment of the future from us, becomes another element in the mercy of God, which furnishes yet another argument for the confidence and abandonment of ourselves to God's good providence which our Lord here teaches. And when we look back over the past, we are able to see how lovingly God has guided us along our path, bringing us across many a very unexpected danger, and often defeating our most cherished and most certain anticipations, and, among other things which show wonderful tenderness, shielding us with an infinite compassion from much which it would have torn our hearts to look forward to.

It is often the case, that the counsels of perfection, such as we may consider this doctrine about taking no solicitous thought for the morrow to be, appear to be almost exaggerations, and to be opposed in some measure to other heads of Divine teaching, while they are in truth only safeguards and supports to the very principles which they appear to contradict. If we look to the Life of our Lord Himself, and to the lives of His saints who have most faithfully followed His example and teaching, we find certain things which seem at first sight to be contrary to this precept of which we are speaking. We find our Lord apparently preparing for what is to come—especially we find Him sometimes spending the whole night in prayer before He does some great action which is to have a lasting effect on the Church, such as the appointment of the Apostles. We find that the saints have been models of forethought, though not of anxious forethought—for they have been the men above all others who have known the immense value of time, and the secret of guarding against its waste by the careful arrangement of their actions for the morrow. This forecasting the order of our engagements, what is to be attempted and what left undone, the portion of our time which is to be given to each action, and the like, is a part of Christian prudence, and of the diligence which we ought to bring to the service of our Master. Such diligence is in no way contrary to the temper of childlike confidence in God which our Lord is here inculcating. Indeed, it may, on the contrary, be said to be necessary for that temper in its perfection, for without it we might have to reproach ourselves with negligence, the consciousness of which must of necessity chill our reliance on the assistance of God. Nor is the force of this truth at all impaired by that of another truth, namely, that our best laid plans are liable to defeat, and that the morrow, when it comes, is certain to bring us a number of unexpected incidents to deal with, which may take from us, either wholly or in great part, the opportunity of using the careful preparation which we have made for what we have calculated upon. There is a fallacy lurking in the inference which seems to follow from this objection. For it is a fallacy to think that the preparation which the children of God prudently and humbly make for anything that concerns His service, can ever be thrown away, any more than the intentions which they form of serving Him, or the designs which they conceive for the advancement of His glory. Such preparation is not thrown away, even if death come suddenly to intercept them in the execution of their plans. For in that case they will have the merit of their diligence, and God will credit them with the service which they intended to do for Him. Nor is it thrown away, even if, as so often happens, the morning places them in a set of circumstances altogether different from those which they expected, which impose on them duties and exertions of which they have never thought. The preparation of the soul, which they intended to fit them for what they thought was coming but did not come, fits them for what does come though they did not expect it. The grace and blessing of God are won for the service which they have actually to undertake, instead of for that which they thought of undertaking. Thus it often happens in mental prayer— the servants of God prepare it, night after night, according to the rules which are laid down for this purpose, and then, morning after morning, God leads their thoughts in some direction altogether new to them, and fills them with light and strength which seem to have no connection with the subject of their preparation, while yet, if that preparation had been omitted through carelessness, the favours to which they are accustomed would be denied them.

Again, we constantly find that the saints and great servants of God have been of all men the most remarkable for the far-reaching aims which they have entertained, the vast plans which they have conceived, the immensity of their designs, and the greatness of the resources which they have required for their execution. The undertakings of the saints often require long and combined efforts on the part of various persons, material means which it takes long to collect, the consent of potentates of the world, the devotion of many souls, long studies, the conquest of many difficulties, the union of a number of discordant wills. Such are many of the works for which God selects those who are most detached from earthly things, and who have attained high perfection in the culture of their own souls. It can hardly be conceived that such undertakings do not call for much forethought, or that the forethought which they require is forbidden by the precept of not being solicitous for the morrow. The truth is, that the example of the saints throws fresh light on the true meaning of this precept. In the first place, the forethought and care which is necessary at this moment, whether for to-day or some future time, is a part of the duty of to-day and not of to-morrow. It may be the business of a merchant to send a ship away for a long voyage to a distant part of the earth, and the provision of all that is necessary for the sustenance of the crew, until its supplies can be renewed, is the duty of the present moment. In like manner, in the life of each soul there may be moments when some decision has to be made on which a long course of action, or even the tenour of the whole remainder of that life may depend, and it is at such times our duty to take into consideration the future as well as the present, and to form our choice under the guidance of God according to the best rules of Christian prudence. That is indeed being thoughtful for the morrow and for many morrows; but such a choice may be and ought to be made without solicitude, as a part of the duties of to-day. Whatever difficulties and evils—in the sense in which the word is used in this passage—beset the chooser, they are a part of the evils and cares of to-day. And as such, we are to give ourselves wholly to them, leaving to the morrow to bring its own cares and solicitudes. In the second place, those only who have thus taken due thought, when thought was to be taken, will be able to meet the further difficulties as to the execution of the projects thus provided for when they arise. This has always been the characteristic of the saints, and of all who have had the secret of doing great things, in whatever kind or order, that they have been able to throw their whole power and attention upon the work on which they are for the moment engaged, as if there were nothing else in the world for them to think or care about. This concentration and method, of which we sometimes see great instances in the men with whose achievements the world is astonished in the line of science, government, or war, is but an image of the calm and deep serenity of the saints, whose whole soul is bent on the duty of the hour, because that it is which at the present moment God demands of them to attend to, that by attending to which they can at this moment please Him most and give Him the most glory. The probabilities and dangers of the morrow have for them absolutely no existence, or if they think of them at all, it is only in the way in which the holy women in the Gospel thought of the stone at the mouth of the sepulchre—that is, they did not know who would roll it away for them, but they went on just the same, as if it was quite certain that rolled away it would be. And they were rewarded by finding that God had already provided for the difficulty which they did not see how to meet, but which in no way deterred them from the enterprize which they had undertaken for His service.

We thus see that an utter absence of solicitude for the morrow is not inconsistent with the rules of Christian prudence and forethought, but, it may almost be said, a part of that very virtue of prudence to which it seems at first sight contradictory. It is a part of that magnanimity of the servants of God which enables them to conceive and execute great design for Him. It is a part of that absolute confidence in Him of which our Lord is here speaking. It sets them free to attend with all their powers to the task which is for the moment before them, and to undertake joyously, and almost playfully, the works from which human wisdom would have dissuaded them, and before the difficulties of which human courage would have shrunk into despair. For it is a part of their forgetfulness, so to speak, of the morrow, not to quail before the highest enterprizes or the beginnings of works which, like the great mediæval cathedrals, will certainly task generations to execute them. They are themselves but the children of a day, but they work for Him in Whose sight a thousand years are but as one day, for One to Whom the sun never sets, to Whom the morrows of the whole span of the existence of mankind are as present as to-day.

CHAPTER IX.

Judge not.

St. Matt. vii. 1, 2 ; *Vita Vitæ Nostræ*, § 34.

WE have already pointed out that the course of our Lord's Divine discourse, on which we are now commenting, seems, in the part on which we are occupied, to have some reference to the order of the petitions which He has taught us to make in His own prayer. If this be admitted, we hardly require any further reason for the connection of the words of which we are now to speak with those which immediately precede them. The precept about taking no anxious thought for food or raiment, or for the cares of the morrow, reminds us easily of the petition for our daily bread. Next to that petition comes the prayer, that our trespasses may be forgiven by God as we forgive those that are committed against ourselves. And so we find, in this part of the Sermon on the Mount, that after the precept as to abstinence from solicitude comes that against judging our neighbour, and that this precept, like the petition of the Lord's prayer, is cast in a form which distinctly reminds us that our own treatment of others is to be the rule according to which we are to be treated by God. In the prayer the words are 'Forgive us our trespasses as we forgive them that trespass against us.' And here the words are, 'Judge not, that you may not be judged. For with what judgment you judge, you shall be judged; and with what measure you mete, it shall be measured to you again.'

Another way of explaining the connection may be this. In the precept about absolute confidence in our Heavenly Father and His providence, we are, in substance, taught to think well and highly and greatly of God. We are taught to have Him continually before our minds as a most beneficent and thoughtful Master, Who will never let His servants know what it is to want anything while they are devoting themselves to the advancement of His interests. We are to remember His care for the lowest things in His Kingdom, and how much more precious to Him must those be who are made His children by their new birth in Jesus Christ, and to whom He vouchsafes to commit the continuance of the work of His own Incarnate Son. And now in the words which follow, we are taught, as it were, to think as well as possible of our neighbour—to avoid all harsh judgment of him, even when he may fairly seem to be in the wrong. And this we are to do partly on account of our own interest, inasmuch as we have to be judged by God in our turn, and partly from considerations relating to Him, inasmuch as He is the one authoritative and rightful Judge of all, and has determined to make the measure which we mete to others that of His own judgment, severe or indulgent, towards us.

There is one other way of explaining the connection of this passage, which has the advantage of shedding much light on the words which follow the precept about not judging, as well as on that precept itself. According to this way of understanding our Lord's design in the whole context, the thought of God and the rights of God lies beneath all. In the first place, our Lord vindicates the supreme authority of God as our Master. In the second place, in the passage on which we have lately been dwelling, as to the obligation of absolute confidence in God, He presents to us the idea of God as our great Provider and Father, and especially describes Him as charging Himself with the care, as to all temporal necessities, of those whom He calls to any close and exclusive service to Him, or sacrifice for Him. Then our Lord goes on, in the verses which we are now to consider, to insist on the exclusive rights of God as the one sole Judge of men, and on His determination to visit upon us any liberties that we may take, either with Himself in this prerogative of His, or with our fellow-men, with regard to whom He has bound us by the law of charity. The verses which follow after this, set God before us as the author of the graces and gifts contained in His revelation of Himself to mankind, and thus insist on the precept of not giving that which is holy to persons unfit to receive it. Thus our Lord may be considered here as warning us against another infringement of the rights of God. His Divine truth, His means of grace, His wonderful sacraments, the spiritual treasures of His Kingdom, are committed to men, especially, of course, to the ministers of the altar and of the Divine word, but they are to be treated as the treasures of the great King, and are to be preserved from all profanation. We shall presently have to speak of the far-reaching application of this principle in the system and history of the Church. For the present it is enough to have pointed out how we are thus enabled to see one and the same purpose running through these successive precepts of our Lord. And, it may be added, in order that we may not have to return upon this method of explaining the connection of this passage, the verses which follow put God before us as the Hearer of prayer, and the motive and vindicator of fraternal charity. This may serve as an explanation, on the principle mentioned above, of this part of the Sermon on the Mount.

The precept on which we are now engaged appears on the face of it to forbid all judgment of our neighbour. 'Judge not, that you may not be judged.' We find, however, that a great number of holy writers understand is as forbidding what are called rash judgments, and so by implication, at least, tolerating those which are well founded and true. On the other hand, the motive which our Lord assigns appears to point to the former interpretation as most natural. What we desire is, to escape the judgment of God, as far as it is possible to us, and not simply to escape unjust judgment at His hands. The other interpretation is probably mainly founded on the threat, that as we judge others so shall we ourselves be judged. For God can judge us severely or mildly, though He cannot judge rashly. But in this case, as in so many others, we shall find that an investigation of an apparent difficulty leads us to a deeper insight than we might otherwise have attained of the meaning of our Lord, and of the truths which may have been before His mind as He spoke.

In the first place, it cannot be denied that it is true that all judgment one of another is in a general way forbidden to us, and that the cases in which we are allowed to pass judgment are exceptions, for certain definite ends, to the universal law. There are many reasons why our judgments must of necessity be faulty or imperfect. But apart from these reasons, there is the question of jurisdiction, and if these reasons did not exist, we should still be forbidden to sit in judgment, from the simple absence of all right in us to do so. This is implied in the words of our Lord, when He was asked to decide between a man and his brother about a question of inheritance. He asked, who had made Him a Judge or a Divider in such matters? Thus St. Paul, when speaking on this subject, in reference to the question of the different views taken about the eating of meats that had been offered to idols, says, 'Who art thou that judgest another man's servant? To his own Lord he standeth or falleth.'[1] And this principle, that God alone is our Master, and that He alone is in consequence our Judge, is enough to forbid our judging others, even if we are capable of doing so, unless we have some commission, as it were, from the one true Judge to execute, in part, His office. Thus all men will be in some sort judges at the great day of account, for then it will be that God's ways with the whole world and with each several soul will be made manifest for the purpose of His glory, and then all hidden things, which are now unknown to all save God, will be brought to light. Thus St. Paul in another place says, 'Judge not before the time, until the Lord come, Who both will bring to light the hidden things of darkness, and will make manifest the counsels of the hearts, and then shall every man have praise of God'[2]—the praise which he deserves in truth, and not that which you in your blindness may be inclined to assign to Him. Where it may be remarked that the principle of St. Paul forbids our pronouncing judgment as such, and not merely unfavourable or rash judgment.

This principle, of the supreme and inherent authority of God as the one Judge of men, an authority which is invaded whenever we take upon ourselves to sit in judgment on one another, may be considered as the foundation of the Christian doctrine on this subject. But of course it does not exclude the truth, that to a certain

---

[1] Rom. xiv. 4.   [2] 1 Cor. iv. 5.

extent, and under certain circumstances, something of a judicial power is committed to rulers in Church and State, to Superiors, to parents, to priests in the sacred tribunal of penance, to society in general, and to single persons for the common good or for their own protection or that of others. And again, there is a sense in which judgment means little more than opinion, and in which it considers only the external part of the conduct of another, without penetrating to the motive or intention, or even to the deliberation with which he may or may not have acted. And as the facts which meet our eyes or come to our knowledge must make some impression upon us, according to the standard of right or wrong by which our consciences are ruled, the practical commentary which we want on this passage has rightly been made to turn chiefly on what is and what is not a rash judgment. We shall proceed, then, to speak of this, insisting only, in the first place, on the principle which has been laid down, that to judge our neighbours' faults is forbidden to us, just as much as it is forbidden to us to speak of those faults, while, as there are certain cases in which it is right and charitable to speak of them, so also there are certain cases in which we have a right to think of them, both judgment and speech being alike forbidden us when these cases do not exist. And, we may add, it is just as much an invasion of God's rights to canonize a man, without His authority, as to condemn him, to declare this or that person to be a saint, or to affirm that this or that heretical leader is certainly in good faith and the like. The judgment against which St. Paul was warning the Corinthians in the passage just now quoted, was a favourable judgment, and this explains why he says, that in the day of judgment, every man shall have his due praise (and not blame) from God.

The common doctrine on the subject of rash judgment tells us that this sin consists in judging that evil has been done when the proof is not manifest and peremptory. In the face of such evidence, it is not a rash judgment to conclude that there has been a fault. This rule has been very much enlarged and explained by ascetic authors who have written on the subject. Father Lancicius, for instance, who has left behind him a complete treatise[3] on the law about rash judgment, gives the following rules as to the limits of permission which are to be observed. In the first place, what is altogether internal, such as the thoughts and desires and motives, which are manifest ordinarily to God alone, are never to be made the subject of condemnation. The reason which he gives has already been hinted at—that it belongs to God alone to judge the heart, which He alone knows. Even the Church does not judge of internal things. She receives all those to the sacraments who profess the true faith, and dispose themselves according to her rules for their reception. In the second place, our judgment as far as it goes, that is, as to what is before our eyes, is never to be extended to the future. Whether the good thief began by joining his companion in blaspheming our Lord on the Cross is uncertain, but it is certain that it might have seemed a thing safe to predict that he would die as he had lived, and yet that judgment would have been rash. In the third place, as to external things which are not in themselves wrong, but which may be either bad or good, we are never to pass judgment on or to condemn our neighbour. The evil interpretation is not certain, and charity requires that we should form best the opinion that is in our power. Again, when the action which is before our eyes is intrinsically wrong, the thing that is done may be condemned, but the person who does it is to be

[3] *De Vitandis Judiciis Temerariis.*

excused as far as may be. We must suppose that he could not have intended what he did, or that he acted inadvertently and under some strong influence which overpowered him. We must remember that he may rise after his fall, and that we may fall and not rise. Again, we must be on our guard against the danger, which is a part of the miserable pettiness of our fallen nature, of forming a judgment as to the character and disposition of a person from a single bad action which may happen to come to our knowledge. Changeableness and inconstancy are a part of our natural weakness, and as we cannot be certain that a man is always good because he has been good once, at least we may not conclude from a single fault that he has a habit of sin. Again, even when our position and relation to the person who is in fault give us a right to judge and even to reprehend him, this must be done gently and sweetly, and we must always retain the recollection of our own frailty. Such judgment, however, is quite lawful and free from sin, and we may take due precautions against dangers which may happen from the faults of which any one may possibly be guilty, even though we do not judge him to have committed them. Thus it is not wrong to protect ourselves against thieves, even though we do not know that any particular person is a thief.

The very moderate limits within which these rules restrain the liberty of judging others, are enough to show the great severity with which writers such as he whom we have been quoting regard the sin of rash judgment in itself. As is usual with him, Father Lancicius gives a number of quotations from ascetical writers and from the histories of the Fathers of the Desert, which will fill any one who reads them attentively with surprise at the very different measure with which the saints, on the one hand, and the generality of Christians, on the other, seem inclined to reckon the heinousness of this sin. But we must pass on to the reasons, or some of the reasons, which are assigned by Father Lancicius, in the treatise of which we are speaking, for the most careful avoidance of all judgments on others. It will be seen how far they illustrate the great principle of the judicial prerogative of God to which we have already referred.

The first reason against judging given by Father Lancicius is drawn from this passage—for he makes it to consist in this—that God will pass a very severe judgment on those who judge others. This is illustrated by the case of the Pharisee, who was not really a bad man in point of conduct, and who may have spoken the truth in regard to his religious observances, but, because he judged the publican hardly, he was condemned. This severe judgment of God in such cases seems to be grounded, in the first instance, on the simple sin of judgment of others. But it frequently goes on much further, because the soul which gives in to the vice of judgment of others provokes God to withdraw His graces and protection from it, and thus falls into the same sins of which it has been the censurer in its neighbour. There is a story in the lives of the Fathers of the Desert, of a monk who had condemned another who had fallen into sin, and then was taken in a vision to Calvary, where our Lord was hanging on His Cross. But the monk was rejected from His presence, and sent back with the loss of his cloak to his cell, as if such persons were to be deprived of the special guardianship which God otherwise grants to them for the state in which they serve Him. Father Lancicius also quotes the case of the Abbot Machetes, who declared that he had censured others of his brethren for three defects, as he deemed them, and had in consequence been allowed himself to fall into the same, that is, to do the things which he had censured. Another way in which the words of the text come true about the judgment falling on us which we have passed on our brethren, is that God allows men to find fault with us in the very same way and for the same reasons.

It would take us too long to draw out the very beautiful manner in which the writer whom we are following illustrates the duty of passing the most indulgent verdict on others, from the example of God in His dealings with Adam and Eve after their fall, and of our Lord on the occasion of the woman who was brought to Him after having been taken in the act of adultery. In both cases we have a wonderful lesson of tenderness of dealing with sinners. In the same way we can only refer to the long chapters in which Father Lancicius goes through a great many instances in Holy Scripture, showing how easy it would be to find fault with the saints of God, with the words and promises of God, even with the actions of our Lord Himself when on earth, if we were to consider ourselves free to criticize and condemn whatever is capable of a bad interpretation. It will be more to our purpose to consider another set of reasons which he gives against this fault, which may illustrate both what has been said about the sinfulness of judgment, and what may hereafter have to be said about our Lord's remarkable words as to the mote and the beam. The writer whom we are quoting shows that these judgments usually spring from serious faults in our own souls, such as dislike, or aversion, or jealousy, or envy, in regard of the persons criticized, or again from pride, or a certain levity and quickness in coming to an adverse conclusion concerning others, or a want of due respect to God Whose creatures they are as well as ourselves, or from ignorance of our own misery, which ought to occupy us so as to leave little room for censure of others. Again, such judgments are so many internal detractions, by which we sin against justice, which forbids us to deprive our neighbour of the estimation in which we hold him without the gravest reason. Lastly, he shows how they proceed from the malice of the heart. Thus our Lord mentions 'an evil eye'—which may be understood to mean a readiness to look on everything around us on the bad side, and to discover and dwell upon what is bad rather than what is good—as among the many wicked things which proceed from the heart of man and are true sources of defilement to him.

Some other reasons which are given by Father Lancicius amount to this—that we may so often be mistaken, because God often allows those who are even great servants and friends of his own, to have certain external defects of character, or again He permits and even prompts them to certain actions which seem to be dangerous or scandalous or sinful, but which are in truth done from the highest motives, and with the best results for the good of souls. Or again we are ourselves so full of faults, that it is absurd to think of the faults of others. Or again, as has been said, those who judge usurp the office of God, and that is illustrated by Father Lancicius by several passages from St. Chrysostom and others, in one of which the Saint reminds us that the seat of judgment is reserved for the only-begotten Son of God. Father Lancicius also quotes some beautiful stories as to the next head, in which he points out how very dear to God those are who take pains never to judge others hardly. One of these anecdotes refers to Bernard of Quinta Valle, one of the first companions of St. Francis, who was seen in a procession of saints of the Order with his eyes shining with a marvellous light, because it had been his practice always to look at everything in the most favourable way possible.

Father Lancicius subjoins a number of recommendations to enable us to practise this precept of our Lord with greater ease. The first of these is taken from the rule of the Blessed Peter Favre, the first disciple of St. Ignatius, and it is founded on truth which has been more than once insisted on in this chapter, that judgment belongs to God, and that we require some special authority to execute it. This rule is, not to judge even of things which are in themselves wrong, unless it be our business to do so, as for instance, it is the business of a Superior in religion to watch over what passes in the lives of his subjects. There may be some obligation of conscience, even on those who are not superiors, but without this it is not to be done. In the second place, when there is a duty of judging, then we must accustom ourselves to do it without any precipitancy, and without any readiness to find out that there has been wrong. We must only condemn with great difficulty. Another rule is to be very frequent and severe in the judgments which we pass on ourselves, for this will certainly tend to make us less willing to see faults in our brothers. Then we are to take great care to acquire the habit of looking on all things and all persons from the favourable side, to remember how constantly we are and may be deceived in our conclusions, to be diligent not to condemn what we cannot excuse, and to make the judgments which we pass, and the thoughts which we entertain, concerning others, the constant subject of very close self-examination.

In more than one place in this treatise of which we have been speaking, Father Lancicius refers to the wonderful discourse which was delivered by St. Catharine of Siena, on her death-bed, to her spiritual children collected at Rome. The point as to which he quotes it, is that of which we are treating—the immense importance and necessity of abstaining from the judgment of others. St. Catharine is related to have said that she had learnt that it was necessary, in order to gain true purity of mind, to abstain from all judgment of our neighbour, and from all conversation about his actions, and to attend in all things to the will of God, Who permits all things for a good end. And so, says Blessed Raymond of Capua, her confessor and biographer, 'she used constantly to affirm with great urgency, as being certain of this truth, that a man ought not on any account to judge any one, that is to despise or condemn him, even though he should see with his eyes a manifest sin, since God doth not reject such a one nor condemn him, and hath even given His own Blood for him. And she used to add that many were hindered from the perfection of life which they might otherwise have acquired by their good works, because they have not observed this law.'[4] This discourse of St. Catharine, which Raymond relates from the accounts given him by those who were present, is very remarkable as an illustration of this part of the Sermon on the Mount. It is well known that the spiritual doctrine of St. Catharine was infused, as theologians speak, and it is very unlikely that she had in her mind the text of Sacred Scripture when she spoke. Her disciples, as they were called, were made up of persons of different ages, professions, and sexes, and they were bound together by a kind of religious rule, and seem to have lived in common. Thus they were to some extent in the same position, as to the abandonment of the world, as many of the disciples to whom the Sermon on the Mount was delivered. It is very remarkable that in this her deathbed exhortation she insists especially upon three things,

[4] *Vitæ di Santa Catarina de Siena.* iii. c. 4.

which form the subjects of our Lord's exhortations in this part of His Sermon. She insists especially on the necessity of prayer, of entire confidence in God, and abandonment to Him of all secular cares, saying that those who did this, would certainly experience wonderful blessings from Him in reward of their faith. And she also insisted strongly, as the passage already quoted is enough to prove, on the duty of not judging others. Thus we find this Saint of the fourteenth century laying down unconsciously to her disciples the very doctrine of perfection which is found in this part of the Sermon on the Mount, guided thereto, not by knowledge of the text of Sacred Scripture, but by the inspiration of the Holy Ghost, to Whom every word of our Lord and every thought of His Sacred Heart were known. It may be added that, as regards the necessity of not judging in order to attain to perfection, this is not the only passage in which St. Catharine has recorded the doctrine as delivered to her by God. Father Lancicius quotes another place, from her Dialogue[5] in which is taught: 'In order that thou mayest attain to this union and purity, never judge of anything that thou mayest see to be done or said by any one against thyself or another, even shouldst thou see a manifest sin, yet draw from that thorn itself the sweet smelling rose, that is, by offering the persons to Me in true and fraternal compassion, and in that way thou shalt arrive at perfect purity.'

It will be convenient for us, before proceeding further with the doctrine which is contained in this passage of the Sermon on the Mount, to point out the distinction between the first part of it and the second. Our Lord gives two principal reasons against the fault of which we have been speaking—that of judging one another. The first is based by Him on our own good and inte-

[5] Chap. C.

rest. We are not to judge, in order that we may not be judged, for, He adds, the judgment with which you judge others will be the measure of your own judgment by God and by man. 'With what measure you mete, it shall be measured to you again.' This is the first great reason, and when we come to analyze it, and to compare it with other passages which bear on the same subject, we find that it resolves itself into two considerations, each of which again gives room for much thought. In the first place we have the doctrine that the judging of others implies ordinarily some infringement of the rights both of God and of man; of God, because judgment essentially belongs to Him, and is therefore a usurpation of His prerogative, unless it can in some way be said to be a function derived from Him by delegation; of man, because every one has a right to a charitable and kindly estimate at our hands, and the act of judging him, unless it can be said to be done by some right, is a kind of mental detraction of which we are guilty against him. This is the first consideration—the rights of God and man as violated by judgment. This truth underlies the words of our Lord and is implied by them, but He speaks more directly of the consequences to which this infringement of rights leads, that is, of the law of God's providence and of the administration of His Kingdom, by which a severe punishment is inflicted on the transgression of the rights already mentioned. That is, it is a law of God's Kingdom that those who judge shall be themselves judged, and in the same way and with the same measure which they have meted out to others. In the first place, if we are severe to others in our judgments, God will be severe to us. There shall be justice without mercy to those who have not shown mercy. And, again, God will withdraw His graces from us if we judge others, and thus let us fall into the same faults which we have condemned. Moreover, He will not protect us even outwardly, and He will allow men to avenge the severity with which we have treated others by thinking and saying evil things of us, according to the exact measure of retribution which we deserve. Having said thus much as to the first part of this passage, we shall devote the next chapter to the consideration of the second.

CHAPTER X.

Motes and Beams.

St. Matt. vii. 3—5 ; *Vita Vitæ Nostræ*, § 35.

THE second reason which our Lord gives us for this carefulness against judging others, is contained in the verses which immediately follow, and of which we have not as yet spoken in detail. 'And why seest thou the mote that is in thy brother's eye, and seest not the beam that is in thy own eye? Or how sayest thou to thy brother, let me cast the mote out of thy eye, and behold a beam is in thy own eye ? Thou hypocrite, cast out first the beam out of Thy own eye, and then shalt thou see to cast out the mote out of thy brother's eye.' These words presuppose a state of things in which it was an habitual and recognized practice for some persons to point out to others the defects which they observed in them. As regards the rule of not judging others, they add to the motives adduced already the very powerful weight of considerations of moral rectitude and propriety. Both of these are violated by the judgment which is passed without right on another. Such judgment is hypocritical, and so against rectitude and honesty. For the only reason that we can fairly allege for the judging, and much more for the correcting, of another, must be that we have a zeal for the glory and service of God and for the good of men, out of regard for which we go beyond what we should otherwise consider the rule of charity and modesty, which would prevent us from passing an adverse judgment on our brother. But such zeal can only be hypocritical, if it does not first of all force us to attend to the custody of our own hearts, and avoid sin more diligently in ourselves than we reprove it in others. And yet, as has been seen above, the tendency to judge others implies a great amount of evil in our own hearts, which we must have neglected before we could fall into the fault of such judgment. Our Lord speaks with that knowledge of the human heart which belongs to Him when He declares, as He here implicitly does declare, that those who blame others when it is not their office or duty so to do, have in themselves greater faults than those which they criticize. Their own faults are as beams, whereas the faults on which they remark are as motes. This is the reason against these judgments on grounds of rectitude. There is also another ground which we have called that of decency and propriety, and this is contained in the precept to cleanse our own eye first, before we undertake to purify that of our brother. That is, however true it may be that our brother may need cleansing, we are not the people to do it until we have first cleansed ourselves. This is the maxim of equity and decency to which our Lord appealed in the case of the woman taken in adultery, when He said, 'He that is without sin among you, let him first cast a stone at her.'[1] For it is not becoming that we should condemn or correct others,

[1] St. John viii. 7.

when we ourselves are in equal or greater need of correction, and are liable to the same or even a severer condemnation.

Here it may be pointed out that, as in other passages in the Sermon on the Mount, our Lord, in this saying, touches some points of doctrine for which he seems to desire to prepare the minds of His disciples, while He leaves the full expansion of them for a later period of His teaching. It is clear that the precepts here conveyed go beyond the rules which are to be observed, as has been said, as to judging others. It is one thing to judge others, and another thing to correct them. But our Lord, in the passage before us, passes from the judgment of another, which He describes as seeing a mote in his eye, to the correction of the fault thus detected or remarked, of which He speaks as the offering to take the mote out of the eye in which it has been detected. We are thus brought at once to the subject of the correction of others, which is something more than the judging of others in our own mind. But, just as our Lord has left the subject of marriage and divorce to be more completely legislated on in the later times of His teaching, so here also He seems to leave the rules as to fraternal correction for the same period. They are not given, in fact, till the last year of His ministry, when the formation of the Church as a distinct body had proceeded much further than at the time of the Sermon on the Mount.[2] It seems natural, therefore, to leave this subject, on which our Lord here touches lightly, till we reach that part of the Gospel history, adding meanwhile what is enough to explain the bearing of our Lord's present injunctions upon it.

In the present place, then, our Lord is speaking of the moral aspect of the discharge of what may be, in

[2] See St. Matt. xviii. 15, 16.

some cases, as we shall see, a positive duty, in the way of the admonition of our neighbours. It cannot be asserted that, when that duty exists, it is altogether barred by the fact that the person on whom it may be incumbent is himself in need of correction. For there may be cases in which this duty has to be performed, even by sinners. It is a duty, when it exists, of the highest moment, and some holy writers have said very strong things indeed of the mischief which results when it is neglected, as if this neglect alone were a cause as fruitful of spiritual ruin in the world as almost any other cause that can be named. The loss which may result when it is disused may be estimated by the care with which the masters of the spiritual life insist upon it, and the advantages which are to be gained by the faithful and courageous following of the rules which they have made for its observance. But there is an obvious moral unfitness about the discharge of a duty like this by a soul which is itself in a state of sin. It is not only intrinsically unfit for such an office, but it cannot discharge that office with heartiness and simplicity, nor can it hope for any great blessing upon its discharge. And it is to this that our Lord draws attention in the words before us. And He seems to tell us, that, that readiness to judge others of which He has been speaking is an almost certain sign of interior imperfection and faultiness, and that one of its worst results may be to incapacitate us for the due discharge of so important a function as that which may become incumbent upon us under many circumstances, of admonishing a brother of a real fault which meets the eyes of men, the natural provision for which, in the ordinance of God, may be his correction by us according to the law of charity. Our Lord's words seem to imply not only that the souls which are so lynx-eyed as to the defects of others, are themselves very frequently chastised by an abandonment on the part of God in time of temptation, so as to fall themselves, but that the temper against which He is warning us is punished by the permission to indulge in habitual faults, which are more grievous than those of which we have to correct others. For it must not be supposed that our Lord used, without a special purpose, the image of the mote and the beam—placing in the soul of the critic of others a defect a great many times more serious and more conspicuous than that which He allots to the person who is to be the subject of correction.

Our Lord, throughout the whole passage, is clearly speaking of private and unauthorized judgments and corrections. To these the reasons which are set forth here apply with especial fulness. But the cogency of the argument is increased when we consider how miserable a thing it is, when those who are by office and calling rulers and teachers of the people, the pastors of souls, and the like, a part of whose duty it is, either publicly or privately, to rebuke vice and injustice, are themselves liable to the very blame which they are obliged to administer to others. It is miserable enough to teach people what we do not ourselves practise, and to enjoin what we do not ourselves obey. It is miserable enough to counsel the higher exercises of the spiritual life when we are ourselves grovelling in the mire of passion, or without taste for the delights of God's service, because our hearts are lost after earthly objects of ambition. But of all the miseries which can befall us in this kind, none can be so great as that of having to reprove faults of which we are ourselves guilty, or which perhaps are not so bad as those of which our conscience reproaches us. And yet there may be cases in which those who have the duty of teaching have no other alternative before them, but either to leave the duty of reproof unperformed, or to reprove what they are themselves guilty of as well as those whom they reprove. It may be said in such cases, that there is something in the line of duty which forbids them to be silent, and yet, if even in this case there is so much internal shame and misery in the conscience, how much greater must there be in the case of those who have no duty and no right in the matter, and who yet assume without commission the responsibility of pointing out faults, which rankle undisturbed and unmolested in their own hearts!

We may thus learn that our Lord has most carefully provided, in the passage before us, for the practice of fraternal correction, which He was about to establish in the Church, and for which He gave, at a later time than this, very detailed regulations. His language here might seem to imply that, after all, we were never to find fault with one another, even for the purpose of charitable correction. It might seem that when He said, 'First cast out the beam that is in thine own eye, and then thou shalt see clearly to cast out the mote out of thy brother's eye,' He meant us to understand that we should never be fit for the discharge of this duty. But it is not so. The principle that those only who are perfectly free from sin should undertake in any way to help to the spiritual improvement of others, has not been enacted by our Lord. He has left the sacraments of the Church to be administered by those who have this treasure, as St. Paul says, in earthen vessels, and He commits the preaching of His word to men who are themselves compassed by imfirmity and misery. It it true that these and all other ministrations of grace in the Church may have a special and particular blessing when they are discharged by saints, and it is constantly the case, on the other hand, that the Word of God becomes unfruitful in the mouth of persons who are displeasing to Him, from their vanity, or their jealousy of others, or other defects of the same kind. But He has not made the effect of all these things depend on the sanctity of the person who may have to administer them. Here He is speaking mainly, as it seems, to such ministers themselves, for, though His words are directly concerned with the discharge of a duty which cannot be limited to priests or others who have some kind of authority in the Church, still the principle which they involve applies especially to those who have the charge of others. It is not that He requires them, or any simple Christian, on whom the duty of correction may devolve, to be immaculate. What He says is, 'First cast out the beam out of thine own eye,' that is, cleanse your own soul before you undertake the office of correction. But the soul may be cleansed in a moment by an act of contrition, or by the reception of the Sacrament of Penance, and, in the case of lighter stains, by a number of means which are in the reach of all of us. So that our Lord's counsel comes practically to this—that we should never undertake anything in any way, which has the character of the administration of rebuke, reproof, the healing or correction of the soul of another, whether by the sacraments or in any other way, without first reminding ourselves of our miseries, without remembering that we are ourselves, it may be, worse sinners than those with whom we are to deal on the part of God, and without, then and there, cleansing our souls in the best way within our reach, just as if we were about to administer one of the sacraments for which it is necessary first to go to confession, or to attempt to discharge the office of exorcist, on some occasion when we might expect the devil to reproach us with our sins in the face of all, if we had not first reconciled ourselves to God. And we may understand our Lord's words in a yet more fruitful sense, if we see in them a sort of promise that, if we do our best to cleanse our own souls, we shall have a special grace given to us to help others out of the same miseries. He says, 'Then shalt thou see clearly to take the mote out of the eye of thy brother.' The more then that we exercise ourselves in contrition and all other practices which have a direct tendency to the purification of our own souls, the more may we hope for the help of God to enable us, not simply to correct the faults and defects of others, but to see clearly how this is to be done. For the careful cleansing of our own souls is a process which God blesses with an ever-increasing gift of spiritual light, not only for ourselves, but for those also whom in His providence He may address to us for aid of this kind. It is not easy to extract an evil principle from a soul in which it has taken root. It is not easy to free a soul from an evil habit, or from some false intellectual maxim which may vitiate a large portion of its practical conduct. No physician's art is so difficult as that art which has for its patients the diseased in the spiritual order. Those who have in any degree or measure to practise this art, have to perform the very highest services, to God and man, that can be rendered in this world. Their illumination must come from God, and God will illuminate the humble—those especially who have practised that humility which is the condition of the purification of their own hearts, and which has that purification for its direct object.

CHAPTER XI.

Pearls and Swine.

St. Matt. vii. 6; *Vita Vitæ Nostræ*, § 35.

IT has been thought by some commentators, that the precept which we are now to consider holds the place which it does hold in the Sermon on the Mount, on account of the need which might arise of some corrective to the indiscriminate confidence in our neighbour which might follow from a literal observance of the warning against rash judgments which has just been considered. They have thought that our Lord meant to warn us, that, although we are not to think evil of our neighbour, still we are to be cautious in trusting to all without discrimination the heavenly treasures of the sacraments and other means of grace, the sublime and unearthly secrets of the Divine Word and doctrine. But it seems better to explain the connection of this passage in the other way which has been suggested above, that is, by supposing that after we have been taught to reverence God in His providence and in His faithfulness, by casting aside all solicitude for the morrow and all anxiety about the supply of our daily wants; after, in the second place, we have been instructed as to the reverence we are to pay to His judicial power and prerogative, by a careful abstinence from that interference therewith which is contained in the act of passing judgment on our neighbour—who has also on his own account, a claim of justice and charity on our thoughts concerning him—we are, in the third place, to be warned that we must treat the things of God which are committed to our administration with all due reverence, a part of which is to consist in great prudence and circumspection as to the persons to whom we are to communicate these precious gifts. The last injunction on which we have commented, which seems to warn us as to the purity of conscience which is required in those who have to administer the Word of God, in the way of correction, to others, may be considered as very naturally preparing us for this head of instruction as to the persons to whom sacred things are to be administered. For there is scarcely anything which requires more delicacy and prudence, in the whole range of spiritual ministrations, than the beautiful and precious medicine of fraternal correction. The same kind of instruction is contained in our Lord's famous words to the Apostles about their being simple as doves, and yet prudent as serpents; and this precept, and the Christian prudence which it recommends, may be constantly traced in its effects and fruits in the discipline and practice of the Church in all ages of her history, as well as in the lives of and personal conduct of her saints. The foundation of this whole system of religious prudence is to be found in the principle which breathes through the whole of this passage, the principle of the reverence due to God, to Whom belong the sacred treasures which are intrusted to the Church. And this principle is here for the first time expressed by our Blessed Lord in that clear and pregnant way which was familiar to Him, of setting forth great truths in the form of simple proverbs or parables. The whole doctrine, as far as it is here given us, is contained in the images which He uses to convey the lessons He would teach.

'Give not,' He says, 'the holy thing to the dogs, neither cast ye your pearls before the swine, lest perhaps they trample them under their feet, and, turning upon you, rend you.' Here we have two images used for the persons who are unfit to be trusted with what belongs to God. They are first called the 'dogs,' and then, 'the swine.' That which is not to be trusted to them is also spoken of under two names—first, as the holy thing, and then as pearls. The reason which our Lord assigns is also two-fold—lest the holy thing, or the pearl, be trampled under foot, and lest the ministers who have imprudently exposed it to such profanation should be themselves torn to pieces or rent by the 'dogs,' or by the 'swine.' It may very well be thought that the persons of whom our Lord is speaking are the same under both images; but that only implies that there are different aspects under which our Lord would have them regarded. And, certainly, the consequence of imprudence is different in the two statements. It is one thing to trample the holy thing under foot, and another to turn and rend the ministers to whom it has been committed. Thus we seem to have three principal subjects of thought set before us in these words—the dignity and preciousness of the holy things, the character of the persons to whom they are not to be committed, and the results, both as to the treasures themselves, and their official guardians, in the case of imprudence in this respect.

The words in which our Lord describes the persons against whom He would warn us in this passage, seem chosen for the purpose of pointing to two distinct characters, which are not to be trusted with holy things. The image of the dogs suggests to us savage anger, irritation, pride, and rage, not so much sullen and brooding, as loud-voiced and aggressive threatening. The image of the swine suggests, on the other hand, sensuality, voluptuousness, filthy coarseness of life, an entire devotion to the indulgence of the lowest appetites, eating and drinking, and the more carnal pleasures. Thus we arrive at once at the truth, that persons whose character is of either of these two kinds, or even persons who for a time and partially are under the influence of these two forms of passion, are either wholly, or for the moment, and as far as they are the servants of these concupiscences, unfit for the reception of the Divine things of which our Lord is here speaking. Anger raises a cloud before the eyes of the soul, and it makes the ears of men incapable of drinking in the still calm accents of the Holy Ghost and of those who speak in the name of God. There can be no reception of Divine truth in its sublimer manifestations when there is no peace in the soul, and anger is inconsistent with peace. Much more are men whose whole character is violent and who are always, as it were, at war with themselves and all around them, incapable of sacred teaching and of the sweet and life-giving sacraments and means of grace. Passion of this kind invariably proceeds from intense pride, and the Gospel light and life are not for the proud. It is probably from some sort of connection between pride and intellectual darkness and obstinacy that the image of the dogs seems to be appropriated in Scripture to heretics, under which head we may include all those who are voluntary aliens from the Church and the faith. Thus our Lord, in His famous words to the Syrophœnician woman, who was outside the covenant of Israel, speaks of taking the food of the children and giving it to the dogs. In the last chapter of the Apocalypse, St. John, when he speaks of those who are excluded from the heavenly Jerusalem, puts in the first place those whom he calls 'dogs,' and then adds sorcerers, and the unchaste, and murderers, and others, while in the parallel passage in the preceding chapter the title unbelievers answers to that of dogs in the catalogue of those who are shut out.[1] Thus, some of the Fathers, when they wish to speak of the manner in which heretics are always criticizing and finding fault with the Church, use the image of the barking of dogs.

On the other hand, it needs no statement by the way of explanation to make it clear how altogether unfit for the reception of holy things are those who are the miserable slaves of lust and sensuality, even in their most apparently refined forms. Wisdom, we are told in the Sacred Book which bears that name, will not enter into a malicious soul—this may refer to the irascible character of which we have just now spoken—nor dwell in a body subject to sins—this seems to refer to the unchaste and sensual.[3] Our Lord says nothing about the slaves of Mammon in this passage, because, as it seems they are included under the two other heads which He does name. It must be remembered, as has been already hinted, that the caution of our Lord does not apply only to the cases of those who are altogether given up to sensuality. Here the doctrine of St. Paul may well come in, which has been the foundation of the whole system of the religious and contemplative life in the Church, as well as of her practice in securing for the direct service of the altar and of the administration of the sacraments and of the Word of God, those who have renounced even the lawful indulgence of the married state in order to follow our Lord in His virginal purity. There will always be certain holy things and certain secrets of that wisdom of which the Apostle speaks in the First Epistle to the Corinthians for which the 'chaste generation' is especially chosen by God, and though it would be entirely wrong to apply to any lawful state of life in the Church the opprobrium, which is

[1] Apoc. xxii. 15; xxi. 8.   [2] Wisdom i. 5.

contained in the epithets which are here used in the Sermon on the Mount, still, the principle of which our Lord speaks may apply in a certain way to those who are entangled in the ordinary cares of life and who do not deny themselves the lawful gratifications of domestic happiness. The proof of this may be found in the fact that when, as frequently happens, such persons are called by God to great familiarity with Him and raised to high spiritual favours, they at once begin to withdraw themselves, and to persuade others to do the same, from even innocent enjoyments. There is something analogous to this in what St. Paul tells the Corinthians, in the same part of his Epistle with that which contains his exhortation to virginity, on the ground that it is the state which favours most especially what he calls attending on the Lord without distraction. He declares that their spirit of party and their habit of drawing comparisons between one favourite teacher or priest and another, was a reason which was enough to prevent him from communicating to them the higher and more Divine truths of the Gospel system, that wisdom of which he says that he and the other Apostles used to communicate it to the perfect. The divisions among the Corinthians, such as they were, generated some kind of jealousy and rancour, and could hardly have been unproductive of anger, and thus we find in this part of the Apostle's remonstrances, a commentary on the warning of our Lord about those whom He calls dogs, as well as an illustration of His doctrine about the purity which is required in those who are to be the recipients of holy things and spiritual pearls.

If we ask ourselves what more especially and definitely may be signified by the double image which our Lord uses concerning the sacred things which are not to be handed over to those unworthy of them, the holy thing and the pearls, we find that our Lord's own example, the practice of the Church from the earliest times till after the cessation of persecution, and the manner of dealing with souls which is familiar to the saints, afford us a very ample commentary by which to explain the precept. In the first place, we find our Lord all through the three years of His preaching, to the very end, observing a very great reserve and reticence as to the sublime truths concerning His own Person and the Godhead in which He was One with His Father and the Holy Ghost. We shall see how He adopted the system of teaching by means of parables with the express and declared intention of setting forth certain great truths in such a way as to be intelligible only to some of those who heard Him. It was the complaint made against Him on the part of His enemies, that He would not tell them Who He was. When at the last they forced from Him an avowal of this, it was indeed a fulfilment of His own prophecy here made, for they trampled the truths of His Divinity and of the future judgment of which He warned them under foot, and turned upon Him with the cry that He was guilty of death. And all that time we cannot help being struck with the number of truths concerning His own Person and His Church which He held back from them. It was the same with the great central truth on which our faith, as St. Paul's tells us, depends, the truth of His Resurrection. It was kept back from the people and their rulers, and committed to certain chosen witnesses. When we turn from our Lord to His Apostles, we are in the same way struck with the reserve with which the whole range of truth concerning the Church, the sacraments, the organization and government of the Christian body, and the like, are withdrawn, and the little space which they fill in the Epistles of the New Testament. St. Paul was writing to those who were members of the bodies which he and others of the Apostles had founded, and yet he seems sometimes on the point of alluding to things, which if he had mentioned openly, the ground of numberless modern questions would have been cut away. Passing on in the Christian history, we find ourselves in the presence of a whole sytem of reserve, the persons from whom the secrets of the Church were hidden so carefully being just those whom the Scripture here as elsewhere seems to speak of as 'dogs'—that is, the unbelievers. A very slight knowledge of the history of the early centuries is required to make us see the necessity of this discipline. It is clear from the Apologists that the grossest misrepresentations were common concerning the Christian mysteries, which were spoken of as Thyestean repasts and orgies in which immoralities of the worst kind were committed. Under the circumstances of the time, it was necessary to be extremely cautious in admitting catchumens to the knowledge of the mysteries, and thus we find that at a certain time of the Holy Sacrifice they were told to depart, and that it was only after long trial that they were entrusted with the teaching about the sacraments, especially Baptism and the Holy Eucharist. Thus these mysteries were spoken of in public in a manner which was intelligible to those who knew the doctrine, and which did not convey any revelation of it to those who did not. There is much witness to this system in the Catacombs, and other monumental and artistic remains of the early Church. The dogma of the ever Blessed Trinity, and even the *Pater Noster* itself, were kept back from the imperfectly trained catechumens. We know, moreover, the extreme care which was taken to prevent the holy books of the Church from falling into profane hands, and how great a crime it was considered to have betrayed them to the enemies of the faith. In all this, both in the conduct of our Lord and His Apostles, and in the customs of the early Church, we have a very clear commentary on His words about not giving that which is holy to the 'dogs.'

Although the special circumstances which forced the early Christians to so close an observance of this precept may have passed away, still the principle remains always in force, for it is founded in truth on the incapacity of our nature in its lower moods to grasp Divine truths without danger to them and to itself. At the present day, the Catholic Church is open to all the world, her doctrines and ceremonies are committed to books which any one may possess and study, her schools and teaching, even on the most sacred subjects, are thrown open without any reserve. If the blasphemies which were common in the early ages are not exactly repeated, there are still as many and as foul forms of misrepresentation current as ever. It may fairly be questioned, whether the heathen of the days of Diocletian had a less accurate knowledge of the Catholic Church on the whole than modern Protestants. So true is it, that a certain disposition is necessary for the reception of Divine truth, and another certain disposition incompatible with that reception, which in any case must require the active assistance of the grace of God working upon the heart to which the truth is addressed. Again, there are certain parts of the Gospel teaching which are more fitted for some dispositions than for others. We have a striking instance of this in these very heads of teaching with which we have lately been occupied. Indeed the whole Sermon on the Mount may be considered as belonging to that portion of our Lord's teaching which may be counted among the 'pearls' of which He speaks. We have remarked on the contrast between this teaching and that which is summed up the words, 'Do penance, repent, the

Kingdom of Heaven is at hand.' The beauty and majesty, indeed, of the Beatitudes and of the subsequent teaching are so great, that we can hardly imagine any one who could listen to them and not be at least charmed, if he were not converted. And yet when we consider the state of soul of those whom our Lord designates as 'the swine,' persons who are given up to sensuality, grovelling in the mire of the lowest animal enjoyments, we can suppose that the preacher who would address them most effectually would not be he who began about the blessings of poverty, or of the pure in heart, or of the mourners, or of those who are persecuted for the sake of justice, while the irascible and high-spirited worldling, even of the nineteenth century, would not be easily approached and won by the teaching of our Lord about humility, meekness, and the peacemakers who are the children of God. The same may be said of other truths of the same sublime character. These have sometimes been exaggerated by teachers who may have thought that they were serving God, but who have certainly made it more difficult practically for the ordinary mass of Christians to serve Him. An instance of this may be found in the false teaching which in the last century infected a great part of the clergy of some Catholic countries, whereby nothing but contrition founded on the pure love of God, or attrition containing in it the love of God above all things, was laid down as the essential condition of the pardon of sins. The Jansenist teaching insisted upon putting what may be called the pearls of Christian doctrine before all men, whether immersed in the mire of vice or not, and it excluded a motive of fear which is so constantly insisted on by our Lord. But when people are laden with sin and are but just emerging from its snares, they require more cogent arguments for conversion. They know little about the love of God, it would be useless to talk to them about confidence in Him who clothes the lilies of the field and feeds the birds of the air, and about taking no anxious thought for the morrow. These men are to be moved by the great truths of our faith, the certainty of death, the inevitable judgment, the severe punishments which await the wicked in the next world, the fires of Hell, the eternity of torments—nay, as St. Francis Xavier teaches us, they are sometimes most cogently moved by threats of the Divine judgments even in this life, the calamities and miseries with which God sometimes visits those who persist in offending Him deliberately. When they have been brought to penitence, when they have made their peace with God in the Sacrament of Penance and restored their ill-gotten gains, repaired their injustices against their neighbour, learnt to lead a virtuous life in the keeping of the commandments of God, and persevered in this reformed state of life for a length of time, then it may be well to teach them the secrets and the delights of mental prayer, the exercise of the love of God, the beauty of perfect charity, the blessedness of the life of obedience, the glory of the virginal state, the anticipated heaven of contemplation and of sufferings for God. All these things may be classed among the pearls of heavenly doctrine. To those who can appreciate them, it is the greatest possible charity to set them forth. The words of our Lord as to the counsel of virginity hold good here—'He that can receive it, let him receive it.' But to those who cannot rise to this level, it is better not to address the teaching which relates to these things. We have our Lord's authority for saying that, to these and other truths of His Kingdom, men are led chiefly and ordinarily by the teaching and drawing of the Father in His Providence, and to run as it were in advance of that teaching may issue in disrespect to the heavenly doctrine itself, and in danger to those who imprudently urge on others the truths for which the grace of God has not as yet fitted them.

When we consider how many things there are in the system of the Catholic Church which are in themselves holy, and the appointed means of promoting or restoring holiness in her children, it is plain that the warning of our Lord cannot be limited to points of doctrine and the like. From the very first it has been understood that the sacraments of the Church have been included in the number of those choice treasures which our Lord here bids us protect from profanation. The conditions on which it is lawful to receive absolution in the Sacrament of Penance, or to receive our Lord in the Blessed Sacrament, or indeed to receive any of the other sacraments, are laid down in the catechism and other books of practical instruction, and these rules must be the guides by which the priests of the Church must be regulated in their administration of these sacred mysteries. There have been times when an excessive strictness prevailed in this matter, and there may be in some cases a natural reaction which may issue in over-indulgence. These words of our Lord may be remembered as furnishing His priests with an additional motive for great exertion and carefulness in the administration of the sacraments, the admission to which practically depends on them. For it may often be in the power of the priest, by the blessing of God, Who is always especially ready to cooperate with efforts that are made for His glory and the greater good of souls in the working of the sacramental system, to change a dog, in the sense of this passage, into a worthy sheep of the fold, and to convert one who has been living after the fashion of the swine into a continent and contrite penitent before he is admitted to the sacraments. The hardest part of the priest's work is that in which he is brought into contact with souls one by one, and the part of the office of a confessor in which the saints differ most from ordinary men, is that in which they have to form in the hearts of their penitents the dispositions which enable them to receive the Sacrament of Penance with the most complete fruit. It is theirs to change, if it may be, attrition into contrition, to lead the soul to the discernment of, and sorrow for, sins which before it thought light of, and to fortify the purpose of amendment into a resolution which, by the grace of God, may not only be sincere at the time, but also strong enough to abide the storms of temptation and the influence of old habits and associations without a relapse. In doing this they are in truth acting on the principle which our Lord here lays down—not that their penitents were before altogether unfit for the treasures of the Kingdom, but that the security of those treasures against profanation is indefinitely increased by the increased fitness of the subject to receive them and profit by them. Much more are the ministers of God acting on this precept when they refuse, as they sometimes must refuse, to allow the sacraments to those who are not likely to profit by them. For though it is well always to bear in mind that the sacraments were made for men, and not men for the sacraments, and that they are designed by God not to find men saints but to make them such; still there is a duty to God in this matter as well as to man, and we are strictly bound to keep off those who are truly and evidently unworthy. Some holy writers have considered that our Lord Himself had left us a beautiful example of this in His silence before Herod, as to the not opening the treasures of Christian truth to the utterly unworthy, and in the case of the danger of an unworthy Communion, by His contriving that Judas should leave the Cenacle without any suspicion on the part of the other Apostles, before the celebration of the Holy Eucharist. The truth of this last inference must of course depend on the view which is adopted as to the order of the events at the Last Supper. However that may be, still it remains indisputable that it is the duty of those who are in charge of the sacred mysteries to look to the preservation of the honour of God in the readiness with which they impart them, and the care they take in preparing people for them.

Our Lord adds to His injunctions as to the reverence with which the sacred truths and the gifts of grace which God has committed to His Church are to be handled and administered, a reason for this, which amounts to a prophecy, "lest perhaps they trample them under their feet, and turning upon you, rend you." In giving this warning our Lord again speaks with that perfect knowledge of men which was one of the essential endowments of His Sacred Humanity. The 'perhaps' which He inserts is not meant to imply any doubt as to the possible result of imprudence in communicating Divine things to those who are unworthy of them, but to signify that, after all, this result depends on the free will of men. This warning, together with the few words at the end of the series of the Beatitudes in which He applies the blessing of those who are to be persecuted for the sake of justice to the disciples personally, as well as the passage which follows about the false prophets in sheep's clothing, and the like, shows that clear insight which our Lord possessed as to the reception which His Church, like Himself, was to meet with at the hands of men in general. And indeed, it might be asked, why is this so to be, as He foresaw it would be, and as we from the experience of history know that it has been?

What is there in the blessed message of peace through Jesus Christ, and in all the details of the method of salvation and perfection which that message embodies, to excite anger, violence, and resentment? Even the animals, to whom our Lord compares those who are unfit for His Divine favours, may indeed reject the delicate and refined food which is not to their taste, but they neglect it, and turn away without being infuriated by its offer. Men themselves do not treat in this manner other secrets and boons which they still do not care to accept. The discoverer of a new remedy for some common disease, the inventor of some new machine for the advantage of trade, or for the greater convenience of life, the men who have the first dreams of new continents, or of the means of making steam or electricity the servants of man, may meet with neglect and contempt, they may find it very difficult to gain a hearing with the powers of the world, or an opportunity of putting their discoveries or theories to the test of practical trial, but they do not find that what they profess to have to impart in the way of benefit to mankind brings on them hatred or persecution. But when it is a question, not of some new instrument of destruction in warfare, or of some new mechanical contrivance for the common use of their fellow-creatures, but of something which relates to the eternal welfare of the soul, and makes it easier to gain peace of conscience and admission to the Kingdom of Heaven, then the whole world is up in arms as if an enemy were at the gates of a city or a pestilence in the air. The precious gift is trampled under foot, and the bearers thereof are torn to pieces. We may endeavour to consider what reasons may be found for this strange fact, to which the whole of the history of the Church bears witness.

In the first place, it must be remembered that there

are elements in our fallen nature which are set in revolt by the near approach of the supernatural, and by anything that recalls the truth that our nature is fallen. We had occasion to speak of these elements in a former chapter of this volume, when we had to explain the Christian doctrine of the necessity of mortification. Unfit as men may be for the reception of Divine truth and of the gracious means of reconciliation and restoration and elevation which the Church has to administer, the mere offer of these things reminds them of their degradation, and touches the wounds which they would fain altogether forget. They are not ready to rise, but they have an instinctive feeling that they are in danger if they remain as they are, that their present state is not that for which God meant them, and that they will have to give an account for remaining in it. No sinner is so hardened but he feels uncomfortable when the keen air of Heaven is breathed in upon the unhealthy atmosphere in which he lives. No one who has rejected some high vocation and resolutely chosen to live a worldly life, but feels himself rebuked and brought to book, as it were, when the higher teaching which he has neglected is brought back to his mind, or thrust upon him by the example of some one who has been more faithful than himself. No teacher of heresy, who has turned away from the path along which he was being guided to the Catholic Church and set himself up as a prophet in a sect outside the Church, but feels angered when the eternal question of the claims of the Church on the allegiance of all Christians is brought before him, time after time, by persons whom he would fain persuade to accept his personal authority instead of hers. It is the same with all who have ever rejected grace. This is the reason which accounts for the savage and unnatural domestic persecution of which we see so many instances before our eyes, the victims of which are the converts to Catholicism in many English families. The persecution is often waged by men of violent tempers and overbearing pride, who have no personal religion at all; but it is often also justified and counselled by those Anglican teachers who are themselves, as they think, the nearest in their doctrines to the Catholic Church. In any case, it is true that there is usually a sense of personal rebuke and reproach about those who cannot close with the offers which are made by the teaching to which our Lord refers, and that this sense shows itself in anger and hostility.

Again, the Church and her teachers always speak, as our Lord always spoke, with a certain tone of authority which grates upon the ears of the children of the world. Nothing is dearer to our fallen nature than its independence, because it feels instinctively that it has a Master Who does not recognize the claims which it would fain make in that regard. But every message of peace, even the most loving offer of pardon and reconciliation on the easiest terms, even the news that God has loved the world so much that He has died on a Cross for its redemption, implies the whole truth of the rebelliousness of man, and that God alone can fix the terms of pardon and order the method of restoration. Again, the pride of man shrinks with dislike from that which is one of the very tenderest and most thoughtful instances of God's condescension in the economy of the Incarnation—namely, the mercy by which the ministry of reconciliation is committed, not to angels or any class of beings superior to ourselves, but to men to whom we are to listen as in the place of God. Thus, when the treasures of grace and of truth are proffered to men whose state prevents them from accepting the offer willingly, all the evil passions which dominate the heart are arrayed against the messenger, on account of the first reason just now assigned, and all the natural pride of man on account of the second reason.

To these two reasons for this fact we may well add a third. In the case of the persons of whom our Lord is speaking, the powers of evil are more or less in undisturbed possession of the soul. They are like the 'strong armed man' of whom we hear later on, who is guarding his hall in peace. The approach of the Divine message and supernatural gifts of the Gospel, especially in the case of its more sublime doctrines, is felt by the powers of evil, like the landing of an army of invasion. It warns them that their usurpation may be brought to an end, their tyranny overthrown, their slaves set free. The footsteps of the Master are heard, the brightness and fragrance of His presence strikes them as with the chill of death. Their best chance is to repel the attack at once, to turn the poor deluded will, over which they have set up their dominion, away at once from all desire even to parley with the advancing grace. This is the case in instances when the extent of the dominion of evil is far from being quite universal over the soul, when persons whom the devils do not care to tempt to the fouler vices are yet deluded into an aversion to a life of perfection, or a call to follow our Lord in the evangelical counsels. Much more is it the case when the soul has been led far away from God, and when it lies at the feet of its enslavers in almost absolute bondage.

CHAPTER XII.

The Precept of Prayer.

St. Matt. vii. 7—11 ; *Vita Vitæ Nostræ*, § 35.

THE connection of the passage on which we have now to speak, with the words which immediately precede it, is not at first sight quite evident. It may be thought that the injunction concerning the prudence and reserve which are necessary in the imparting of Divine truths and gifts, suggests the difficulty of the Apostolical ministry, and that the weapon of prayer is here given us by our Lord, as if that were the one source which remains, after it has become evident that men must in many cases be left to themselves, or rather to God, instead of being directly addressed with the Gospel message. The hard and obstinate heart, the soul sunk in the mire of lasciviousness and sensuality, the angry and proud enemies of the faith, the arrogance of heretics, the conceit of the so-called men of science, and the like, cannot be reached by preaching or argument or authority, but they can nevertheless be won by the grace of God, and that grace may be set in motion by prayer. We can do nothing ourselves, but we can win for such the mercy of God, in Whose hands are the hearts of all. But it is perhaps better not to seek too close a connection in every link of this great chain of precepts. It is clear that our Lord is now drawing towards the close of this series of wonderful instructions, which He addresses in the first instance to those whom He calls to a very single and entire service in His Church. These are the persons whom He invites to an absolute renouncement of earthly cares, and to the most perfect dependence on the providence of His Father. These are the persons to whom, in a special manner, the precept of taking no anxious thought for the morrow is given, and who are then warned to practise the most perfect reverence to their neighbour, in the way of refraining from all judgment, and also the most perfect prudence in the administration of the sacred gifts which are entrusted to them for the rest of His children. Now, it may be said, they are fit to receive the great, all-powerful weapon of the Kingdom of God; for they are prepared, by the precepts already imparted to them, for the use of prayer in all childlike confidence. 'If you abide in Me,' He said to them later in His course, 'and My words abide in you, you shall ask whatever you will, and it shall be done unto you;'[1] and the Evangelist who records these words says, in his First Epistle, as if referring to them, 'Dearly beloved, if our heart do not reprehend us, we have confidence towards God, and whatsoever we shall ask we shall receive of Him, because we keep his commandments, and do those things which are pleasing in His sight.'[2] And thus now, at the close of His instructions to His intimate friends and disciples, our Lord seems to speak of this great boon for which He has been making them fit. Here again, as has been already mentioned, we have the same connection of thought as in the discourse already referred to of St. Catharine of Siena on her death-bed. 'A person cannot give his heart to God without prayer founded on humility, which acknowledges itself nothing, and devoid of all self-confidence. A general application to mental prayer is requisite, because it increases and strengthens virtues which, with-

[1] St. John xv. 7.   [2] 1 St. John iii. 21, 22.

out that aliment, would become weak and come to nought. She taught all her followers to devote certain hours to vocal prayer, and to give themselves continually to mental prayer, either actually or in heart.'[3]

Thus the words on which we are now to dwell may be understood as referring to the whole of the precepts and counsels delivered in the Sermon on the Mount, and as furnishing the one great means by which these are to be carried out. That is, the one great instrument and power in the Kingdom of God, as it has been sketched in the beatitudes and in the precepts which have followed, is the use of prayer. This is the great law of the Kingdom. There are states in which everything is to be gained or brought about by the moving of public opinion, by means of agitation, discussion, argument, and the like. There are states where money is the motive power; others where that power is the favour of courtiers; or again, the force of military despotism. The Kingdom of God is the kingdom of prayer. As other kingdoms depend on public opinion, money, or brute force, everything in this kingdom depends on the will of the Sovereign, and the will of the Sovereign is moved by means of prayer. In its highest and widest sense, prayer is the intercourse between the subjects of the King, the children of the one Father, and their Father and King. He has created them such as they are, He has given them the faculties of knowledge, reason, will, love, which they possess, in order that they may know Him, love Him, serve Him, and converse with Him in prayer. In this sense prayer is the end for which rational souls are made. It is not wonderful, therefore, that it should be the means by which everything is to be obtained, eveything done, all desires accomplished, all tasks and undertakings executed.

[3] *Vita*, part iii. c. 4.

Again, the beatitudes, and the instructions which have come after them, have opened an almost boundless field of desire and labour for the children of God. They are invited to be poor in spirit, to be mourners and meek, to hunger and thirst after justice, and the rest. They are to be the salt of the earth and light of the world. Their justice is to rise far above that of the Scribes and Pharisees, the most learned and religious persons of the holy nation, and they are to keep the commandments of God with the highest purity of observance, so as to refrain from the interior movements of anger and desires of lust. They are to love their enemies, to imitate God in His perfections, to address to His eyes alone their deeds of almsgiving, their prayers, their mortifications. They are to be occupied in laying up treasure in Heaven, they are to serve Him with the utmost singleness of service, and to rely on His providence, as the birds of the air or the grass of the field. How is all this perfection to be won? Where are they to get the strength which will make them all that they are told to be, and enable them to do all that they are commissioned to do? Hitherto our Lord has not said. Now He tells them— it is to be found in prayer. None of these things, our Lord seems to say, are out of your reach. They do not depend on your own strength or ability, they depend only' on your asking for them—'Ask and it shall be given you, seek and you shall find, knock and it shall be opened to you. For every one that asketh receiveth, and he that seeketh findeth, and to him that knocketh it shall be opened.' It is not always so indeed, it might be replied—it may be that no one who asks not receives, and no one who does not seek finds, and no one has the door opened to him who does not knock. But in all earthly things we may ask without receiving, we may seek without finding, we may knock again and again and yet not gain admittance. But in this case of the goods of the Kingdom of Heaven it cannot be so, on account of the character of Him with Whom we have to do. This our Lord goes on to urge, as He has before used the character of His Father and ours, to make us secure when we depend on His providence—'Or what man is there among you, of whom if his son shall ask bread, will he reach him a stone? or if he shall ask him a fish, will he reach him a serpent? If you, then, being evil, know how to give good gifts to your children, how much more will your Father Who is in Heaven give good things to them that ask Him?'

The threefold form in which our Lord has cast His exhortation to prayer, has been understood of the different ways in which we are to assail the loving mercy of God by simple petitions, by adding exertions and industries of our own to obtain what we desire, and by a sort of violence and clamour, by which the obstacles which shut us out from what we are bent on attaining, may be removed. Others consider that the threefold expression is used by our Lord in order to represent the earnest and persistent prayer which must be used with God. It must also be remembered that the things which are set before us in the Sermon on the Mount as the objects at which we are to aim, are of various kinds, some of them simple gifts, others virtues which require practice and exercise on our own part, others belong more to the class of truths and lights concerning our position here with respect to our Father and the work which He has set us to do, others are conquests which must be achieved over flesh and blood or against the spiritual enemies of our salvation and perfection. Indeed it may be said that the acquisition of any of the virtues which reach their perfection in the beatitudes is a work which requires the use of the threefold weapons which are spoken of in this Sermon, the three great acts of religion, prayer, almsdeeds, and fasting or mortification. To gain poverty of spirit, or purity of heart, for instance, prayer will not be enough unless we set ourselves to seek for the virtue which we desire by practising its acts, and by doing violence to ourselves. And if we wish to gain any favour from God, as for instance, the spirit of charity which reaches to the perfect love of our enemies, we must not only ask it in prayer, but seek it by good deeds, and knock violently at the door of the Divine mercy by mortification. In such cases the exercises of good works of charity, which are done for the intention which we have before us, are turned into prayer by that intention, and the same is to be said of the mortifications of any kind which we may use for the same purpose. Thus our Lord may mean to remind us that we have this threefold armoury, and that we must use all three of these means of bringing down the mercy of God on ourselves and others, if we are to obtain the boons which we desire. We are to do all that we can do—and thus this explanation of the words before us falls in with that of those who consider that our Lord means simply to signify the need of the most continuous and urgent prayer of which we are capable.

It must also be noted, that our Lord does not put this doctrine about the efficacy of prayer simply in a conditional form, as if He had said, if you wish to receive, ask, if you wish to find, seek; if you wish to be admitted, knock. That conditional form would have expressed the truth, but it would not have put so directly the injunction which our Lord lays upon us. We are the servants of the one Master, the children of the Great King; we have a certain work to do for Him, unless we are to be unprofitable servants and degenerate children, and for this work prayer is essential. We are not, therefore, free not to pray—prayer is as incumbent on us as is the salvation of our souls, the obedience to the commands of our Creator and our Lord, the accomplishment of the work which He requires of us in our own souls and in those of others. Whatever call we may have to the formation in ourselves of the virtues of the beatitudes and to the accomplishment of the other precepts and counsels of the Sermon, that call binds us to the acquirement of the habit and virtue of prayer in the sense in which it is here used, in which it embraces all the weapons we have at our command for the attainment from God of the graces to which we are called.

It would seem as if our Lord were meeting an objections in the words which follow on this injunction to prayer, when He says that every one that asks, receives; and he that seeks, finds; and that to him that knocketh it is opened. The objection would be that common complaint, even of persons who serve God and are earnest and instant in their petitions—that they ask and do not receive. We may put aside the cases in which the prayer that is ineffectual is unpleasing to God, as in the cases which are mentioned by St. James in his Epistle,[4] when faith does not accompany prayer, or when the prayer is made amiss because its object is the satisfaction of concupiscence. In these cases it would not be according to the laws of God's Kingdom that the prayer should be granted, for faith is necessary in order that God may be pleased, and God would not be a good Father if He gave us things evil for our souls. Again, it may be that, as has been said, it may be necessary in many cases that we should not only ask, but seek and knock also, and that it is only to the force of the three together that the mercy of God will yield. Thus, at the end of this passage, our Lord, after speaking of God as compared to an earthly

[4] St. James i. 6, 7.

father, says that He will certainly give good things to those who ask Him, without mentioning the other two conditions, as if the true asking included the other two. But it may be that all these three means have been used, and the prayer made in the perfect way which is required by the conditions which are laid down as necessary, that is with piety, and with perseverance, and as to matters which concern our souls and their salvation or perfection. Such we cannot doubt was the prayer which St. Paul addressed to our Lord, when he desired to be delivered from the painful and annoying temptation which he speaks of in the second Epistle to the Corinthians, and which he calls 'a thorn in his flesh, a messenger of Satan to buffet him.'[5] We cannot certainly suppose that the prayer of the Apostle can have been wanting in any condition requisite to make it acceptable to God, and yet he tells us that he was refused the particular boon which he had asked, and on which his heart was set. The reason was given him that it was, in effect, better for him to suffer that molestation and to overcome the temptation by the grace which was promised to him, for thus he was preserved in humility, and gained continual victories thereby: that is, his prayer was heard, but he did not receive what he asked, but something else which it was better for him to have.

This opens to our thoughts the whole subject of the conditions which are required in order that prayer may have the kind of right to be heard which is, as it were, implied in this promise of our Lord. These conditions are commonly laid down as four. First, that is, we must ask for ourselves and not for others—for our prayers for others, as will be seen presently, are liable to impediments arising from those for whom they are made,

[5] 2 Cor. xii. 7.

even if all the necessary conditions have been fulfilled on our part. In the next place, we must ask piously, and in this condition is included the requirement that we are in such a state as to be heard by God, and that our prayer is made with all the reverence and modesty and attention which such an act requires. In the third place, we must pray with perseverance, not asking once or twice and then desisting, which shows inconstancy or want of confidence, or impatience, or some other fatal defect, but continuing earnest and instant until our prayer is satisfied. Lastly, the things which we ask must be things that relate to our salvation, the good of our souls, and the glory of God. The saints understand our Lord's promise, in the passage before us, of such prayer as these conditions imply, and of such prayer they understand our Lord to say that it shall be heard. But even here it is to be noted that He does not say that they shall have exactly that particular thing which they ask for, but they shall receive, and shall find, and that it shall be opened to them. And when He goes on to use the comparison of an earthly father, who will not give his child a stone when he asks for bread, nor a serpent when he asks for a fish, He does not say that our Heavenly Father will give exactly what we ask—for that would often be to give us a stone instead of bread, or a serpent instead of a fish—but that He will give good things to those who ask Him. And in the similar passage in St. Luke He says simply, He will give His good Spirit to those who are his petitioners.[6] For all good things and graces are but various ministrations and imparting of the Holy Spirit of God. This, then, is what is promised to prayer—not that the actual request will always be granted, for in that case God would have to abdicate the government of the world, and put it into

[6] St. Luke xi. 13.

the hands of men of short sight and most imperfect wisdom. His own glory would suffer immensely, and the good of our souls would be lost to the same extent.

It remains to say a few words about the manner in which God answers prayers which He does not directly grant. There are some things, in the first place, which may be won by prayer, but not by every prayer—as when our Lord spoke of the demoniac boy after the Transfiguration, that the evil spirit by whom he was possessed did not go out but by prayer and fasting. There are some things which require not only prayer in its most restricted sense, but the prayer that is joined to mortification and sacrifice. There are some things which require the prayers of the Church as well as private prayers, though, by the mercy of God, the private prayer of every Catholic Christian is in a true sense the prayer of the Church. There are some things for which the prayer of the saints, so much more powerful than ours, is necessary, and for which recourse must be had in a special way to her through whose hands, as it were, all our prayers pass to God and all boons come to us from Him, the most Blessed Virgin Mother of our Lord. In the next place, we must remember that God as a good Father is bound to consider the good of the person who makes the prayer, as in the case already mentioned of St. Paul; on this account it is that a great number of prayers are not granted as they are made. Again, God is bound to consider the good of others also, as well as of the person who prays, and He may see that the direct granting of a certain petition may be injurious to the Church at large, or to some particular persons. Thus it may have been that David's prayer for the life of the child of his sin with Bethsabee was not granted, because his life would have been a perpetual witness to the world of the fall of a great friend of God. Again, it must be remembered that God is bound to preserve untouched the general laws of His Kingdom and government, unless He sees good, in some particular case, to work a miracle. This is the reason why He does not at once set His servants free from the molestation of evil thoughts when they pray against them—for such thoughts have often some right, as it were, to be there, on account of negligence in the avoidance of what may give them occasion, or on account of past habits of carelessness or worse, or of the physical condition of the body, or of something else. And in such cases God sees it better to give grace to resist them in answer to the prayers that are made, than to work a sort of miracle by removing them. It is not that He is chary of His power in favour of His saints and children, but that He reverences His creation and the laws which He has given to it, and prefers assisting His servants in the way of grace, which is the law which He has laid down, than in some extraordinary way which sets common laws at nought. For He has chosen the way of dealing with us which He adopts, out of consideration for what is best on the whole for our souls as well as for His own glory, according to the inscrutable counsel of His most holy will. And, in the same way, He does not grant all the desires of His saints, even when He has Himself inspired them. It is His will that they should have the merit and the spiritual benefit of designs and plans for His glory which He does not intend them to execute. He lets some of them pine with longing for martyrdom, while he makes them work for years without meeting with an occasion of it, and then die in peace. They are sanctified and made more pleasing to Him by their desires, and that is what He wills. In other cases He delays for long years the granting of the boon for which they besiege Him, as in the case of St. Monica, who became a saint by having so long to wait for what was the great object of her prayers. In other cases, the reason why prayers are not granted, as they are made, may be something in the eternal counsels of God in the government of the Church, as when He would not grant to St. Francis Xavier the power to enter and preach in the Kingdom of China, or as when He told the Venerable Marina of Escobar that the time for the conversion of England to Catholicism could not be yet. In this case there were absolute impediments, as it appears, in the character of the reigning King, Charles I. We find the same in other cases when the object of the prayers of the saints has been the conversion of some single sinner, as in the case of the miserable son of Vasco di Gama, who opposed the embassy to China on which St. Francis Xavier had built his hopes of entering that kingdom, though we may suppose that the charity of the Saint availed his persecutor in obtaining him the grace of penitence at the last.

But we are here entering on a very wide, though a very beautiful, subject, and enough has been said to show that there are many ways of explaining the apparent difficulty as to the answering of prayer. Like other difficulties about the government of God, it is found at last to lead us to highest and nobler thoughts about that government than we should otherwise have conceived. For, although God does not answer prayer in the way which poor short-sighted mortals might expect and even hope, still He answers it in a way of His own, the study of which reveals fresh glories of His wisdom and love and power. We may be sure that when all things which concern the government of the world and of each soul by God are made plain, we shall find endless reasons for glorifying Him in what we come to know as to this subject-matter.

The Precept of Prayer. 217

We shall see, in the first place, how entirely the Kingdom of God is the Kingdom of prayer. It will then become manifest that prayer has been the main agent in the government of God—the prayer of the Sacred Heart, the prayer of Mary, the prayer of the Saints and Angels and of the Holy Souls, the prayer of the Church and of her children one by one. We do not mean to set any limit to the free mercy and bountifulness of God—indeed, it is manifest that the creation itself is a free act of God, which could have been preceded by no prayer of creatures, and that the gift of prayer itself is something which no one could ask or earn. But it is not the less true that prayer is the great ordinary means by which the mercies and graces of Heaven are drawn down upon the Church on earth, and on her children. The light of Heaven which will reveal all God's doing with our race, and with each child of Adam, all His providence in the Church, and over each single soul, will lay bare the history of what has been done by the Holy Mass, by the regular prayers of the Church, the Orders, and contemplative souls who have been hidden from the eyes of the world, and yet have been its great benefactors. It will show us what we owe to the prayers of the saints and angels, and to those on earth who have interceded for us while we thought little of them. It will show how the course of human events, the fortunes of the Church and of the Holy See, the preservation of kingdoms, and the conversion of nations, have been ruled by prayer. We shall trace its influence with our own lives, the graces it has procured, the dangers it has averted, and the thousand various sources of good which we have never known. Another thing that will become clear in the daylight of eternity will be how no prayer of whatever kind has ever failed of its effect, according to the ordinance of God. Every single aspiration of the faithful soul will then be seen to have been noticed by its Father, and counted to it for good, and fruitful of reward and impetration. The marvellous providence of God in arranging the fruits of prayer, when He has granted it at once, when He has delayed to answer it, when He has given what was asked, when He has given something better, the substitution of grace of a higher order for what He was asked in a lower order, of spiritual strength for temporal relief, of patience under suffering for the removal of that suffering, His denial of boons which would have led to pride, His sending of wholesome chastisements instead of granting prosperity, His preparing the soul for Heaven when prayer was made to keep it on earth—all these things and a thousand others which they suggest as belonging to the same department, if we may so speak, of His ineffable wisdom and charity in the governing of the world, will then become plain. We often think of St. Paul's words where he says that the history of the Church, as it unfolds to the heavenly powers the many-sided and many-coloured wisdom of God,[7] is the delight of the angels and saints in Heaven, and surely each soul of all that blessed multitude will rejoice in the particular contemplation of the mercy of God in this respect towards itself. And then also it will come to be known what prayer had it in its power to effect if it had been duly used; how all the difficulties which have beset the work of God in the world—committed, as it is, to human hearts and hands, and which have increased, as it seems, as the Christian centuries roll on, until at last it appears as if the designs of God had almost been defeated,—are to be accounted for by the simple truth that prayer has not been made as it ought to be, that

[7] Ephes. iii. 10.

the faith, as a grain of mustard seed, of which our Lord spoke, has not been fostered in our hearts, and that so the mountains which might have been moved and cast into the sea are still standing in their place, and the conquest of the world to the kingdom of our Lord has not been accomplished.

It may be added, that the threefold form of expression which our Lord has chosen in this place, seems to extend the promise far more widely if He had only said that what we ask shall be granted to us. When we consider how wide is the extent of what may be called the kingdom of prayer, we see how much we have gained by this threefold promise. Asking is not quite so much as seeking, nor asking and seeking as knocking; nor is receiving the same as finding, nor as being admitted to the place at the door of which we have knocked. Our Lord seems to tell us that the whole magnificent range of the Christian virtues and graces is laid open to us if we will—that we shall find knowledge and wisdom and spiritual powers, the riches which satisfy the intelligence, and the delights which answer to all that the affections can long for. He tells us that the palace of the King of kings, the inclosed garden of contemplation, the anticipated heaven, which consists in close familiarity with God—all shall be laid open to those who have the courage to ask and seek and knock. Not merely this or that boon, but the Giver of all boons, shall be ours to know and possess, if we are persevering and indefatigable in prayer. The secrets of the Kingdom, the hidden things of the Divine counsels, the mysteries of theology, those things which the Holy Spirit alone can know, shall be revealed to us, because He will teach us to pray as we ought. The treasures which are thus in store for us may require long petitioning, and much seeking, and painful knocking, for they can only be won by those who do violence to themselves and die to earthly delights and interests, and lead on earth a life which has its conversation in Heaven. But their worth is such and the enjoyment of possessing them so great, that no one who has known them will count any labour that he has had to undergo, as worth thinking of in comparison with the blessings which he has won thereby.

But the teaching of this passage can never be thoroughly mastered by us, unless we understand in how true a sense it contains a positive precept as well as the declaration of a privilege of untold value. The precept of prayer is like the precept of the love of God, as prayer is, indeed, the exercise of the love of God. We are sometimes surprised at some of the language of the Apostles on this subject, as when St. Paul bids the Christian be 'instant in prayer'[8] or 'pray without ceasing;'[9] or when he lays it down as a rule for the Church in which Timothy was Bishop, saying, 'I desire that first of all supplications, prayers, intercessions, and thanksgivings (Eucharists) be made for all men . . . , that men pray in every place, lifting up pure hands, without anger and contention.[10] The pagan view of prayer is that it is a resource when we are in need and can obtain relief in no other way, as men will pray when they are in a sinking ship, or when some one whom they love is in unusual danger of death, and then, if their prayer should be heard, never think either of thanksgiving or of praying again. Too many Christians, unfortunately, are pagans in their views of prayer. The Christian view, as set forth in the New Testament, is that prayer is the first duty of men who know God—not merely the key of Heaven, the safeguard of salvation, the all-powerful weapon of defence against danger, the treasure by which

[8] Rom. xii. 12.   [9] 1 Thess. v. 17.   [10] 1 Tim. ii. 1, 8.

all blessings here and hereafter can be purchased, but the positive duty of all who are capable of it as far and when they are capable of it. It is not fixed for one time rather than another by the commandment of God, because it is incumbent on us at all times when we are not prevented from practising it by other obligations; or rather, all our duties, the obligations of our calling in life, our needs, our rest, our recreation, our social intercourse, our public business, and the like, are forms of indirect prayer, and when these do not press on us, we are to fall back on the general duty of praying always, besides going certain times to direct prayer and converse with God. Thus Christians have a great variety of callings, but the calling to pray is the calling of all. They have a great number of duties to attend to, but the one duty to which they are bound at all times is prayer. Circumstances which they cannot help may keep them from all things rather than this—from the active exercise of good works, or the assistance at Mass, or the frequentation of the sacraments, or from hearing the Word of God—no circumstance, except that of mental incapacity, can excuse them from prayer.

CHAPTER XIII.

The Law and the Prophets.

St. Matt. vii. 12 ; *Vita Vitæ Nostræ*, § 35.

THE considerations of the last chapter set before us the vastness of the extent of the realm of prayer in its widest sense. They show us how every function of our life, as the children of God, may be summed up in prayer. They show us how the whole of our duty to God as our Father may be said to be contained in its exercises and their fruits. But has our Lord nothing of the same kind to say as to our duty to one another? If this is so complex as to embrace a great number of precepts, may it not at all events be brought under some one general rule, which can be expressed by some formula easily remembered and applied, and which may furnish us with practical guidance like that in which our Lord has cast the duty and the privilege and the efficacy of prayer? Some such formula seems to be given us by our Lord, as the conclusion of this part of His Divine Sermon, when He says, in the words which are now to occupy our thoughts, 'All things, therefore, whatsoever you would that men should do unto you, do ye also unto them, for this is the Law and the prophets.' The words themselves are simple enough, and seem to put within easy reach the performance of the whole Law and of the counsel of the prophets, who in many respects, as we have seen, completed and developed the more perfect principles contained, but not unfolded, in the Law itself. The words of our Lord are founded, as it seems, on the instruction given to his son by the elder Tobias, except that in the Old Testament the instruction is cast in the negative form—'See thou never do to another what thou wouldst hate to have done to thee by another.'[1] Between the negative and positive form of the precept, there is all the difference between the Law and the Gospel. For it has already been remarked how the main precepts of the Law were prohibitions rather than precepts, while the Gospel enjoins positive and active virtues, instead of the simple refraining from the indulgence of evil appetites.

This precept of our Lord's is introduced by a particle which connects it with the preceding words of which we have lately spoken. For our Lord says, 'All things, therefore, whatsoever you would that men should do unto you, do you also to them,' as if He was giving the precept as a reason for something which had gone before. What has gone before is the direction about the power and duty of prayer, as the great exercise of the love of God. He seems, then, to say that prayer will have the power of which He speaks if we put no impediment in the way to that power on our part, if we fulfil all the conditions which are requisite in order that God may give us what is here promised. And therefore it is that we must do to others all things that we would have them do to us, for that is the condition on which God will do for us all that we ask and seek for in prayer. Or, in other words, if we wish our prayers to be heard, if we desire to have the benefit of the magnificent promises about asking and receiving, seeking and finding, and the like, we must practise that fulfilment of the Law as regards our neighbour which is expressed in the injunction to do unto others all things that we desire they should do unto us. Thus the connection between these two precepts is just the same as that between the two parts of the

[1] Tobias iv. 17.

petition in the Lord's Prayer, for the forgiveness of our trespasses as we forgive others, or as that which we have lately noticed, between the precept not to judge others and the reason which our Lord gives for that precept. We have thus a first declaration on the part of our Lord as to the indissoluble union between the two great commandments, as to which He afterwards spoke in His last teaching in the Temple. In the same way the words seem to lead on to the doctrine which is contained in the parable of the unmerciful servant, namely, that if we wish God to forgive us we must forgive others, if we wish God to hear our prayers we must be ready to listen to the entreaties of others. Thus the words before us are not simply a summing up of our whole duty to our neighbour, but they are a declaration that the performance of our perfect duty to our neighbour is required by God, as a manifestation of our love towards Himself, and as a condition on which may depend the fulfilment of the promises which He has made to us, as a crown of that duty which we owe to Him.

These thoughts naturally suggest the consideration of those other places in which the idea here set forth in a few words is more fully developed either by our Lord or by the Apostles. The first of these places has been already referred to, where, in the course of our Lord's last teaching in the Temple in Holy Week, He answered the famous question as to the great commandment of the Law—' Thou shalt love the Lord thy God with thy whole heart and with thy whole soul and with thy whole mind. This is the greatest and the first commandment. And the second is like unto this: Thou shalt love thy neighbour as thyself. On these two commandments dependeth the whole Law and the prophets.'[2] In this place our Lord seems to enlarge most on the first of the

[2] St. Matt. xxii. 37—40.

The Law and the Prophets. 225

two great commandments, as containing in itself, as it were, or involving, the second. In the passage in the Sermon on the Mount, the second is spoken of as involving the first. In the passage in the Epistle to the Romans, which reads like a commentary upon the words before us, it is the same. St. Paul fills up the part which our Lord, in the Temple, left undeveloped, that is, our duty to our neighbour is put forward in detail, as if that included our duty to God. St. Paul says: 'Owe no man anything but to love one another, for he that loveth his neighbour hath fulfilled the law. For, thou shalt not commit adultery, thou shalt not kill, thou shalt not steal, thou shalt not bear false witness, thou shalt not covet, and if there be any other commandment, it is comprised in this word, Thou shalt love thy neighbour as thyself. The love of our neighbour worketh no evil, therefore love is the fulfilling of the law.'[3] And the same Apostle says in the Epistle to the Galatians, 'All the law is fulfilled in one word, Thou shalt love thy neighbour as thyself.'[4] In these passages, then, we have the twofold truth asserted, that of the close connection between the two tables of the law, and that of the summing up of our duty to our neighbour in the single commandment to love him as ourself. This precept itself, as we shall presently have to point out, is taken from one of the Books of Moses, and it is as old as the Decalogue itself.

Little is required to show that the love of God is included in all true love of our neighbour. For our neighbour is only truly to be loved for the sake of God, Who is the Creator, the Father, the Lord of all alike, Who, as St. Paul says, 'hath made of one all mankind,'[5] Who has given to every man a command concerning his neighbour, Who is the Founder of natural society, Who

[3] Rom. xiii. 8—10.   [4] Galat. v. 14.   [5] Acts xvii. 26.

has also united us in the supernatural society of the Church, which is the Body of His Son, in Whom He has made us partakers of the grace of a new supernatural filiation to Himself, and so united us to one another in a new and heavenly brotherhood, and Who has further enacted that our love to Himself, Whom we do not see, is to be shown and proved by our practice of the love of our brother whom we do see.[6] And there can be no true charity among men, no true supernatural tie, which is able to bear the strain of passion and self-interest and lust and covetousness, unless it be in some way charity, that is, the love of man founded on the love of God. On the other hand, wherever there is true love of God, there is of necessity a burning desire to show Him love and to do Him good and, if possible, to benefit Him in every way. But as God himself cannot be in any way benefited by us, all true love of Him is unsatisfied until it can find something that belongs to Him and represents Him, on which it can vent and lavish itself. This is the principle of the love of the holy angels for men, whom they know to be the poor and feeble creatures and children of Him, our great Lord and Father ; and thus they regard it as a prize, to use the expression of St. Paul in a different connection of thought, to be allowed to have the care of us and to show their love to God thereby, more especially because our nature fits us also to know Him and to love Him. We see the working of the same principle in all Apostolical charity in the Church, in whatever form it manifests itself.

The other point, that is the summing up of the whole law of man's duty towards his neighbour in the precept of charity, is also easily understood. The notion of a law as exterior to man himself, involves a certain necessity on his part for direction or prohibition, which

[6] 1 St. John iv. 20.

necessity is in itself a weakness. In a perfect state of society, such as that of the blessed angels in Heaven, there can be no need for any such code. They are a law to themselves, that is, they carry in their hearts the light and love of charity, which reflects on all around them the tender love for their own good which is part of their nature, and which is the pattern of their love for others. But in that blessed society of the inhabitants of Heaven there is no self-love, in the sense which the word usually bears, there are no partialities and no coldnesses or dislikes, there are no rivalries or jealousies, and consequently no wishes for the lesser good of others, no rejoicings in that lesser good, if such there can be, but rather a perfect and simple delight in all the good and all the joy that each one possesses on the part of all the rest. Thus there can be no need of any law which prohibits this or that as against the good of others. Thus far does their intense mutual love provide for the negative part of the law of their conduct one to another, and it is the same with the positive exercise of all that is good and kind, that further and more active part of the law of love which our Lord enjoins on us, when He bids us do to others all things whatsoever we would that they should do to us. For the love of God and of all others in and for God is, as has been said, a fire burning in their hearts which cannot be restrained. It is for ever breaking forth in desires and acts of charity, charity guided as to its exercise by the illumination of the wisdom and counsel of God. No need then for any external law of prohibition, exhortation, or instruction, when they are borne along in their free and happy course of mutual love by a principle within them, as the heavenly bodies are guided unerringly and unfailingly along their paths by the law of their nature. There can be no need of the negative part of any such law as that of which we are speaking in a society in which perfect charity reigns and rules. And for the exercise of the positive part of the same law a simple standard is enough. All God's creatures are bound for His sake to love themselves for Him, in order that He may be perfectly glorified and pleased in them, and that, as our Lord says of His Apostles, 'their joy also may be full,' that is, the joy for which He has created them. This love which the angels bear to themselves is the standard and pattern according to which they love one another, wishing to each other all the good of which they are capable, in the true Divine sense of good, according to the ordinance and the providence of God.

The society of mankind, of which God is the Author, and Founder, and Father, and bond, was intended by Him to be governed, as to the whole intercourse between man and man in which its life as a society consists, by the same interior law of perfect charity, forbidding on the one hand everything that can in any way injure the rights of another, and, on the other hand, enjoining the same kind of love for all others as a man is bound, by the law of His Maker, to bear to himself. In the happy state of innocence, and in the preternatural elevation of that state to which man was raised before sin and evil came into the world, there would, again, be no need of separate prohibitive and enjoining precepts to enforce this blessed law of charity, for the Spirit of God then dwelt and reigned in the hearts of men. When men went forth into their exile from Paradise they took with them the tradition of this interior law, both negative and positive, and, but for the manifold evil and wickedness which so soon overspread the earth, there would have been no need for any law other than the interior law of charity, at least for any law other than such as could have been enacted by society for itself, to meet the requirements of all the complicated demands of justice, obedience, equity, and the like, which its organization made necessary. The wickedness of man, his selfishness, his lust, his cruelty, the tyranny of the strong over the weak, the power of covetousness and of ambition, and other like passions, made a more positive law necessary, as St. Paul tells us that the Law was added 'because of transgressions.'[7] When the family of Noe left the ark after the Deluge, and became dispersed over the earth, they are believed to have taken with them the positive enactments of natural precepts which are called after the name of that second father of mankind. When in the process of centuries a fresh and far more solemn declaration of the Law was made on Mount Sinai, it was of immense benefit not only to the holy nation, but to the world at large, because it preserved, in the form of authoritative prohibitions, the great precepts of the natural and Divine Law, which might have been entirely forgotten and obliterated long before our Lord came, but for their formal enshrinement in the Decalogue and their committal to the Jewish nation as to their appointed and special guardians. The precepts of the Decalogue, however, do not contain, except in germ, the commandments of charity which were already in the possession of mankind. Certainly, as far as their letter is concerned, they do not rise above the principles of charity which are to be found in the Book of Job, which represents a state of society living under the primitive dispensation, when as yet there was no chosen people of God at all. Yet it is very remarkable, when we consider in what state, so to speak, our Lord was to find the traditions as to mutual charity, that the very words in which He here sums up, as He says, the Law and the Prophets, are to be found in the Book

---

[7] Galat. iii. 19

of Leviticus, 'Thou shalt love thy friend as thyself.'[8] But the Jews had limited the meaning of the word 'friend' arbitrarily, till it had come to signify those of their own nation, and then the adjunct had been invented, which our Lord mentions, to reprobate it, in this Sermon, 'Thou shalt love thy neighbour, and hate thy enemy.' We see the struggle, as it were, of the old tradition, in the question put to Him before He delivered the parable of the Good Samaritan—'But who is my neighbour?'—whereas, as has been remarked before in this work, the Book of Proverbs had enjoined certain special acts of kindness in the case of the misfortunes of personal enemies.'[9]

Later on, the prophets, (especially the Evangelical Prophet) gathered up and developed many principles of perfection and charity like those to which Job witnessed, thus keeping alive, on the one hand, the primitive traditions which sprang from the first ages of the human race, and, on the other hand, preparing the way for the full development of the law of charity which was to be given to the Church by our Lord and by His Apostles. All that was thus to be found in the Old Testament was, in the first place, but a witness to the original law of charity which bound man to man as brother to brother by virtue of their common origin and their common Father and Lord in Heaven, and in the second place, a prophecy of that more perfect and heavenly law which was to rest the precept of charity on a new foundation, and enforce it by a new sanction, when God Himself became Man, when men became the sons of God in a higher sense by virtue of their regeneration and adoption through Jesus Christ, and when the supernatural tie of oneness in our Lord as members of His Body the Church was to be

[8] Lev. xix. 17. See also 18, 19.
[9] See *Public Life*, vol. iii. p. 151. The text in Proverbs is xxv. 21, 22.

added to the natural bond by means of which men were already one.

Thus we may compare together what may be called the offices of the Law and the prophets as to the two great laws, the tradition concerning which had been among the chief treasures with which the human race started on its long pilgrimage after the Fall. One of these laws was the law of belief concerning God, the other was the law of conduct towards men. The knowledge of God became gradually obliterated as to almost all its chief features in the pagan world, as the long centuries which were to intervene before the coming of our Lord rolled on their course. The unity, the spirituality, the holiness, the mercy, the justice, the providence of God over His creatures—all these truths and many more concerning the Divine Nature, were lost to the heathen. Nor did the enemies of God and man, to whom it was all important to hide Him from His creatures, do their work by halves. They took care to raise in the place of the truth concerning Him a whole fabric of lies, by means of which they were themselves worshipped in His place, and by means of which also all the vilest passions and vices were deified, and the filthiest moral degradation sanctioned and enacted by the example of what was worshipped, and by the rites of religion itself. Yet all that time the heathen world was never so entirely abandoned by God that there was not a continual witness—as St. Paul points out in his speeches which are recorded in the Acts,[10] and in the first chapter of the Epistle to the Romans—from which men might have learnt the great truths concerning Him for which their minds and hearts yearned and 'groped.' On the other hand, we find scattered over that part of antiquity with which literature makes us acquainted, a

---

[10] At Lystra, Acts xiv. 17 ; and at Athens, Acts xvii. 22, seq.

very large amount of natural piety, devotion, religiousness, a certain trust and faith in God, a certain belief His holiness and purity as well as in His justice and in Fatherly love, which show that there were always, as we may hope, a large number of human hearts that were worshipping and honouring Him well, according to their poor lights.

We now turn from the heathen to the chosen nation, to which, as the same Apostle says, the 'oracles of God' were confided, and we find that the truth had there been preserved intact, as it was delivered to man at the outset of his history, though it was still to receive an immense fulness of development and explanation in the Christian theology which was confided to the Apostles by our Lord. The difference between the Jews and even the Samaritans, the nearest to them of all other nations, was so great, that our Lord could say to the woman by the well, 'You adore that which you know not, we adore that which we know'—a saying which may have arisen to the mind of St. Paul at Athens, when he came across the altar 'to the unknown God.' Thus it was in heathenism and Judaism respectively, as to the great law of belief as to God. We find the history, so to speak, of the law of charity exactly analogous to that of Divine truth. It was given to man at his start in life, together with the commandment of the love of God. Without the guardianship of the appointed nation, and the code committed to it, this law was soon practically lost among the heathen, though among them we find glimpses of charity as we find gleams of Divine truth. It was shrined in the Law of Moses, but it was not originally declared in that Law, nor did the negative precepts by which it was therein defended correspond accurately to the extent and depth of its requirements. It was witnessed to by the prophets, who did not learn it only from the Law, and then, in the fulness of time, it was brought into the world almost as a new revelation by our Lord, Who based it on a new foundation, enforced it by a new sanction, and made its practice, in all its marvellous fulness and magnificent variety of development, possible by the grace which He won for us, and obligatory, as it were, by the intrinsic power of its own beauty, and by the irresistible magic of His own example.

These thoughts sketch out very briefly the truths on which many of the beautiful sayings of our Lord, concerning the precept of charity, rest, as when He says that He gives the law of charity as a new commandment, as His own commandment, as a law which was to be carried out after His own perfect example, and again, as when He makes the visible execution of this precept the badge by which those who are His are to be known to the world, the great evidence of His Church and of the truth of His Mission. We may use them here as explaining how it is that the precept of active, and not negative, charity here laid down by our Lord, is said to sum up the Law and the Prophets, the whole teaching of whom, as far as it regarded the conduct of man to his neighbour, had for its object to keep alive this law as it had originally been given to man, and to look forward to its still further development by our Lord, and in the Church. It was the character of the commandments of the Mosaic Law to limit their actual injunctions to the prohibition of the actions by which they were openly and most flagrantly violated, as is seen in so many of the prohibitions of the Decalogue itself. Even the precept given to his son by the elder Tobias, to which reference has already been made, is stamped with the character of negation, and it does not literally reach to the will or the intention, but only to the act. And yet it may be said to include the principle of active charity, even of the heart and the affections, in the same way as the prohibition of murder contains the principle of benevolence, and the prohibition of adultery the principle of purity. As, then, these two great commandments of the Decalogue are fulfilled in the perfect Christian practice of the virtues to which they refer, so may the whole teaching of the Law and the Prophets on the subject of charity and brotherly love be said to be fulfilled in the precept which our Lord here gives. This may be illustrated by the parable in which our Lord Himself has drawn out the picture of His own charity to man, considered as a pattern which they are to imitate in their conduct one to another. This parable is that which we call the parable of the Good Samaritan. The Priest and the Levite, who did neither harm nor good to the poor victim of the robbers, as he lay by the wayside, may be said in one aspect to have fulfilled the precept of not doing to another what they would have hated to be done to themselves, because, as has been said, they left him no worse than they found him, and had no active share in the ill treatment which he received. But in another sense, the Christian sense, they broke the law most outrageously, because under the circumstances of the case to neglect him was almost to cooperate to his death. The whole difference between the two precepts is expressed in the contrast between their conduct and that of the Samaritan. He did all that he would desire to be done to himself if he were in a similar case, and they did nothing positive which they would have hated to be done to themselves.

The importance and the novelty of the principle thus introduced by our Lord may be gathered in a beautiful way from the extent to which it seems to fill the minds of His Apostles in the Epistles which form so large a part of the New Testament. The Epistles vary very greatly in their doctrinal teaching, because they were occasional in their object, that is, they were addressed to the temporary needs of particular Churches, which were seldom altogether the same. They were addressed to Christians in all stages, so to speak, of ecclesiastical development, some to Churches hardly yet fully formed, as the Thessalonians, others to Churches which were beset by special forms of error, as the Galatians, others to communities requiring practical guidance as to daily arising questions, as the Corinthians, while others are almost doctrinal treatises, as the Epistle to the Hebrews, in particular, and, in great part, that to the Romans. The Epistles of St. Paul's captivity, as they may be called, those which the Apostle wrote from his prison at Rome, such as those to the Ephesians, the Colossians, and Philippians, are addressed to Churches which had already made great progress in the spiritual life. Yet all breathe the same strong exhortations to brotherly charity as the beginning and the end of Christian perfection. The Thessalonians had not been many weeks converted to the faith when St. Paul wrote to them, 'As touching the charity of brotherhood we have no need to write to you, for you yourselves have learned of God to love one another.'[11] At the beginning of his Second Epistle to them, a little later, he declares that he is bound to thank God for them, 'Because your faith groweth exceedingly, and the charity of every one of you to each other aboundeth.'[12] The Epistle to the Galatians is mainly occupied with the controversy which occasioned it, but St. Paul cannot part, even from that question, without reminding those to whom he writes that they have been called to liberty, 'only make not liberty an occasion to the flesh, but by charity of the spirit serve one another, for all the law is fulfilled in one word, thou shalt love

[11] 1 Thess. iv. 9.　　[12] 2 Thess. i. 3.

thy neighbour as thyself.' And after a short interval he gives that beautiful description of the works of the Holy Ghost with which we are familiar, the whole of which seems to illustrate our Lord's precept: ' Charity, joy, peace, patience, benignity, goodness, longanimity, mildness, faith, modesty, continency, chastity,' and he adds, 'against such there is no law.'[13]

The Epistle to the Romans was written about the same time, and in part deals with the same question, as that to the Galatians, but it contains a wonderful passage in illustration of the subject before us. No sooner has St. Paul got free, so to say, from the difficult discussion as to the reprobation of the Jews and the call of the Gentiles to the Church, than he turns with a certain air of relief to precepts of conduct, at the beginning of the twelfth chapter, where he introduces for the first time his favourite image of the limbs of the body, as applied to the members of the Church, all of which are bound together by mutual needs and offices. The long passage which follows is a sort of commentary on this precept of our Lord, as to doing to men whatsoever we would that they should do to us. Love is to be without dissimulation—the Christians are to love one another as brothers, they are to prevent one another in honour, they are to communicate to the necessities each of each, they are to practise hospitality, they are to rejoice with those who rejoice, and weep with those who weep, they are to bless their persecutors, they are to be of one mind, they are to keep peace with all as far as possible, they are not to return evil for evil, nor to revenge themselves, but to give place to wrath and overcome evil by good. And it is certainly very remarkable how the Apostle, in the next chapter, where he is speaking of giving all men and all ranks their due,

[13] Galat. v. 13, 14, 22, 23.

goes back to the same subject as before, in the place already quoted in this chapter, telling them to owe no man anything but to love one another, 'for he that loveth his neighbour fulfilleth the law,' and after enumerating the commandments of the second table to prove this, he adds, 'the love of our neighbour worketh no evil, therefore love is the fulfilling of the law.'[14]

The two Epistles to the Corinthians belong to the same cluster, so to speak, of the letters of St. Paul at this time, and it is needless to show at length how much witness they bear to the point of which we are speaking. The very occasion from which the Apostle starts is the danger of the decay of charity from the divisions, slight as they were, among the Corinthian Christians, but in which he saw the germ of spiritual ruin and ecclesiastical sterility. One of the faults for which he most severely reproaches the Corinthians was the coldness of their charity as shown by the separation of the several classes among them at the Agapæ. Again, in the first Epistle he repeats and draws out far more fully than before his image of the unity of the members of the human body as applied to the Church, and also gives his famous description of charity, every feature of which is contained in the general picture drawn by our Lord in the few words on which we are commenting. For what is it to be patient and kind, not to envy, not to deal perversely, not to be puffed up, or ambitious, not to seek our own, not to be provoked to anger, to think no evil, not to rejoice in iniquity, but in the truth, what are the other beautiful characteristics which make up this portrait of charity, to bear all things, to believe all things, to hope all things, to endure all things, but simply to carry out into detail and practice the general principle of loving

[14] Rom. xiii. 8.

others as ourselves? We may say much the same of the exhortations to perfection which are found in the later Epistles written when St. Paul was at Rome, as to the Ephesians, for instance, where after laying down the doctrine of the new birth, he proceeds to speak of the developments of charity, 'Wherefore putting away lying speak ye the truth every man to his neighbour'—a command which he rests upon the love which we owe to one another, 'For we are members one of another.' And then he goes on to forbid anger and stealing—this last that men may work with their own hands and have something to give to others—evil speaking, 'all bitterness and anger and indignation and clamour,' and he bids them be kind one to another, merciful and forgiving, 'even as God hath forgiven you in Christ.'[15] He tells the Philippians that nothing is to be done 'through contention or by vainglory,' but each is to esteem others better than himself, each one considering not the things that are his own, that is, his own interests and tastes, but those that are other men's; and he tells the Colossians that they are to put on as the elect of God, holy and beloved, the affections of mercy, benignity, humility, modesty, patience, bearing with one another and forgiving one another, if any have a complaint against one another,[16] and the like. It is impossible to consider all these and the many kindred passages in the Epistles of St. Peter carefully, and not to see how the Apostles caught up this principle of our Lord's, and applied it in a thousand ways for the personal guidance of the faithful. And when we turn to the Epistles of St. John, we find the precept of charity insisted on almost in every line. Such is the magnificent comment on this precept furnished by the writings of the Apostles. And it must be remembered that what is thus insisted on in the

[15] Ephes. iv. 25—32.   [16] Coloss. iii. 12, 13.

Epistles must necessarily be that part of the Christian law which was most new to the converts, and that by which the greatest store was to be set.

But a still more beautiful commentary on these words of their Divine Master is to be found in the lives of the Apostles themselves, and in the maxims which they imparted to their disciples all over the world. We know but little of the personal career of any of the Apostles except St. Peter, St. Paul, and St. John. But we may well gather from what we know of them what was the course of life led by their brethren in that holy choir. St. Paul was not one of those who heard the words of the Sermon on the Mount fall from the lips of the Incarnate Son of God. But no one more completely than he caught the spirit of that Divine teaching, no one more perfectly exemplified it in his own life. His whole life was the carrying out of this one precept. The world had never till then seen men run all over the habitable globe, at the risk of their lives, for the sake of proclaiming fearlessly and without reserve the spiritual truths on which the salvation of man depended. It had never seen man teach without a selfish end, and at the risk of death. From that day to this the Apostolic Ministry has gone on in the lines traced by its first leaders. Men intrusted by God with the message of salvation have never been wanting to carry the glad tidings of the Gospel to the ends of the earth, at the risk of their own lives, and at the certain cost of the abandonment of all that is dear to human nature in the way of friends and home. With the exception of St. John, whose martyrdom preceded his death, all the Apostles laid down their lives directly for the preaching of the truth to men who knew it not. Nor has the holy race ever died out. It is as ready for the unheard-of torments of modern persecutors in England, or in Japan, or China, or the Corea, in the seventeenth and nineteenth century, as it was in the first century for the amphitheatre at Rome or Ephesus.

But the charity which the Apostles came to teach and practise was not limited to the imparting to men, at the utmost personal risk, the saving truths which opened to them the gates of Heaven and the eternal joys of the world to come. It was also to be a principle of happiness here, and to transform social life into an imitation of the loving companionship which constitutes the life of the saints above. From the very first, without any formal teaching, the law of charity removed the separation and bridged the distance between the rich and poor, between those who had all that they could want, and those who had little. And thus we find the first Church at Jerusalem beginning, as by some heavenly instinct, the practice of the community of goods. One of the measures of persecution which were at once adopted against the faithful by the Jewish authorities, was the excommunication of all who believed in our Lord, who were thus deprived, when they were poor, of all share in the copious alms which were continually sent to Jerusalem by the Jews from all parts of the world. Thus the converts were reduced to great indigence, and the Apostles used, if we may so say, their deep poverty as the occasion to introduce among the various Christian Churches the custom of mutual assistance under such trials, as a fresh bond uniting those who were already one in faith and in hope. This explains the importance attached by St. Paul and the other Apostles to the collections made for the poor Churches in Palestine, as is shown by the commission given to the first-named Apostle when he was sent as the special Apostle of the Gentiles,[17] and by the large space which the execution of this work of

[17] Galat. ii. 10.

charity fills in his apostolic career and in his Epistles. The same care to promote charity among the new communities of Christians was probably the origin of the Agapæ, of which mention is made in the first Epistle to the Corinthians, in which the disciples of various classes and ranks met together after the celebration of the Divine Mysteries, and in which it was, in consequence, a crime to keep up anything like division or separation among the brethren. This is the ground of the severe repremand which St. Paul addresses to the Corinthians on the subject, as if it were a sin against the Blessed Eucharist itself to impair in any way the perfect charity of these meetings after Communion.[18] In this, and in a hundred other instances, we see how seriously the Apostles took up this part of their Divine commission, the introduction of the law of charity, of doing to others all things whatsoever we would have them do to us, as scarcely inferior in importance to the precept of preaching the right faith to the whole world.

But the field which is opened to us by these considerations is limitless in extent, for it embraces the whole history of the manifold developments of Christian charity in the Catholic Church. If we were to attempt to traverse it, we should have to follow the footsteps of all the apostolic missionaries in all ages, to trace the labours of the long line of Pontiffs and their subordinates in the Christian ministry, in the ruling of the Church, the arrangement of her relations with the world, the protection of the weak, the defence of the injured and oppressed, the enlightenment of the ignorant, the banishment of heresies and lesser forms of error, the raising the condition of the poor, the redemption of captives, the abolition of slavery, the mitigation of the horrors of war, the care of orphans, the tending of the sick and

[18] 1 Cor. xi. 18.

the lepers, and the evangelization of the heathen. We should have to recount the lives of a hundred saints, whose mission has been the relief of corporal miseries almost as much as that of those of the soul. From the work of the Pontificate and the Doctorate, down to that of the simple Sister of Charity on the battle-field or in the hospital, from the charity which saves the world from false doctrine about the Blessed Trinity, to that which receives the children of sin or shame into foundling hospitals, the whole range of this beautiful virtue, as we see it in the annals of the Church, is but one long and ceaseless commentary on the words of Him Who said, on the mountain in Galilee, that the whole of the Law and the Prophets consisted in doing to others all things whatsoever we would that they should do to us.

CHAPTER XIV.

The Narrow Gate.

St. Matt. vi. 13, 14; *Vita Vitæ Nostræ*, § 36.

WE have now come to a point in the Sermon on the Mount, at which our Lord seems to change His tone. The last words on which we have commented sound like a summing up of the whole discourse, at least as far as it relates to our duty to our neighbour. The whole of the Law and the Prophets are said to be contained in the single precept of doing to others all things whatsoever we would that they should do to us. At a later point in His preaching, our Lord spoke of the Law and the Prophets as having lasted in their ministry until that of St. John the Baptist, and then He added, that since his time the Kingdom of Heaven had been suffering violence, and the violent had been bearing it away.[1] It is remarkable that here also, after the mention of the Law and the Prophets as summed up in the precept already mentioned, our Lord should go on to speak of what is the first principle of that holy violence which secures the Kingdom of Heaven for itself. The beginning of such violence is the conviction that, as a matter of practical conduct, those who seek the Kingdom of Heaven must make up their minds to great difficulties. They must look upon it as a narrow gate, through which it is not easy to enter, and which it is very easy to miss. The sentences which follow, to the very end of the Sermon, are pitched in the same tone. They are sentences no longer of Divine instruction, opening ever new views of spiritual beauty and magnificence raising the mind and heart to thoughts about God as a Father of inexhaustible wisdom, power, and love, delighting in the entire abandonment of themselves to Him of His children, in their imitation of His perfect and most patient charity, in their abstinence from all judgment one of another, and in their diligent devotion to the great privilege of prayer. From this point to the end of the Sermon, our Lord is engaged in warning against dangers, and, by that very tone of caution, prophesying failure and defeat to many a bright scheme and aspiration of charity and perfection. We hear for the first time of the false teachers who come in the clothing of sheep, while they are in truth wolves. We hear of the many who shall claim to have been on our Lord's side, and even high in His service, who shall be disowned by Him, of the many who shall be hearers and not doers of the Word of God, and whose edifice of apparent virtue shall fall with a great fall under the storms of trial and

[1] St. Matt. xi. 12.

persecution. Such is the termination of the discourse which begins with the Beatitudes, and which contains the Lord's Prayer and so much sublime teaching in harmony therewith.

It is certain that our Lord is here using that marvellous knowledge of mankind of which we have already spoken more than once, and that if His manner of concluding His Sermon is at first sight discouraging, it is nevertheless witnessed to by all experience, both of the history of the Church, of those Institutes therein in which special profession is made of perfection in His service, and also of the history of individual souls, even of those on whom He has bestowed the highest calls and the choicest favours. It was His custom, on occasions such as that before us, to look beyond the audience whom He was immediately addressing to those who would be in similar circumstances long after the others had passed away. This He has done, for instance, in His great charge to the Apostles when He first sent them forth to preach, and again in His prophetic discourse on the Mount of Olives after the close of the public teaching in the Temple, and once more in His discourse to them after the institution of the Blessed Eucharist, a discourse which is in a certain true sense a prophecy of the history of the Catholic Church. So here He passes on to the fortunes, so to speak, of the Divine truths and sublime counsels which He has been imparting, their reception in the hearts and their influence on the lives of the great bulk of those to whom they are addressed, and the view which presents itself to Him is such as to make Him pour forth these last strains of loving warning and of implied complaint. The Sermon ends with the image of the man whose house was built upon the sand, and it seems as if this last account of the manner in which so many would deal with the Divine truths of which our Lord has been so prodigal, was taken up almost exactly, though the image was changed, when He began, after the interval of some months, to describe the fortunes of the seed of the Word of God in the first of His parables, that of the Sower. At the same time it may be remarked that the dark picture here painted does not include all the features which are found in later delineations of the same kind. That is, our Lord here speaks chiefly of those causes of failure which are inherent in the weakness, the folly, the carelessness of man, rather than of those which are dependent on the action of forces outside man himself, such as the devils, whom He afterwards describes as the fowls of the air who steal the good seed away, as He also speaks of the thorns of worldly cares and occupations which choke it. Here, indeed, we have the warning against the false teachers, the wolves in sheeps' clothing, but the chief cause of failure on which our Lord now dwells is evidently an internal cause—the instability of man, his great feebleness, the immense want of correspondence to grace and light, which marks his efforts after perfection. There is some danger, against which our Lord warns us, of the deception of false teachers, but the great danger as to which He seems to speak in this passage is the danger of self-deception, the danger of thinking that it is enough to hear the Word of God without doing it, the danger of building the fabric of virtue, which is to be assailed by all the tempests of temptation, on the sand instead of on the rock. And in the description of the winds and rains and floods which are to assault that fabric we have a first glimpse of the external trials of persecution, of which, in His later utterances, He speaks so much more fully. But even these trials are as fatal as they are on account of the foolishness of those who build on the sand, and not on the rock.

It may be worth while to dwell for a moment on this prophetical aspect of these words of our Lord. It is a matter of constant surprise to the sanguine and inexperienced among Christians, that the world remains so much what it has always been after so many centuries of Christian preaching, and we are always, on the other hand, expecting that the time may some day come when things may finally change, and the great promises of the Gospel, as we deem them, be fulfilled in the complete conquest of the human race to the sublime and yet plain truths of the message which the Church has to deliver. Surely, we are inclined to say, nothing but accidents can hitherto have hindered the straight onward march of Christian grace to the empire of the world. It might seem as if the mere proclamation of the Beatitudes would have been enough to bring round at least the cultivated portion of mankind—at least those who could rise to the sublime teaching of men like Socrates or Plato, or whose hearts could be moved by the yearning after truth and perfection which gives its irresistible charm to so much of the poetry of Greece and Rome. The prophet speaks of our Lord as the Desired of all nations, and now He has come in all His beauty and graciousness, full of sweetness and condescension, His hands full of gifts, His lips laden with messages of love and secrets of perfection. What is to prevent Him from at once mounting His throne in the hearts of all men, and establishing that eternal and universal Kingdom of which the Evangelical Prophet is so full? The history of nearly nineteen centuries is the comment on these aspirations. It begins with the scene on Calvary, and it ends—though the story may be yet, for all that we know, far from its close—with the Church still calling in vain on the nations to listen to her voice, and with the Vicar of our Lord dethroned, the flock which calls itself by His name divided, and the greater portion of the inhabited globe as yet a stranger to His sway. The internal aspect of the heritage of our Lord is far from presenting that picture of beauty which might be some compensation for the darkness which reigns outside, and for the ill-treatment of the Church by the unbelieving world. Indeed, it must be said, that the darkness outside, and the rebellion of the world against our Lord, are evidently in great measure the consequences of the shortcomings of those within the fold, the rulers and the ruled alike. Our Lord in this same Sermon tells the disciples to whom He speaks, and in them the many generations of Christians who were to succeed to them, that they are the light of the world and the salt of the earth. But He adds words about the salt losing its savour, and the light being put under a bushel. Those to whom the precious truths of the Sermon on the Mount were to be committed, were placed by Him in His own place, as it were, as far as the enlightenment of the world and the salting of the earth formed the great object of His Mission. They were gifted with these mighty graces and a number more, which were to enable them, if faithful to their use, to carry out into practice the teaching which so much delighted them. But they received these graces not for themselves alone, but, as is implied in the words of our Lord to which we have referred, for the benefit of others also. And the influence of the teaching of our Lord, and of the mighty means of grace by which it was confirmed, was to depend, in the providence of God, in great measure on the faithfulness or unfaithfulness of those to whom it was first committed. These, again, were to hand it on to others, and thus each generation was to inherit the precious commission of evangelizing the world around it. Thus the history of the Church becomes a continual history of the failure of Divine powers to produce on the hearts of men the effects of which they are in themselves abundantly capable, because the salt has not done its work and the light of the world has not shone with its full brightness.

What has happened as to the influence of the Church on the world at large, may be seen on a smaller scale, as it were, in the history of many of the institutes in which special attempts have been, and are continually, made, to carry out to the full the teaching of our Lord as to Christian perfection. These institutes are the glory of the Church, the seed-plots of virtues, the homes in which the most tender communion has passed between our Lord and the souls whom He has loved and who have loved Him best. It is there that, as a general rule, to which there have been numberless exceptions, the example which He has left behind Him of the perfect method of pleasing God by the practice of sublime virtue, has been most closely studied and most successfully imitated. It is there that the work of grace has been allowed its course with the least hindrance and under the most favourable opportunities, and it is from thence that the great champions of the Church have so often proceeded to their work, as well Hildebrand to the throne of St. Peter as St. Francis Xavier to the conversion of nations whose multitudes would have gladdened the heart of St. Paul. Here, if anywhere, we might have hoped for continued and unbroken perfection, the seed growing up to the stately tree, the tree unfolding itself in a crown of mighty branches and shedding its fruit far and wide. Here we might have hoped to see the Beatitudes in their living manifestations, the counsels carried out without let or failure, the absolute charity, the entire service, the complete abandonment of all care to the providence of the Father, which become the character of the children of God as it has been sketched by our Lord. What do we see? Certainly enough to make the heart glow with joy and thankfulness, for the glory of God and the beauty of the human soul as it has been exhibited there. Certainly enough to prove, if there were no other proof in the world to which to appeal, the heavenly character and origin, and the supernatural might, of the teaching of our Lord by word and by example. And yet these beautiful creations of grace are as flowers in a country in which they are not indigenous, and in which they cannot quite make their home without continued care and precaution. The rules of the religious orders are full of maxims and means of perfection, but the number of these rules and the constant need which is found for insisting, over and over again, on their better execution, is a sufficient commentary on the difficulty with which any high standard is maintained, even in an atmosphere which has been created and lived in by a succession of saints. There must be constant reforms; from time to time the religious vigour of the Church must be renovated by fresh institutes. It must be the work of a series of saints to keep up the primitive fervour of the rule of St. Benedict. The Franciscan family must send off, time after time, fresh shoots, as it were, to keep the idea of St. Francis alive in its purity, and St. Teresa must arise to fight a hard battle, against the children of Mount Carmel itself, to restore its former lustre. Everywhere there is the same story of comparative failure, by the side of splendid success.

What is so true of the influence of the Church on the world, which depends, by the law of God's providence, on the faithfulness with which she fulfils the duty of using to the utmost the means of grace which are stored up in her treasures, what is so true in the history of the religious institutes in which the counsels of perfection seem sometimes almost to take refuge, as if nowhere else could they find a home, is true also, as must of necessity be the case, in the history of the influence of Divine grace upon single souls. For the Church has no actual existence outside the souls of her children, and the institutes of perfection live only in their members. It is impossible that all the souls of which the Church is made up should be perfect, and she herself not be perfect, or that the inspirations and movements of grace should be perfectly corresponded to by all the members of an institute, and that institute itself be in a state of imperfection. The history of each order and of every soul is like the history of the Church. And the incomplete manner in which grace has its way in the world at large, or in those who are bound to the observance of a particular rule, can be studied perfectly in the struggle between grace and self-love, the spirit moved by the Holy Ghost and the sensual man, with all its alternations of victory and compromise, which is written in the momory of any one who has any acquaintance at all worthy of the name with the interior life of his own soul. Well, then, may our Lord's wonderful Sermon die down, as it were, in these last strains of almost mournful prophecy and warning, in which we read beforehand the small return which earth was to make for the magnificent charities and prodigal distributions of light and grace which were to be the characteristics of the kingdom of the Incarnation.

We may consider the sentences which now follow, until the end of the Sermon, as containing the warnings and remedies suggested by our Lord for the dangers of which we have been speaking. The first may be said to be contained in the words on which we are now more immediately to comment, about the narrow gate which leads to life and the fewness of those who find it. The

The Narrow Gate. 251

second is contained in the warning against false prophets or teachers, who come to us in the clothing of sheep. The next consists in the declaration that there are many who shall think that they are on our Lord's side and that they belong to Him, whom yet He will finally reject, because they are workers of iniquity. And the last is to be found in the warning with which the Sermon concludes, about the necessity of acting on what we hear of the words of our Lord, in whatever form or with whatever circumstances of abundance or scantiness they come to us, if we do not wish to be like men who build their houses on the sand, when they are to be exposed to all the dangers of rain and wind and tempest and inundation. Salvation, therefore, is far more difficult than we are inclined to think it. There are many false teachers who will aim at seducing with lies the children of God. There is a great danger of self-deception for those who think they are at work on God's side. And the external trials which are to assail us are so great, that their power and fierceness are sure to overwhelm all those whose virtue has not the most solid and deep foundation. These several heads of warning may be made the subject of separate consideration.

It is remarkable, in the first place, that the first of these warnings seems to consist chiefly in the assertion of a fact, to which most men may be supposed to be blind. The fact is, that the entrance to the life of which our Lord speaks is not easy, but difficult. It almost seems as if our Lord were content to impress this fact upon us without more. 'Enter ye in at the narrow gate, for wide is the gate and broad is the way that leadeth to destruction, and many there are who go in thereat. How narrow is the gate, and strait is the way that leadeth to life, and how few there are that find it!' Before we go on to explain what our Lord may mean by these words, we may remind ourselves that the doctrine which they contain is evidently echoed by St. Paul in the passage to the Corinthians,[2] in which he speaks of the difficulty of obtaining the prize. The common idea of the Christian course, which he seems to wish to combat, is that it is not a race of man against man, soul against soul, but that it is open to all to win the same crown, if they all use their opportunities with equal faithfulness. This, no doubt, is true, and yet St. Paul seems to use the other idea as explaining his own line of conduct and his care for his own soul. 'Know you not,' he says, 'that they that run in the race, all run indeed, but one receiveth the prize? So run that you may obtain. And every one that striveth for the mastery refraineth himself from all things, and they indeed that they may receive a corruptible crown, but we an incorruptible.' Here the Apostle seems to refer to this passage of our Lord's, as well as that other in St. Luke in which, at a much later period of His teaching, our Lord repeated these words with greater strength of expression, for He said, 'Strive to enter in by the narrow gate, for many, I say to you, shall seek to enter in and shall not be able.'[3] The Apostle, as is said above, seems to translate these words of our Lord into language which suits the Corinthians to whom he is writing, for it is language taken from the games with which they were so familiar. But the image of the Apostle sets before us a hard contest of many for one prize, as to which, therefore, it is certain that the greater number of the contending persons must fail. St. Paul cannot mean to teach that there is a strict resemblance in this between the contest for eternal life and the contest for the prize at the Isthmian games. But his language is consistent with such a meaning, if there were not other passages of

[2] 1 Cor. ix. 24. [3] St. Luke xiii. 24.

The Narrow Gate. 253

revelation which explain it otherwise, and we are therefore quite justified in understanding him to bear witness, by the image which he uses, to the doctrine here set forth by our Lord, of the great difficulty of entering life.

And now, what is it that our Lord means, by urging upon us so strongly that the gate to life is narrow and the path that leads to it strait? while, on the other hand, He insists with equal earnestness that the gate is wide and the way broad which lead to destruction? It is clear that to understand this we must have a clear comprehension of what He means by life on the one hand and by destruction on the other. In drawing this out, we may have to pass beyond the meaning which these words bear in this particular passage, where our Lord is speaking of that life and that destruction which depend in the main on ourselves. The theological meaning of the words, as we shall see, goes beyond this, and thus it is that we may seem to see difficulties in Catholic doctrine which are, in truth, the results of our own imperfect appreciation of it. The line of separation between life and destruction is always clear enough, but there may be inadequate significations attached to the two words life and destruction. When our Lord's words are considered in their theological meaning we come upon many truths which might otherwise escape us. The life of which He speaks, the true perfect life of the soul of man, to which, in the intention and desire of God, the steps of every child of Adam in this mortal time of probation are tending, and to which He desires that all men should arrive, is the possession of Himself in Heaven. 'For with Thee is the fountain of life, and in Thy light we shall see light,' says the Psalmist.[4] But this eternal life is supernatural to man as such. God is in various ways the life and light of

[4] Psalm xxxvi. 10.

the soul of man. Scripture and Christian theology alike teach us that He may be known and possessed in various ways, natural or supernatural. If it had so pleased Him, He might have left man in the state of nature in which he was created as such, and given him no further revelation concerning Himself and His law that what is continued in the voice of conscience, the natural law, and the teaching regarding Him which is embodied in the physical universe, the providential government of the world, and the like. Under such circumstances God would still have been the only life of the soul, whether here or hereafter, but the life hereafter to which He would have led man, on the faithful discharge of his duty during his time of trial, would not have been the supernatural possession of Himself. That is, it would have had its own beatitude, but not that of which we have hitherto been speaking. The beatitude of such a state would still have been a beatitude worthy of God to bestow, and sufficient to satisfy the very highest cravings of human nature, but it would have been as darkness to light, when compared to the supernatural beatitude to which man became the heir when, at the time itself of his creation, he was elevated to a higher state by the pure mercy and magnificent liberality of God; and to attain it now, and nothing more, would become a fall and a punishment, because it involves a judicial forfeiture of the new rights conferred by that mercy and that liberality. This act of grace on the part of our Creator, has altogether changed our prospects, our duties, the conditions of our probation, and the issues of our conduct under that probation. We are capable of, and destined to, a higher life than that natural felicity of which we have just spoken. Moreover, it is the constant doctrine of our Lord, as for instance, in the parables in which He represents God as a Master Who intrusts certain talents to His servants, that it is not free to man to decline the responsibility of any probation to which his Creator may think fit to put him. Now that the life which is set before him as the prize at which he is to aim, to use the image of St. Paul, is something so inexpressibly higher than anything to which he could have aspired by the rights or powers of his nature, he is not at liberty to decline the contest, and fall back, as it were, on the natural knowledge of God and the beatitude thereto corresponding, for which his creation, apart from the supernatural elevation by which it was crowned, made him fit. God has made him, as it were, the candidate for the ineffable bliss which consists in or is the fruit of the Beatific Vision, and to miss this is now the destruction which awaits him if he is unfaithful, while to gain it and to gain nothing short of it, is the life by which alone he can truly live for ever.

Scripture and Catholic theology speak of that as a loss, a sentence, a judgment, a condemnation, which would not have been so but for the action of God in raising His creatures by a special grace above the original capabilities of their nature. Thus, apart from any elevation of man to the supernatural destiny of which we have spoken, to miss this end would not have involved any loss on the part of man, inasmuch as he had no title to it and no capacity for it. Thus we do not call it a loss or a destruction to one of the lower animals, to miss the life of any kind in the next world for which their nature is not fitted. But now, to man, to miss this supernatural possession of God is a loss and a destruction, even if it be without the fault of the person who so loses it, as is the case, for instance, with infants who die in original sin, without having been capable of the commission of any actual sin. They have not lost it by any personal fault, but they have been placed by God in a state in which they might under other circumstances have attained to it, and in which He intended it for them and them for it. Thus, although the reason why they have missed it lay in the negligence of their parents, if they were born in Christian countries, or in the place and time at which they came into the world, as if they were born outside the reach of the Church or in a period of the world's history when the means of regeneration were not known, still they suffer this great loss on account of the sin of their first parents, in whom for that purpose they were contained, and therefore, in the theological sense of the words, they are punished for that sin which excluded all the children of Adam from Heaven, and the effects of which can only be done away by participation in the redemption of Jesus Christ. And this is the first and largest sense of the destruction to which the wide gate and the broad path lead—the loss of the eternal possession of God supernaturally known and loved. In this sense there is no question involved as to the manner in which the great forfeiture is incurred, or as to the personal fault of those who incur it. And in this sense there can be no difficulty at all about the truth of our Lord's words—for it is certain that a very large number of the human race must be for ever excluded from that possession of God of which we speak, for want of that regeneration by means of which it is to be procured, as by a condition the absence of which is fatal to their admission to that felicity.

The next sense of loss or destruction, for the word used by our Lord signifies both, the latter because it signifies the former, is far more appropriate to the passage of which we are speaking. Our Lord is here

The Narrow Gate.

speaking of the loss and the destruction which can be avoided by our own exertions and faithfulness to grace, whereas the loss which is incurred by those who are excluded from Heaven solely on account of original sin, cannot be avoided by those who suffer it. Thus the sense in which we have been considering this loss and destruction applies very well to the statement about the wide gate and the broad way, but not to the warning to enter in at the narrow gate and by the strait way. Those who lose the possession of God, of which we have spoken, by their own fault, are those who, having had the means of gaining life offered to them, have yet neglected them, and incurred destruction by their own sin unrepented of. It is of these, then, that our Lord's words are to be primarily understood. He tells us that of these the greater number do not, as a matter of fact, enter the narrow gate. It is true that under every one of the successive dispensations of God by which He has dealt with mankind since the fall of Adam, it has been possible to please Him and to gain a share in the redemption wrought out by our Lord. It was possible to do this under the primitive dispensation, as is seen in the case of Job, to mention no other of the great saints and friends of God who were not partakers of the covenant which He made with His chosen people, the descendants of Abraham. In the case of Job, who may have lived after the time of Abraham, we have an instance of an earlier dispensation subsisting side by side with a dispensation later than itself in point of time. The same participation in the one Redemption was possible under the Mosaic Law, and it is possible now under the dispensation of the Gospel. In all these cases it has been possible to gain this inestimable gift of life, on the condition of faith and of obedience to God's law, according to the light which was imparted in each case to those who were called on to believe and to obey. If either of these conditions was wanting, the condition of faith or the condition of obedience, in those capable thereof, the life of which our Lord speaks could not be gained, though the grace of God was always ready to assist men, under any of these dispensations, to gain that life and so to escape destruction. Destruction, in the case of adults, therefore, from the beginning of the history of man, has, in its fullest sense, been the penalty, not simply of original sin, as in the case of infants who die unregenerated, but of wilful disbelief and disobedience.

And yet, with reference to the words of which we are speaking, it cannot be doubted that under all the dispensations which had succeeded one to another, until the time at which our Lord spoke, the majority of mankind had chosen destruction rather than life. They had either disbelieved the truths about God which were presented to their acceptance by such witness as was vouchsafed to them—always sufficient, though not always equally overwhelming in evidence—or, 'knowing God,' as St. Paul says of the heathen who had kept their knowledge of Him 'captive, as it were, in injustice,'[5] had followed the law of their own passions rather than the law of nature and conscience, and, in the case of the more favoured nation, the moral law as additionally proclaimed to them by the legislation and the whole system which goes by the name of Moses. This is the witness of history as to the great mass of the heathen world. It is the witness of Scripture, as quoted by St. Paul, in the Epistle to the Romans, as to the mass of the Jewish nation itself.[6] Thus in this sense also, the words of our Lord are evidently true, that the gate is wide and the way broad which lead to destruction, and that they are many who walk therein, while on the other hand,

[5] Rom. i. 18. [6] Rom. iii. 9, seq.

the gate is narrow and the way strait which lead to life, and that those who find them are few.

When our Lord came to preach to the chosen nation, the flock of the house of Israel, the new truths which He proclaimed, especially concerning His own Person and authority, then the new law which He taught, the formal promulgation of which we are considering as made in the Sermon on the Mount, amounted to a fresh call on the faith of those to whom He addressed Himself, as well as on their obedience. The conditions of life remained the same as from the beginning—faith and obedience: but the truths to be believed became more particular, the law to be observed became more interior and sublime. In this sense the Gospel would have made the finding of life even more difficult than before, had it not been that it had brought more than new truths and new commandments into the world, —it had also brought new light by which these truths might be perceived, and a new armament, so to say, of grace, by which these commandments might be fulfilled. It was our Lord's own presence and example, and His marvellous gifts of spiritual power, that made His yoke easy. If this had not been the case, the Gospel law would not have been unlike, as to the assistance which it gave to mankind for the finding of life, to the Mosaic code. 'The law was given by Moses, but grace and truth came by Jesus Christ.' It follows that the gaining of life was immensely facilitated by our Lord, but only to those who gave Him their faith and obedience.

The same may be said, as far as the subject before us is concerned, of the Catholic Church and her influence on the world. Life is made easier of access, and an immense power of vigour and perseverance is communicated to the will by means of the sacraments and other means of grace. The treasury of Heaven is opened, the way is made more clear, the yoke becomes light to those who take it up, the burthen more easily borne. We have more helps and aids and means of strength and recovery. But all this increase of power is at the disposal of those only who give themselves to the keeping of the law of God with a good heart. Again, it is not our Lord's purpose here to draw out the marvellous resources for the recovery of those who have gone astray from the right path, by means of which it becomes indefinitely easier than before to pass from the way of destruction to the path of life. All this is true, and more that might be said here to the same purpose. But still it remains true, that the new call made by our Lord, on the people to whom He was especially sent, involved a strain on the part of those who were to become His true followers which was more than the majority were prepared for. For it involved their adhesion to new truths of faith, as has been already said, and their obedience to a stricter code and a loftier view of life than any which they had before entertained. Thus, as a matter of fact, though our Lord was at the time of the Sermon on the Mount followed by an enthusiastic crowd from the cities of Galilee which He had passed through in the course of His preaching, still the greater part of that very crowd was perhaps not to persevere in His school, while His teaching was to be rejected with scorn and hostility by the religious leaders and authorities of the holy nation itself.

The Gospel involved the Cross, and our Lord's cross can never be the attraction of the multitude. Partly from difficulty as to belief, but much more from the influence of human respect, and, again, much more still from the purity and severity of the Christian law, the great part of those to whom the way of life was proposed by our Lord, did not walk therein. It has been the same

The Narrow Gate.

with the teaching of the Church in the world, which is the continuation of the ministry of our Lord, and must be expected in the main to have the same reception. At this moment the Church has been so many centuries in the world, and we see with our eyes the immense fruits of her sojourn upon earth. We see a number of results which prove beyond all doubt her Divine power and mission, as has so often been said. One of the favourite arguments of her defenders in the days in which we live is most truly drawn from her influence upon the world, and from the inestimable benefits which she has conferred upon society, which owes to her, first its preservation in life, and then all that is its greatest boast and ornament. And yet, with all this, the world remains unconverted, the majority of the human race are not yet even nominally children of the Church, while of those who call themselves Christians a large proportion either deny some of the vital points of her creed, or are rebels against her government and separated from her Communion. The want of a true and perfect faith, and the want of obedience to the commandments of God—the very same causes which operated to exclude the generations before the coming of our Lord from the path of life—are still the influences which debar the greater portion of mankind, now that He has come and died and established the Church, with all her panoply of celestial powers and weapons, from closing with the offers of His love and turning away from the broad road which leads to destruction.

It may seem a hard and a discouraging doctrine that, as it appears reasonable to conclude from the statement of our Lord, the greater part of mankind are to walk along the path which leads to perdition. And so many thoughtful minds are driven back to seek an escape from the consequences which this doctrine seems to involve.

We can only answer, that the Church does not exaggerate the force of our Lord's words, nor does she lay down anything certain as to the ranges of fact which lie beyond the sphere of the teaching committed to her. She affirms certain truths as to the conditions of attaining the supernatural bliss of Heaven; and she affirms the unchanging doom which is the punishment of wilful incredulity and disobedience in Hell. It does not follow that there are no questions as to the future state of man which she leaves to theologians, reasoning on principles of faith. Nor does she dogmatize on the question of fact which relates to the actual issue of the probation to which this or that class of souls is subjected. These are some of the most engrossing questions on which our speculations can be occupied, though we have only practically to deal with them so far as they affect what we are bound to believe. Thus it may be wrong to be over-inquisitive as to all the possibilities of the future, while it is right or useful to set our minds free from embarrassment as to the goodness or wisdom of God. It is in this sense alone that we need deal with the most salient of these questions. Thus it may be asked, in the first place, are we to understand that there is no middle lot between the highest form of life on the one hand, that life which consists in the eternal possession of God in Heaven, and the extreme perdition of Hell on the other, of Hell, that is, as we commonly speak of it, as the place of eternal torment and misery? And it may be asked in the second place, are we to think that these words of our Lord, about the broad road of destruction and the narrow path of life, are to be extended in their application to the children of the Catholic Church, so that we are to suppose that, even in their case, it is true that few are to be saved?

We must first answer in general that our Lord is here

speaking practically and not speculatively, and that when, later on in His ministry, the question about the fewness of those who are to be saved was put to Him directly, He did not answer it in so many words, but only by the exhortation to "strive and enter into the narrow gate, for that many would attempt to enter it and not be able." So we seem to have His authority for declining to discuss such questions, and for thinking of them chiefly in the practical bearing on our own conduct, which is exactly the lesson which we gather from what St. Paul says about his own rule. But, to speak a little more in detail about these questions, it may be said that, as regards the first, what has already been said about the effects of original sin in excluding souls from the blessed vision of God in Heaven, the felicity altogether above our nature, and to which we should have no right or claim at all, even for the most perfect service of God according to the precepts of the natural law, may serve to show that there are various degrees, if we may so speak, of the life and the perdition which are here spoken of. For it is clear that there must be many millions of souls which depart from this world in the state in which they can never have been guilty of wilful and conscious sin, because they have never reached the age of reason, after which alone it is that the human soul becomes capable of moral choice, for which it is personally responsible to God. Such souls as those of which we speak, if they have been regenerated in holy baptism, go at once to Heaven for the sake of our Blessed Lord's merits, which have been communicated to them, while, if they have never been made partakers of Him and His new birth in baptism, they must be for ever excluded from the beatific vision in Heaven. These souls, then, cannot enter Heaven, and yet we cannot think that they are doomed 'to the eternal torments which were prepared, as our

Lord says, for the devil and his angels, that is, for spirits who have deliberately risen in the most heinous rebellion against God in His very presence, and before His very throne. Thus, if we extend the realm, so to speak, of perdition to all those who cannot enter Heaven, or if, speaking untheologically, we extend the realm of salvation to all those who are not doomed to Hell, we must in either case use the words perdition or salvation in a variety of meanings, and we must mean that some who are in one sense lost are in another sense saved, while some who are in one sense saved are in another sense lost. If all were to be considered saved who are not to suffer the torments of Hell in the strictest sense, then would many be saved who do not reach Heaven, and if all were to be spoken of as lost who do not enjoy the beatific vision of God for ever, then would many be lost who do not suffer in Hell. These are truly lost, because they lie under the sentence of God's justice passed on the human race. Less theologically they are saved, for no sentence of condemnation has smitten them for deliberate and conscious sin. What the number of such souls may turn out to be at the great day of account we have no means of knowing. For it would not be enough, in order to arrive at a knowledge of this, to know the number of infants only who have died in original sin, it being certain that none can be condemned to Hell except for a mortal sin unrepented, and it being possible that adults as well as infants may thus escape that extreme perdition. Nor, again, have we any certain declaration as of faith as to the conditions under which such souls are to exist hereafter. It is enough to know that the great Day of Judgment will not only justify the dealings of God with every soul of the children of Adam, but will also show how infinitely merciful He has been in His dealings with the whole race as well as with each member of it. And this is enough, not to satisfy all speculations, but to show us the folly, as well as the wickedness, of questioning the goodness of God because all His arrangements are not explained to us beforehand.

With regard to the second of the questions just mentioned, whether the statement as to the fewness of those who enter the narrow gate is to be understood of the children of the Church in her best days, it may at first sight seem that our Lord is speaking directly of the generation to whom He was Himself sent. And on the other hand, it is clear that, if that generation was exclusively privileged in having Him for its teacher, and in the marvellous effusion of graces which accompanied the foundation of the Church, still it was a time of very severe tribulation and trial, especially to those among the Jews who embraced the faith which our Lord preached. Such a time was very unfavourable to the acceptance of the Gospel truth by the multitude. It may be said that the Church has not a full opportunity of bringing home to the souls of men the whole variety of her means of salvation except in quiet times, and in places where she is more or less in peaceable possession. We can only see truly the effects which she can produce upon mankind in general, when she is able to preach the word of God freely, when her worship is unimpeded in all its magnificence, when the sacraments can be freely administered, when she has her schools for the young at her command, and when she can cultivate sacred learning, and the training of her ministers for the service of the altar, the preparation of fit instruments for the conquest of new realms to her peaceful empire, and when she has leisure to shed the light of Heaven upon all the various fields in which the far-searching mind of man can wander and occupy itself. We cannot doubt that the Church can do indefinitely more for the world when she enjoys peace, and yet we can hardly find a period in her history, since she went forth from the Cenacle at Jerusalem, when the world has been so blessed as to let her work her utmost for its good. But we are speaking of states of things which are not merely ideal but actual. There are disadvantages as well as advantages in quiet times, there are blessings as well as trials in times of persecution. Still, it may be said that the blessings for which the Church so constantly prays when she begs for days of peace, are very great indeed, and that it is hard indeed not to think that, when and where she is in full possession and in comparative tranquillity, if the great majority of her children do not always walk along the path of life from their birth through the whole course of their pilgrimage, at least a very large proportion of them are brought back to it by the manifold provisions for pardon and reconciliation with which God has made her system abound. For there is no imperative need which compels us to understand what our Lord here says of the best days of the Church and of the most faithful generations of her children. On the other hand, the language of the Epistles of St. Paul and the other Apostles, while it is full of warning and of exhortations to holy fear, is still such as to give the impression that they considered that the greater number of those to whom they wrote would not miss the everlasting blessedness of which they so often speak.

These, however, are speculative questions, only important to us in so far as the answer which we give to them helps us on to make our own 'election sure,' as the Apostle speaks. What is certain is, that our Lord here urges on us the immense importance, in order to the carrying out of the heavenly precepts of which His Sermon on the Mount is full, of gaining that true idea of salvation which represents it to us as a difficult task. It is difficult in itself, for it requires a constant conflict with ourselves, a constant denial of our lower appetites, and of what is often far more hard to conquer, our self-will and love of independence. The precepts of the Sermon on the Mount are entrancing in their beauty, but it is a heavenly beauty indeed. We live in a dull atmosphere, and carry about with us many a load which presses us to the earth. And then, after all, our Lord seems to tell us, the difficulty for which we must prepare ourselves is not merely the intrinsic difficulty, great as that may be, of the lofty path of perfection to which we are invited. He tells us that the immense influence of the greater part of those with whom we live, will be on the same side as our own weakness and inclination to evil. We shall always have the multitude against us — the example of the majority, even of Christians, and much more the pressure of the human respect which the world exacts from us, with a tyranny which it costs us much to resist. We are creatures of society, for God has so made us, and sometimes the pressure from without will be more powerful for evil, than the conflict waged against us within ourselves by the lower parts of our nature. We must make up our minds to have always to fight against the multitude. It is the example of the multitude of Christians which keeps back a thousand souls in every generation from the pursuit of perfection. It is the example of the multitude of Catholics which is always the most powerful argument, in the minds of those outside the Church, to deter them from entering her pale. It is at this moment the example of the multitude of so-called Christians, which steels the hearts of millions of unbelievers against all the evidence of the Gospel dispensation.

This truth is supported by the language of the masters of the spiritual life, writing even of that part of the flock which is most shielded from danger. Nowhere can we be safe from the danger of following the example and adopting the principles of the majority. If there could be found a place in the Church in which the weight of this great influence is turned in the direction of good and of what is most perfect, it would be in the holy homes of the religious life, which are set up for this especial purpose, among others, that there at least the influence of example, companionship, public opinion, and common practice, may be on the side of what is not only good, but perfect in the service of God. We may thank God that this is always so in a very great degree, and that the fruit of it is seen in the comparative ease with which many a weak soul is helped on along a lofty path, to which it would not otherwise aspire. But even here the danger of the example of the multitude sometimes creeps in as an influence which tends to destroy perfection. We find such writers as Father Lancicius and Father Lallemant, warning their disciples against the comparative relaxation in light matters which may be learnt by following the example of the multitude, even though that multitude may be made up of men who are on the whole faithful to the calling which they have embraced. Nor is it quite enough to say, in answer to this, that those who become in the sense of these writers relaxed, will still most probably be saved, although they may miss many great rewards which might otherwise have been in store for them. For relaxation in a high vocation must certainly be punished in Purgatory, and it is, moreover, an evil which involves so much of unfaithfulness that it is impossible to say at what point it may stop.

It follows from this that, in order to gather the full fruit from our Lord's words in the passage before us, we should make up our minds, not only that the salvation at which we are aiming is a difficult thing, but further that it is a thing which we must gain by following the few and not the many. The true import of lessons like that before us is caught by such souls as St. Antony, who went round the Hermits of the Desert, all of them famous for their perfection of virtue, and studied in the example of each the practice of the special virtue in which each excelled; thus seeing in one the master whom he was to follow in humility, in another his teacher in the spirit of prayer, or of mortification, or of purity, or of fortitude, and the like. And thus that blessed soul was enabled, by the grace of God, to unite in himself the excellences which were scattered over the desert, so to say, one here, another there, but which were all mirrored in Antony, because in regard of each single virtue he did not content himself with the example of the multitude, even of the choice servants of God, but sought out what was singular in the perfection of each saint and of each virtue. If we take this practice of St. Antony as a supplement to the doctrine of St. Paul as to striving for the prize which one alone, out of many, could gain, we shall understand the sense in which the saints of God in all ages have taken these words of the Sermon on the Mount about the narrow gate and the strait way. They have not troubled themselves with speculations as to the number of those who are to be saved, or as to the multitude of the chances which may favour, in any particular case, the hope of salvation. The gate of life has been narrow to them, because they have feared the falling short in any particular of the perfect service which God expects of them. The way of life has seemed to them strait, because they have looked on the path along which they are bound to walk as a simple onward path along the most direct line to their great reward, every step of which must be taken at the right moment if the whole distance is to be accomplished, while to diverge even an inch on either side was so far to endanger their ever arriving at the goal which was before them.

CHAPTER XV.

The False Prophets.

St. Matt. vii. 15—20; *Vita Vitæ Nostræ*, § 34.

THE first warning which our Lord gives, in this last portion of His Sermon on the Mount, has been considered in the foregoing chapter. The lesson which it teaches us practically, is to pray for and seek, in every possible way, such a strengthening of our faith as may enable us very clearly indeed to see the truth on which the vigour and unceasing perseverance of our exertions after perfection must depend, that is, the truth that salvation is a difficult task and one in which a great many fail. Our Lord now turns to another head of danger which He foresaw as likely to cause immense mischief in His Church, and in the battle for salvation, which was to be the great occupation of His children. This second danger, quite as formidable as the blindness as to our spiritual perils to which we are so prone, was to come from without. It was to be a chief feature in the Christian system, as it had been in the Jewish system, that men were to be trained and instructed, in the way of life and of the service of God, by others like themselves, who had received commission to be guides, pastors, and teachers. The Church was to be very jealous and careful in the selection of such guides. She was to train them very carefully, she was to confer on them a sacred commission, guaranteed by solemn rites and sacramental grace, and she was to watch continually and most vigilantly over their lives and their doctrine. But all this would not be enough to shield the faithful from the danger of false teaching and erroneous guidance, whether from the defection of her real ministers or the usurpation of their office by others. For it was to be one of the prime devices of Satan to corrupt the teachers, to send his own emissaries in their place, to pervert, if he could, first their hearts, and their doctrine, and then their lives, so that they might teach falsehoods, instead of truth, or at least contradict by their examples the holy doctrine which their lips conveyed. Later on, when our Lord was taking leave of His teaching office among men, and predicting the latter days of His Church on earth, or at least what was to happen after His own departure, He added other lines to the picture which He here draws; as for instance, the circumstances of persecution, betrayal, dissension, and other calamities which were to try the children of the Church. But now, so soon after the beginning of His Ministry, although a great part of the fulfilment of what He is saying was not to take place immediately, still He warns them at once of this terrible danger, and gives them at once the remedy which would enable them to defend themselves against it.

'Beware of false prophets, who come to you in the clothing of sheep, but inwardly they are ravening wolves. By their fruits you shall know them. Do men gather grapes of thorns, or figs of thistles? Even so every good tree bringeth forth good fruit, and the evil tree bringeth forth evil fruit. A good tree cannot bring forth evil fruit, neither can an evil tree bring forth good fruit. Every tree that bringeth not forth good fruit, shall be cut down and cast into the fire. Wherefore by their fruits ye shall know them.' There are a number of points for consideration presented by this passage, but we may first of all dwell for a moment on the persons of whom our Lord may have been immediately thinking when He gave this warning to the multitude of disciples to whom the Sermon on the Mount was delivered. Our Lord had already warned His followers that the justice which would be required in them, as citizens of the Kingdom of Heaven, must exceed the justice of the Scribes and Pharisees. These persons, as has often been said, were the most religious and learned of the sacred nation of the Jews, and were held on that account in the greatest veneration among the people. Up to the time of which we are speaking, they had not very openly taken a part against our Lord. He had retired from the neighbourhood of Jerusalem, less than a year before this time, on account of some apparent tendency to hostility on their part, and this was the human reason which seems to have brought about the fulfilment of the prophecy which St. Matthew quotes, about the land of Galilee, as the scene of the shining of the great light which Isaias had foretold.[1] But our Lord's retirement from the immediate neighbourhood of the capital had had some effect in securing for Him, during the months which had since elapsed, a time of quiet though most active preaching, in Galilee, which had led to the formation of the large body of disciples who followed Him from place to place, as well as to the great effect which His preaching and miracles had produced upon

[1] St. Matt. iv. 15, 16; Isaias ix. 1.

The False Prophets. 273

others. To all human appearance, He was likely to gather around Him the materials of a flourishing Church out of the inhabitants of Galilee, and to continue His term of preaching without serious molestation. But all this was only appearance. Already He foresaw the storm which burst on His next appearance in Jerusalem, at the approaching feast of the Pasch, and the relentless malice with which, from that date onwards, He would be pursued. The words in which the warning in the text is conveyed were literally fulfilled in the case of His Galilean disciples, though they are true in every age and under all circumstances of the Church. Between the time of which we have just spoken and His next ascent to Jerusalem, and thus, even before He had clashed, as He was then to clash, with the prejudices of the Pharisees and others about the Sabbath, we find a number of Scribes and Pharisees sent down from Jerusalem with the apparent object of watching Him, and taking note of the character of His teaching. This may not have been with any definite purpose of hostility, but we find that soon afterwards, when He had openly broken with their traditions about the Sabbath by the cure of the man at the Probatic Pool,[2] it became the object of the rulers at Jerusalem to bring about His destruction, and that when He again retired to Galilee, they pursued Him by their emissaries, who gave Him no peace, and even went so far as to form an alliance with the Herodians to put Him to death. During the whole of the second year of our Lord's teaching, He was continually haunted by the active opposition of these enemies of His, who were represented by priests and Pharisees sent down on purpose from Jerusalem, and of whom we cannot doubt that their main object was to turn away from Him the favour and admiration of the

[2] St. John v. 1, seq.

people. For this purpose they used every effort to calumniate Him and lower Him in the public estimation. For this purpose, as we may judge from the statements of the Evangelists concerning them, they used the authority which their religious character gave them; they alleged objections of a religious kind against His teaching and practice, thus representing themselves as zealous of the law, and as desirous of keeping the people from falling into the snares of false doctrine. To the very end their malice against Him was cloaked under the name of zeal for the law, and at last they put Him to death as for blasphemy. Our Lord may well have seen the immense danger to the souls of His disciples among the multitude, from this false teaching, veiled as it was under the appearance of religion and strictness of practice as to outward observances. He never seems openly to have denounced the priests as such, but only under their titles of Scribes or Pharisees, which did not involve of necessity their sacred character. At the present time their assaults on the faith of the disciples were as yet future, and He therefore in this passage speaks of them in still more general terms, such as suit not only their case, but that of the thousands of others who were to succeed them in all ages, in carrying on the work of Satan against the Gospel teaching of the Church. He describes them as false prophets who come to solicit the confidence of the faithful in the clothing of sheep, being all the time ravening wolves, eager for the destruction of souls and for their own satisfaction in what they might gain by making them their dupes.

These men, then, seem to have been in the first instance present to the mind of our Lord when He spoke these famous words about the wolves in the clothing of sheep. But it has been already said that it is our Lord's wont, in discourses like this before us, which were to last for all time and to serve the needs of all generations in the Catholic Church, to look far beyond the immediate occasion on which He was speaking, and to embrace in His view the future history and trials of His children to the end of the world. And certainly here also we might well claim for the words on which we are commenting the character of a prophetical denunciation, the prediction of a state of things which human foresight could never have divined. It might have been thought, indeed, that the Chief Priests themselves, and the rulers of the sacred people, would have been the first to be moved by the marvellous cogency of the various heads of evidence which witnessed to our Lord's Divine mission, by the beauty of His teaching, by the majesty and heavenly sweetness of His character, by the fulfilment of the prophecies and types in His Person, by the splendour of His miracles, the manner in which He satisfied in His doctrine all the wants and needs and questions of the human soul. Our Lord expressed His astonishment at the blindness of the teachers of Israel in His discourse to Nicodemus, and it may well seem one of the problems of history that the ecclesiastical rulers did not at once seek a place in His Kingdom—or at least, it might well seem such a problem, if we did not know how the human heart is hardened by ambition and blinded by jealousy, and how difficult it is, beyond all other difficulties, to turn the hearts of priests of impure life, or full of pride and ambition, in whom true interior religion has long died away. But granting that the immediate reception of our Lord by the priests at Jerusalem might have been expected, and their persecution of Him predicted, what mind, however versed in the malignity of which our nature is capable, could ever have seen the depravity, the malice, the cunning, the restless perversity and ingenuity which have been displayed in the subsequent history of the Church by the false teachers to whom His words are meant to apply!

Thus the words of our Lord of which we are here speaking are full of prophecy, of which we have the fulfilment even in His own lifetime, in the attempted seduction of His disciples in Galilee, on which we have been speaking. He seems to refer to attempts of the same kind in the last year of His teaching, in the discourse which He delivered after He had wrought at Jerusalem His great miracle on the man who had been born blind. This man had been excommunicated by the Jewish rulers for believing in our Lord, and thus the official representatives of God in the holy nation had set themselves in direct opposition to Him present among them, the True Shepherd of the fold, to be separated from Whom was the truest, the only true, excommunication. This fact is to be borne in mind in reading the discourse of our Lord in the tenth chapter of St. John, where our Lord declares that He is Himself the door to the fold, and that all that did not enter through Him were thieves and robbers. Thus His enemies had pretended to have the authority to exclude His followers from the fold, whereas it was only through Him that any one could enter it, much less exercise any authority or jurisdiction therein. In the sequel of the same discourse He uses the other images of the hirelings and the wolf, and of the rapacity of the false teachers, to steal, to kill, and to destroy, to catch the sheep and scatter them.[3] This appetite for destruction, which is characteristic of a teacher of falsehood, is noted by our Lord in the passage of the Sermon on the Mount on which we are commenting by the epithet of 'ravening,' which He applies to wolves in sheep's clothing. We shall have occasion hereafter to speak of its meaning more fully.

[3] St. John x. 1—13.

The False Prophets.

The Church had hardly been founded, when the evil on which our Lord here, as it were, puts His finger, became manifest. From the very beginning, there were attempts made to usurp the authority of the Apostles and of those delegated by them, and to lead the faithful astray by false doctrines. The letter sent by the Apostles after the first Council at Jerusalem to the Gentile converts begins with complaining that 'some going out from us have troubled you with words, subverting your minds, to whom we gave no commandment.' Here we have the twofold evil, the assumption of authority and the propagation of false doctrine. As we proceed in the history of the Acts, we find continual instances of the immense activity with which the teachers of falsehood beset the onward progress of the Gospel on every side. They fill a large space in the history and in the Epistles—a space which they have seen since held in the annals of the Church. They attacked not only St. Paul, who was, of course, the object of particular animosity to the Jews and the Judaizing party among Christians, but the other Apostles also. We find St. Paul warning the priests of the Ephesian Church in the discourse which St. Luke records in the twentieth chapter of his history, against the 'wolves' that were to enter in among them, not sparing the flock, and against those among themselves who were to arise, speaking perverse things, to draw away disciples after them.[4] We find the same Apostle in conflict with false teachers in the Epistle to the Romans, and, still more evidently in that to the Galatians, written also at the same time. We see in this last named Epistle how bitter the attack on him had become, and how it aimed, as such attacks have continually aimed in the subsequent history of the Church, at the separation of Christians

[4] Acts xx. 29, 30.

into sects and parties, and at the usurpation of the apostolic chairs of teaching. The Epistles to the Corinthians bear witness to the same tendency, although in them St. Paul is engaged in combating more directly the spirit of division as such, which would break up the body of Christians into a number of personal followings, than that of separation on account of diversity of doctrine. It is needless to point out how the later Epistles of the same Apostle witness to the growth of the sectarian spirit, from mention of which hardly one of these Epistles is free, even those which are written with such overflowing openness of heart and with such a glow of charity as to intimate friends, as those to the Philippians and Ephesians. The First Epistle to St. Timothy contains the passage in which St. Paul sketches the heretics of the coming ages of the Church. 'The Spirit,' he says, 'manifestly saith, that in the last times some shall depart from the faith, giving heed to spirits of error and doctrines of devils, speaking lies in hypocrisy, and having their conscience seared, forbidding to marry, to abstain from meats, which God hath created to be received with thanksgiving by the faithful, and by them that have known the truth.'[5] The Second Epistle to the same Saint, written when St. Paul was near the time of his martyrdom, speaks yet more strongly. 'In the last days shall come on dangerous times, men shall be lovers of themselves, covetous, haughty, proud, blasphemers, disobedient to parents, ungrateful, wicked, without affection, without peace, slanderers, incontinent, unmerciful, without kindness, traitors, stubborn, puffed up, and lovers of pleasure rather than of God, having an appearance of godliness, but denying the power thereof.' These words seem to describe a state of society in which men shall be nominally Christians, but

[5] Tim. iv. 1, seq.

The False Prophets. 279

in truth, almost pagans in their manner and principles of life, and yet the Apostle goes on to speak of the evil teachers even of his own day as included under the same description. And he adds that the evil is to be ever on the increase: 'Evil men and seducers shall grow worse and worse, erring, and drawing into error.'[6] In his Epistle to St. Titus, St. Paul tells his disciple to be very short in his dealings with heretics. 'A man that is a heretic after the first and second admonition avoid, knowing that he, that is such an one, is subverted, and sinneth, being condemned by his own judgment.'[7]

The other Apostles are equally plain in the evidence which they furnish of the immense growth in the Church of the danger of which our Lord here speaks for the first time. In the warnings which St. John addresses, at the beginning of the Apocalypse, to the seven Churches of Asia Minor, we see how large a part of his apostolical anxiety was caused by the existence or even the toleration of false doctrine. The Angel of Ephesus is commended because he cannot bear those that are evil, and has tried those who say they are apostles and are not, and has found them liars, and even after the faults that are pointed out in him, he is finally commended: 'This thou hast, that thou hatest the deeds of the Nicolaites, which I also hate.'[8] Of the Angel of Smyrna it is said that he is 'blasphemed by them that say that they are Jews and are not, but are the synagogue of Satan.'[9] The next two Churches are blamed, that of Pergamus, 'because thou hast them there that hold the doctrine of Balaam, who taught Balac to cast a stumbling-block before the children of Israel, and also them that hold the doctrine of the Nicolaites;' while that of Thyatira is censured, 'because thou sufferest the woman Jezabel,

[6] 2 Tim. iii. 1—8, 13. [7] Titus iii. 10, 11.
[8] Apoc. ii. 2, 6. [9] Apoc. ii. 9.

who calleth herself a prophetess, to teach and seduce my servants to commit fornication, and to eat of things sacrificed to idols.'[10] The 'synagogue of Satan,' and 'those who say they are Jews, and are not, and lie,' are also mentioned in the charge to the Church of Philadelphia.[11] It would be foreign to our purpose in this work to attempt to explain the particular heresies of which St. John here speaks, but it is clear that in each one of these addresses he is thinking of the special dangers which beset these particular Churches, and it is a sad commentary on the words of our Lord that he should find so much to say of this kind at the time at which he wrote.

But the strongest testimony furnished by the New Testament to the fulfilment of this virtual prophecy of our Lord concerning the danger from false teachers, is to be found in the Second Epistle of St. Peter, written, like that already mentioned of St. Paul to St. Timothy, not long before the martyrdom of its author. It seems to have been the chief object of this Epistle to warn the faithful of the peril of which we are speaking. The language of the Prince of the Apostles is of such a kind that we may fairly consider it as striking the earliest note of those plain and severe denunciations of heresy which have so frequently issued from the successors of St. Peter. If this Epistle had been lost, and if it were discovered for the first time in the present day, it would certainly be described by the press of our time as an example of the 'insolent and arrogant language of the Roman Curia.' St. Peter comes to the subject of the false teachers at the beginning of the second chapter, although almost all that precedes it may be considered as having no distant reference to what is to follow. 'There were also false prophets among

[10] Apoc. ii. 19, 20. [11] Apoc. iii. 9.

The False Prophets. 281

the people' of Israel, St. Peter says, 'even as there shall be among you lying teachers, who shall bring in sects of perdition, and deny the Lord Who bought them, bringing upon themselves swift destruction. And many shall follow their riotousness, through whom the way of truth shall be evil spoken of, and through covetousness shall they with feigned words make merchandise of you. Whose judgment now of a long time lingereth not, and their perdition slumbereth not.' Then the Apostle goes on to say that God, Who did not spare the apostate angels, nor the antediluvian world, nor the cities of the plain, would not spare these fresh enemies of His, although He would deliver the just from among them, as He had delivered Lot from Sodom. 'The Lord knoweth how to deliver the godly from temptation, but to reserve the unjust unto the Day of Judgment to be tormented, especially them who walk after the flesh in the lust of uncleanness, and despise government, audacious, self-willed, they fear not to bring in sects, blaspheming.' He then speaks of the modesty of the angels, 'But these men,' he says, 'as irrational beasts, naturally tending to the snare and to destruction, blaspheming those things which they know not, shall perish in their corruption, receiving the reward of their injustice, counting for a pleasure the delights of a day.' Then St. Peter, as it were, pours himself out in describing these men as 'stains and spots . . . having eyes full of adultery and of sin that ceaseth not, alluring unstable souls, full of covetousness, leaving the right way for the path of Balaam,' who counselled the seduction of the people of God, 'fountains without water, clouds tossed with whirlwinds, speaking proud words of vanity, alluring by the desires of fleshly riotousness, promising liberty, whereas they are themselves slaves of corruption,' and the like. And he ends this part of his Epistle by applying to them the proverb of the dog that returns to his vomit and the sow that was washed to her wallowing in the mire. And, again, in the third chapter of the Epistle, as it is now divided, he seems to speak particularly of false teachers who shall argue from the stability and unchangeableness of the laws of nature that there can be no such catastrophe as that which the Church teaches us to expect at the second coming of our Lord, and that these teachers shall encourage licence of living. 'In the last days,' he says, 'there shall come deceitful scoffers, walking after their own lusts, saying, "Where is this promise of His coming? for, since the time the fathers slept all things continue as they were from the beginning of the creation."'[12]

If anything could enhance the weight of this warning of St. Peter, it would, perhaps, be the manner in which his thoughts and words are taken up and enforced in the canonical Epistle of St. Jude. This Epistle, again, it may be said, would be railed against, if it were published in our time, as a choice specimen of intolerance, as if it were a powerful Pastoral Letter promulgating and insisting upon the condemnations of an Encyclical or a Syllabus. St. Jude professes that the false teachers have furnished the occasion which compels him to write, 'Dearly beloved, taking all care to write to you concerning your common salvation, I was under a necessity to write unto you, to beseech you to contend earnestly for the faith once delivered to the saints, for certain men are secretly entered in (who were written of long ago unto this judgment), ungodly men, turning the grace of our Lord God unto riotousness, and denying the only sovereign Ruler and our Lord Jesus Christ.' St. Jude reminds the faithful, as St. Peter has done, of the judgment which God has executed upon the fallen

[12] 2 St. Peter iii. 3.

angels and upon Sodom and Gomorrah, but he begins by inserting a new instance, how our Lord 'destroyed those that believed not' among the Israelites after their deliverance from the bondage of Egypt. Then the case of the heretics is most exactly described; they have been delivered by our Lord from the bondage of Satan, their sin is unbelief and disobedience, and their punishment not only severe, but public and immediate. St. Jude gives exactly the same description as St. Peter of these false teachers; they are men 'who defile the flesh, despise dominion, and blaspheme majesty,' that is, their teaching and example tend to laxity, and they rebel against the constituted authority of the Church. He explains St. Peter's allusion to the modesty of the angels by mentioning the tradition about St. Michael's contention with the devil about the body of Moses, when the glorious Archangel used no stronger language than 'The Lord rebuke thee.' Then follow several verses in which the images applied to the false teachers by St. Peter are repeated, with a few additions, and which end with the famous citation from the Book of Enoch, in which the future coming of our Lord is predicted, 'To execute judgment upon all, and to reprove the ungodly for all the works of their ungodliness, whereby they have done ungodly, and for all the hard things which ungodly sinners have spoken against God.' Then St. Jude returns to the persons whom he is attacking, 'These are murmurers, full of complaints, walking according to their own desires, and their mouth speaketh proud things, admiring persons for gain's sake;' and he reminds the faithful to whom he is writing of the warnings of the Apostles, 'who told you that in the last time there should come mockers, walking according to their own desires in ungodliness. These are they who separate themselves, sensual men, having not the Spirit.'[13]

[13] Epistle of St. Jude.

Before we pass on to the consideration of the test which our Lord gives us as the means of discerning these false teachers, it may be well to pause for a moment on the picture which is drawn for us in the Gospels, and in the passages to the Epistles to which reference has been made, of the heretical teachers of the Apostolic age and of all subsequent ages in the Church. No other collection of men in human history presents the same features, especially if we include among the heretics men like the founders of Mohammedanism and Mormonism, and of all false religions and systems of life outside the Church. The several characteristics which are summed up in passages like those which have been quoted from St. Paul, St. Peter, and St. Jude, are certainly found in different proportions in the persons of the various heresiarchs and masters of falsehood, but there is always a family likeness between them, which is found also in the false philosophers of modern, as well as of ancient times, in the men who teach materialism or rationalism, systems of physical science which exclude God, or mind or freewill, or the truth of the creation of the Universe, in England, France, or Germany, as well as those who provoked the scorn of Socrates or Plato in Athens. For many of these men there is the excuse that they have either never known of the Church and her doctrine, or have been brought up in absolute antagonism to her—an antagonism produced by the foulest misrepresentation. Or again, the representative of the truth of God to them has been some impiety, like the doctrine of Calvin, or some system of comfortable worldliness, like the less Catholic phase of Anglicanism. Thus the picture is sometimes more mournful than absolutely hateful, for the teachers of falsehood have been groping after truth, and assailing it, under immense misconceptions, while they were so groping.

The False Prophets.

But, setting this consideration aside, there have been among the teachers of evil who have sprung up inside the Church herself, men most entirely different in character, in talents, in position, in learning, in the motives which urged them along their fatal course, in the doctrine which they have perverted, in the speculative character of the tenets which they have advanced. They have assailed every article of the Creed, they have sought to defile every portion of the great field of the theology of the Church. They have attacked the Most Holy Trinity itself, the Persons of the Father, the Son, and the Holy Ghost, they have waged war against the Immaculate Mother of God, the Angels, the Saints, the Church, the Roman Pontiff, the Sacraments, the Sacrifice, the Priesthood. They have not left man his free-will, nor the grace by which it is elevated and assisted, nor the truth of the virtue which that grace can enable him to practise, nor his power to keep the commandments of God, nor the merit of his good works, nor his hope of eternal reward, nor the resurrection of his flesh, nor the spirituality and immortality of his soul. They have risen up in the sanctuary itself, they have sat on Patriarchal or Episcopal thrones, they have come from the cloister of the monk or the friar, or from the cave of the anchorite. All sexes, all ages, all ranks and callings of life, have contributed to swell their numbers, and they have as often appealed to the passions or prejudices of the multitude, as to the avarice of nobles, or the licentiousness or ambition of monarchs and their counsellors. They have been different among themselves in every way, and no two of them have ever agreed together, or even tolerated the idea of any alliance, except against the Church. And yet the portrait drawn of them by our Lord when He described them as wolves in the clothing of sheep, when He further spoke of them as evil trees whose fruit was like the stock on which it grew, as thorns and thistles in their sterility and wounding power, is found, after the experience of so many centuries, to suit them all. It is practically the same picture as that which is drawn in the passages of the Epistles already quoted.

The image of the wolf, which is the first which our Lord here uses, is kindred to that of the dog, of which we had lately to speak when commenting on a former verse of this same Sermon. But it conveys the idea of aggression and hungry rapacity, as well as of destructiveness, more than that former image. This is one of the chief characteristics of the heretical spirit. It might have been thought that persons like those of whom we are speaking might have contented themselves with their own thoughts on matters of religion without any great craving to propagate them. At the first sight, an heretical doctrine is usually some derogation from or paring off of Catholic truth, and when we consider such cases as those of the false teachers of our own time, the most important of whom are those who advocate systems of philosophy which tend to materialism or pantheism, or those who deny the spirituality of the soul, free-will, the creation of the world by God, Providence, the future separate existence of each single soul, and the like, we find that their creed, if we may use such a term of their opinions, becomes more and more a simple negation both of religion natural as well as revealed, and of any obligatory morality. There can obviously be no duty to propagate such tenets, even when they are supposed to be true, nor can their propagation tend to anything but the dissolution of all social bonds and the denial of all morality as ruling by right the public and private concerns of men. It is not even supposed that to hold these opinions tends in any way to increase the happiness or the well-being of the philosopher himself, unless a man is better off for having no restraint at all in the thought of God, or the authority of conscience, to prevent him from the indulgence of his passions on every possible occasion. The same remark holds true, in a less degree, of a great many less fully developed forms of error, whether in the strictly theological sphere, or in that of the essential philosophy of human life. And yet there never yet has been a heretic or a teacher of falsehood of any kind, who has been content to keep his tenets to himself. The true wolfish instinct always overmasters them; the appetite for the destruction in others of that simple faith which they have lost themselves, which can be compared to nothing more truly than to that hatred of the happy works and creatures of God which prompted Satan, when he first assailed in Paradise the father of the human race. The action of the devil in his desire to lay waste the innocent peace of Paradise is set down in Holy Scripture to his envy—his inability to bear the sight in others of that happiness and favour with God which he had forfeited for himself. Heretical teachers, using the term in the largest possible sense, seem to be driven on by the same hateful impulse, as if the faith and obedience of others were a reproach to themselves, as if the perversion of others might be some secret consolation, perhaps some salve to the troubles of their own conscience, which writhes under the sense of isolation and rebelliousness which is in itself a condemnation of such a position in every Catholic mind. Certain it is, that the activity of all heresies and sects in multiplying their proselytes is one of their chief characteristics. In the case of the false teachers of whom the New Testament speaks, whether in our Lord's time or in that of the Apostles after Him, there were other and sordid motives to whet their zeal. The Jewish rulers were responsible to the Romans for the tranquillity of the whole nation, and their position as to temporal influence and gain was highly prosperous. But only prosperous so long as the people rested its confidence upon them as its spiritual guides. The power of our Lord over the multitudes filled them, as we see in the speech of Caiaphas, with envy and fear. The earliest heresiarch of whom Christian history tells us is the Simon mentioned in the Acts [14] as seducing the people of Samaria, and he was so struck with the advantages which might accrue to him if he possessed the spiritual powers which he witnessed in the Apostles, that he offered St. Peter and St. John money if they would impart those powers to him. We see the same motives of self-interest in the teachers of error mentioned later on in the Acts and in the Epistles. They are said to 'love pre-eminence,'[15] to 'creep into houses and lead captive silly women, laden with sins, who are led away by diverse desires,'[16] and the like.

There were personal motives of this kind, as St. Paul hints, in those who disturbed the peace of the Galatians and the Corinthians respectively. The love of personal influence, of having a large following, is usually one of the marks of the teachers of error in all times, and when their private lives come to be known, it is constantly found that the lust for the gratification of lower appetites, those of avarice and even sensuality, has not been without its effect upon them. It cannot be denied that a position of influence and usefulness, such as that which belongs, more or less, to all the ministers of the Church where she is flourishing as the mother of a large population, has attractions for the weaker side of human nature, and it is on this account, as well as on others, that she is so severe in the selection and training of her

[14] Acts viii. [15] 3 St. John 9. [16] 2 Tim. iii. 6.

priests, and in her watchfulness over them in the discharge of their sacred duties. It is almost always the aim of a teacher of heresy to gain a position of the same kind, in which, of course, he is free from all the restraints and deprived of all the safeguards which hedge in and shield the Catholic bishop or priest. Thus we find it very common for heretical teachers, not only to usurp the functions and the authority of a truly commissioned priest, but to exaggerate that authority very largely, and to convert that which our Lord intended to be one of the most delicate and most helpful relations which can exist between soul and soul, into a spiritual despotism and tyranny which could not exist within the pale of the Church. In these and other features of the character of the heresiarch, we see the full truthfulness of our Lord's account of them when He called them wolves.

The circumstance of the sheeps' clothing added to the character of the wolves, is full of significance. It has often been remarked that even the most wicked of mankind, the enemies of all religion and virtue, always pay so much of homage to those two principles that they never profess to attack them as such. It is always in the name of God that His Church is assailed, it is always in the name of good that evil is planned and carried out, the plea of conscience is always alleged for its most flagrant violations, the rights of humanity are always put forward when the grossest tyranny and injustice are to be exercised. But the false teachers of all ages who rise up in the Christian fold do not merely allege the principles of faith, the traditions of antiquity, the language of Scripture, for the falsehoods which they circulate, and they do not affect that open carelessness as to the evident falsehood of their allegations which has characterized the political and military brigandage of the generation in which we live. Heresiarchs do really

T 24

disguise themselves under the garb of holiness and strictness, and they do really conceal the poison which they disseminate under the appearance of true doctrine. No doctrine whatever can have any vitality or attractiveness, any success among Christian people, unless it wears the garb of truth and seems to have the stamp of authority. Thus, even the novelties which these miserable men invent are dressed up to look like old truths, and the innovators themselves always appeal from the living authority, the Church of their own day, which alone can speak in their own day, to other authorities to which they claim to interpret better than she does, in some cases reason, in others Scripture, in others antiquity, in others history. Each century in the life of the Church has its own modes of thought and expression, its own prominent subjects and questions, the solution of all of which is contained in the Creed, the depositum of the faith, but which still wear a colour of their own and require for their complete elucidation the action of the Church, not of any other century, but of their own. Thus, it is hardly ever impossible to raise apparent difficulties against present developments from the teaching or language of one or two writers of the past, men who, if they were now alive, would be the first to submit to the unchanging authority to which they bowed in the days in which they actually did live. In this way, again, the clothing of the sheep is used by the wolves. And again, once more, no false system is wholly false: if it lives at all, or if it seems to live, it must have some elements of truth to sustain its existence. As a matter of fact, heretical and schismatical systems are usually true, except on one or two points; indeed, it is possible to conceive a schismatical community which is wrong only in the single point of unity. Heretics uniformly begin by objecting to one point of the faith, and in process of time, discard more and more, besides giving up the principle of faith itself. Nor is there any more remarkable proof of the ravening and destructive character of false teachers, as our Lord here describes them, than the manner in which, as all experience shows us, a Christian community which begins by rebelling against the Church on one single point goes on in the course of a very few years to sacrifice almost the whole of the Creed. But at the outset, there is perhaps but one single error of doctrine mixed up with all that, on other points, Catholics believe and practise, and in this sense also it is most true that the wolves present themselves in sheeps' clothing.

CHAPTER XVI.

Trees and Fruits.

St. Matt. vii. 16—20 ; *Vita Vitæ Nostræ*, § 36.

WHAT has already been said as to the characteristics of heretics and false teachers of every kind and in every age, may be enough to illustrate the language in which our Lord describes them in the passage on which we are engaged. It now remains to draw out the various truths which are contained in the words which immediately follow, and in which He goes on, as has been said, to furnish His disciples with a simple, practical, and unfailing test, by means of which the lurking wolves may be detected, notwithstanding the sheeps' clothing in which they have concealed themselves. In order to furnish us with this test in a few pregnant words, our Lord now changes the image under which He has been conveying the warning against the false teachers. We shall see how appropriate is the new image which He adopts to the truths which He intends it to teach.

'By their fruits you shall know them. Do men gather grapes of thorns, or figs of thistles? Even so every good tree bringeth forth good fruit, and the evil tree bringeth forth evil fruit. A good tree cannot bring forth evil fruit, neither can an evil tree bring forth good fruit. Every tree that bringeth not forth good fruit, shall be cut down and cast into the fire. Wherefore, by their fruits you shall know them.' The images of grapes and figs suggest the most delightful and wholesome fruits on which man can be fed, and this is the characteristic effect of good and sound doctrine that it alike refreshes, delights, strengthens, and enlightens the mind. The images of the thorns and thistles suggest sterility, uselessness, the destruction of fertility in the land on which they grow, and which they occupy to the exclusion of useful plants, which they choke and stifle. And, again, thorns and thistles wound the hand that touches them. Thus we have many of the characteristics of bad teaching conveyed in the simple words of our Lord, its hardness, its cruelty, its unfruitfulness, its darkening and withering power over the soul and the heart, and the uneasy combativeness and aggressiveness which are found in those who maintain and propagate it. But our Lord remembers the former image, from which He is now passing, according to which the false teachers made their approaches, not undisguised and in their natural garb, but in the clothing of sheep, that is, under the guise of teachers of the truth rightly commissioned and duly authorized. It would be easy enough without any fresh criterion to detect a wolf in the skin of a wolf. It would be foolish enough to expect a thorn to yield grapes, or a thistle to bear figs. We must, therefore, remember the truth conveyed in the former image, and carry it still in our minds while we are considering the present image. What our Lord is teaching us is that the tree may seem to be a vine, and be in truth a thorn, and so incapable of bearing grapes; or it may seem to be a fig-tree, but be in truth a thistle. Such being the case, we are to judge, He tells us, not from the appearance of the tree or of its leaves, but from the fruit which hangs thereon. Then the image is tacitly once more changed, and the trees are spoken of as 'good' and 'evil,' that is, as sound or unsound trees of the same kind. A thorn cannot disguise itself as a vine, nor a thistle as a fig-tree, but a tree may be healthy and in good condition, and then its fruit will be sound and wholesome, while another tree in the same garden or orchard may be rotten to the core, and the fruit which grows upon it will then be rotten also. And He tells us without hesitation or restriction, that the true test between the good and evil teacher is the soundness or unsoundness of their doctrine, whether we consider it in its speculative or practical aspect, and that the teacher whose teaching leads to evil results in either of these ways is to be rejected as a wolf in the garb of a sheep.

Although our Lord does not always use His familiar and parabolical images in exactly the same sense and with reference to exactly the same truth, we may still find great light as to one instance of their use from other places in His discourses in which also they occur. This image of the trees and their fruits occurs in two other passages in the Gospels. The first is in the Sermon on the Plain, of which we shall have to speak in a future volume, and which consists very mainly in an adaptation of the thoughts and instructions contained in this Sermon on the Mount to an audience and an occasion in many respects different. In the passage of the Sermon on the Plain,[1] to which we refer, our Lord connects this image of the trees and their fruits with the admonition on which we have lately commented, which forbids us to correct the faults of others before we have cleared our own consciences of the same or greater faults. 'Hypocrite!' He says, 'cast first the beam out of thy own eye, and then shalt thou see clearly to take out the mote from thy brother's eye. For there is no good tree that bringeth forth evil fruit, nor an evil tree that bringeth forth good fruit,' and the rest. Here the meaning may be, that a hypocritical correction of another will certainly not

[1] St. Luke vi. 43, seq.

succeed, because the successful use of such a weapon of charity must depend on the grace of God and on the purity of intention with which it used, while, as we have seen, corrections which proceed from impenitent hearts, in which there is not even an attempt to get rid of their own guilt, cannot have a pure intention, and the grace of God cannot be expected to cooperate with them. Thus a hypocrite is placed, so far, on the same level with a teacher of falsehood, and the principle of God's Kingdom to which our Lord appeals is the same in each case, that is, the principle that any rottenness of heart or unsoundness of thought in the person by whom a moral effect is to be produced, infects the whole operation of the production of that effect. The other occasion on which our Lord used this same image was not long after the delivery of the Sermon on the Plain, when, as it appears, His enemies for the first time put in circulation their detestable calumny about His league with Beelzebub, being driven thereto by the splendour of His miracles, the truth of which they could not question. Our Lord then, among other severe things which He said of them, used this image in the sense of a reproach to them for attributing results so obviously and confessedly good to an evil principle. 'Either make the tree good and its fruit good, or make the tree evil and its fruit evil. For by the fruit the tree is known.'[2] That is, they should either have called Him evil and His works evil, or called Him good and His works good. To say that He did good things by the power of the Evil One, was to contradict the laws of God's Kingdom, as much as the attributing good fruit to a rotten tree was to contradict the laws of nature and experience.

But further consideration will show us that there is more in this argument than may be at first sight discerned.

[2] St. Matt. xii. 33.

The Author and Governor of the natural world is the same God Who has created and Who governs the spiritual world also. In nature there is nothing fantastic, unreasonable, fickle, mischievous, such as might have been the case if the Author of nature had been evil in character, and had made His world in a capricious, thoughtless, or desultory way. There are many wonderful analogies between the works of God in various orders, and the beauty and fitness, the perfection and harmony and wisdom of the physical world may well prepare us for the display of qualities of the same sort in the arrangement and government of the moral and spiritual realm of the same God. Disrespectful and irreverent as it would be to expect to find nature governed by cruel, mocking, and spiteful laws, it would be far more so to imagine that rules of the same kind could be allowed to prevail in the far higher spheres of the spiritual and moral universe. It would, however, be an error of this kind to think that God could fail to prosper and bless with fertility and power for good the truth on which He sets so much store, and the lawfully authorized and holy teachers who are commissioned by Him. And it would be the same error to think that He Who has done so much to proclaim to the world His love of truth and His hatred of lies, would allow the evil doctrine of usurping and vicious teachers to produce effects evidently good as to their moral and spiritual character. In the passage to which we are now referring as an illustration of the words before us, our Lord utters some of the most severe things which ever passed His lips about the blasphemy against the Holy Ghost, words which have led many to think that it is a sin too great and heinous for God ever to pardon. And yet, by comparing the two passages together, we see that this sin was committed by those who attributed good fruits to an evil tree. For the Christian doctrine reveals

Trees and Fruits. 297

to us the truth that the good fruits of which our Lord is speaking in the Sermon on the Mount are the work of God the Holy Ghost Himself, the Third Person of the Adorable Trinity, without Whose action no spiritual good whatever can be produced, and who cannot possibly lend Himself to cooperate in the imposing of falsehood upon the people of God, as would be the case if He were to bless the false doctrine of the teachers of whom our Lord is speaking with the beautiful fruitfulness of His graces. If the tree of which our Lord speaks be good, it is because the Holy Ghost dwells with the teacher who is thereby represented; if his fruit be good, it is because the Holy Ghost works in and with him. If a teacher be bad, the Holy Ghost cannot be with him, and he is like an evil tree on that account, and his fruit evil, because the Holy Ghost will not and cannot work with him or make him His instrument.

The doctrine on which this rule of our Lord is founded is thus seen to rest upon nothing short of the unchangeableness and holiness of the Divine Nature itself. But the practical application of the rule does not appear so easy, especially if it be remembered that it is given as a rule the application of which must of necessity be very frequent. We have already to some extent glanced at the multitudinous and heterogeneous swarm of false teachers of every kind who have beset the children of the Church from her earliest years, and now we have to understand from our Lord that the touchstone by which all these impostors and usurpers are to be detected is to be found in the simple rule, 'By their works you shall know them.' This is one of the cases in which a great truth is brought out in its full beauty and proportion by examining the difficulties and objections which may be raised against its reception. It is certain, it may be said, that many good men do evil things, and that many bad men do good things. It is certain, and, indeed, it is the doctrine of our Lord in this very Sermon on the Mount, that many an outwardly good and religious action is not such in the eyes of God, because it is spoilt by some false intention of vanity, the seeking of human applause, and the like. It is certain that we are told by our Lord to hide, as far as possible, our good deeds from the eyes of men, who therefore cannot be able to see in them the fruits of a good life. Again, we are not to judge the actions of others, and how, then, are we to discern the false teachers by their conduct? Nay, if we leave aside the question of persons as such, and consider that our Lord's words here are limited, as in truth they appear to be, to doctrine and teaching, of which we are to judge from their fruits, still it remains true that, as has already been said, all false teaching has a large admixture of truth in it, by means of which it lives and flourishes, and that therefore it may happen that the true and Catholic ingredients, so to speak, in a system of teaching which, as a whole and fundamentally, is false, may produce good fruits, which meet the eye, and which may thus serve to accredit as coming from God what is in truth opposed to Him. And then we may remind ourselves of the virtues and good works for which some of the heretical leaders have been conspicuous, and of the results of fervour and of the renewal of piety, and even, to some extent, of true doctrine, which have followed from their preaching. Again, there have been times of laxity in the Church, when her prelates have been ambitious and worldly, or her clergy indolent and ignorant, while, at the very same time and in the same place with these scandals, there may have arisen men misguided rather than, at the beginning, wilfully heretical, who have originated sects which have started with a great appearance of primitive religion. In the same way, it may sometimes come to be known that ministers of the Church here and there are men of bad lives, and in cases like these the rule of our Lord would seem liable to be used against Himself and against the truth which is so dear to Him.

On the other hand, it must be certain that, rightly understood and faithfully applied, this test of our Lord's must not only be true, but the very best and most perfect truth, for the purpose for which it is given. It must be the one easiest and most infallible rule to say, You shall know them by their fruits. In regard to the objections which have now been stated, and others like them, it may be replied that, in the first place, as has been said already, the rule is directly given for the discernment of doctrine. It is very true, as has been observed by St. Thomas and others, that it is a rule which tries and detects false sanctity as well as false doctrine. What is meant by this is, that false virtue does not stand the test of trial. A man may appear to be humble, and holy, and pure, and devout, and mortified, but if he is taken unawares, as by some sudden insult, he betrays pride, anger, impatience, or if he is disappointed in what he has set his heart upon, he is unable to bear his disappointment with meekness, and breaks out in fury against this or that person whom he supposes to have thwarted him. In the same way, the test that our Lord gives in the Parable of the Sower, of trial and tribulation, reveals, how shallow and without root is the apparent sanctity of many. But this kind of touchstone cannot be easily applied at any moment, and it may be long indeed before the test comes into operation under which pretended or imperfect sanctity gives way. So far, then, there seems to be good reason for the limitation of the words of our Lord to a test of doctrine, to which such a test can be applied, as we shall see, almost immediately.

How this may be done, we may learn to some extent from the Apostle of Love, the Blessed Evangelist St. John, the very intensity of whose charity makes him speak even more strongly than the other Apostles against the false teachers of his own time. 'Dearly beloved,' he says, 'believe not every spirit, but try the spirits if they be of God, because many false prophets are gone out into the world.' The Church had not nearly accomplished her first century of life since the day of Pentecost, and the world was already full of false teaching under the name of Christianity. 'By this is the Spirit of God known. Every spirit that confesseth that Jesus Christ is come in the flesh is of God, and every spirit that dissolveth Jesus is not of God, and this is the Antichrist of whom you have heard that he cometh, and he is now already in the world.'[3] Here we have the test of true doctrine as to the Incarnation of our Lord and all its results, given as the touchstone which is to try the spirits, whether they be of God or not. It is very true that the heresies of the Apostolical age seem to have fastened especially upon the doctrine of the Incarnation itself, the Person of our Lord, His Divine and Human Nature, the reality of His Body or of His death, and the like, and that thus St. John may be giving a rule which, in one sense, applied with particular aptitude to the evils of that generation. But the words of the Apostle embrace the whole of the great doctrine which explains the coming of God in the Flesh, its purposes, and its results, and, if they are thus understood, they contain enough to furnish the rule which may detect any false teaching whatsoever, let us say, for instance, the teaching of the Lutherans as to justification, or the Calvinist and Jansenist doctrine as to grace and predestination. For what is it to 'dissolve Jesus?' The words may apply to the denial of the

[3] 1 St. John iv. 1—3.

Unity of His Sacred Person, or of His twofold Nature, or of His Eternal Godhead, or of His true Sacred Humanity, or of His Reign here as in Heaven, or of His Life in the Blessed Sacrament, or of His working in the Church through the Holy Ghost, or of the unity, authority, and indefectibility of His Church, which is His Body, and which is spoken of by the Apostles as 'Christ.' In all these senses the denial of the true Catholic doctrine is the 'dissolving of Jesus,' and, in an especial way, the teaching of any new doctrine, or any rebellion against the Church's authority, which directly tends to schism, in such a 'dissolving.' There is the same evil effect on the doctrine of the Incarnation in particular heresies, as such, apart from their rebellious and schismatical tendency. Justification apart from any change of heart, in the Lutheran sense, is in itself a dissolving of our Lord, because it separates two operations of His which are indivisible. The Calvinist doctrine of predestination attacks directly the Divine Goodness in our Lord, and imagines another Jesus Who did not die for all men. But these and all other heresies 'dissolve' Jesus in another and a still more evident way, which is discernible at once even by those who are not instructed enough or thoughtful enough to see their effect on the true doctrine concerning our Lord. For they 'dissolve' Him in His Church and they violate her unity, rebel against her authority, they separate the one flock from the One Shepherd, and break it up into various folds.

Here, then, we have a test given us by our Lord which the simplest child of the Church can apply for himself with as much ease and readiness as the most learned among her doctors. Every false teacher, on whatever part of the Creed it may be that he teaches falsely, produces at least the one clearly evil and detestable fruit of separation from unity and rebellion against authority. These are sins in the Christian kingdom in as true a sense as murder and idolatry and adultery are sins; and as we should know a man to be wicked whom we saw with our own eyes commit either of these last-named enormities, so do we know a man to be wicked if we know that he teaches against the doctrine of the living Church of the present day, the unfailing life, power, and authority of which is an article of the Creed. His doctrine may seem to tend to strictness of life, purity of manners, unworldliness, the frequentation of the sacraments, the practice of good works, but if it is not the doctrine which the Church teaches, it is the evil fruit of an evil tree. It contains within itself the destruction of the unity and charity to establish which our Lord has founded His Church.

But it is also true that, apart from this simple sense of our Lord's words, they contain the further truth to which we have already alluded in connection with the passage in which He speaks of the blasphemy against the Holy Ghost. That is, as all the beautiful fruits of virtue and perfection which are His work in the souls of men spring up naturally from the root, so to speak, of the charity which He sheds abroad in their hearts, so when this is wanting, as it is wanting of necessity in all teaching which is against and in defiance of the Church, the ordinary effect of such teaching is to lower the standard of virtue and morality among those with whom it prevails. This result may not be at once discernible, though it follows very rapidly indeed, in some cases, upon the declension from Catholic unity, as has been seen in our time among the unhappy men who professed a few years ago that they would hold the whole doctrine of the Catholic Church as it was taught before the Council of the Vatican, while at the same time they refused to submit to the decrees of that Council. A very few years have sufficed to lead them to the abolition of the celibacy of the clergy and the abandonment of other points of their former doctrine or practice. In the case of the great religious revolt of the sixteenth century, as the work itself, in almost every country where it succeeded, originated in the hearts of men and women of conspicuously evil lives, the rapidity with which the evil fruit manifested itself was almost equally remarkable. The glory of the virginal state, the indissolubility of marriage, the necessity of confession, the practice of works of penance and mortification, the religious consecration of a life to God, and the like, all these vanished from the practical code of the men who denied the Catholic doctrines of the unity and authority of the Church, Transubstantiation, the Eucharistic Sacrifice, the power of the keys, Purgatory, and Prayer for the Dead. False doctrine never prevails, without engendering laxity and opening the door to vice; and the truth of this is more conspicuous than in other cases, when, as with the Jansenists, the false doctrine itself pretends to teach the highest purity and the strictest severity. So that, as a matter of history, it may be questioned whether the great convulsion, which began at the end of the last century in the French Revolution, was more truly the child of the infidelity of the philosophers, or of the tyranny and voluptuousness of the Court, or of the rigour of the Jansenists.

It may be said that the common mass of Christians are too little accustomed to reflection, or too little instructed, to discern the link between the tree and its fruit in such cases as that of which we have been speaking. If that be so, then we should have still greater reason than before for thanking God for giving us the authority of the visible Church and the throne of St.

Peter to tell us in a moment what is the fruit which must proceed from an evil tree. But it must be remembered that men are ordinarily very quick in discerning the moral tendencies of doctrines which present themselves, in the first instance, almost as matters of simple speculation. This is the case both with those who are jealously vigilant against the slightest derogation from purity of doctrine, and with those who are instinctively ready to welcome the slightest relaxation of the moral law. St. John speaks of the quickness with which the loyal children of the Church are gifted in the detection of error, in one of the passages in which he has also mentioned the false teachers. 'These things have I written to you,' he says, 'concerning those that seduce you. And as for you, let the unction which you have received from Him, abide in you. And you have no need that any man teach you, but as His unction teacheth you of all things, and is truth, and no lie. And as it hath taught you, abide in Him.'[4] There are many instances in which simple Catholics will feel that there is a strangeness and unsoundness about a doctrine, without being able to give it a theological exposure or refutation, and this will be constantly the case even when the poison which infects its moral character is not prominent. And there is a keen instinct among those who desire to free themselves from the severe morality of the Gospel, which leads to the same quick detection of heresy and its fruits, though in this case the process cannot be attributed to the unction of the Holy Ghost. Such men easily penetrate the mask which is worn by the unhappy apostles of error. They detect at once a doctrine which represents the commandments of God as impossible, and feel that such teaching tends to set them free from the obligation of endeavouring

[4] 1 St. John ii. 26, 27.

to keep the commandments of God. Tell them that every work which does not proceed from the purest charity is sinful, and they will at once recognize an invitation to unlimited self-indulgence, to eat and to drink, for to-morrow they die. Tell them that no one ought to approach the sacraments except with an almost angelical purity and reverence, and they will understand that they are freed from all moral obligation to approach the sacraments. Teach them that grace, when it is really worthy of the name, cannot be resisted, and they feel that they are told that their will is not free, and that they are not responsible for their faults. These illustrations might be continued almost indefinitely. The revolt against the Church, which was begun by Luther, professed to deliver men from spiritual bondage and superstition, and it led directly to the plundering of ecclesiastical revenues by covetous nobles and princes, to the renunciation of civil obedience on the part of subjects towards rulers, and to the severest tyranny and oppression on the part of rulers towards subjects. The rejection of the obedience due to the Pope and the Church, and the assertion of the right of private judgment, brought about the social miseries to which Europe was subjected in the sixteenth and seventeenth centuries, the loss of civil liberties, and the gradual extinction of belief even in the doctrines of natural religion. The whole history of heresies and their results is but one long commentary on these words of our Blessed Lord.

There is something still further to be noted as to the concluding words of this passage. Our Lord not only says that a good tree cannot bring forth evil fruit, nor an evil tree good fruit, but He adds, before He concludes, some words which are recorded by St. Matthew as used by St. John Baptist in his preaching to the Jews, and especially to those Pharisees and Sadducees who came to listen to him. St. John first used the image of the axe being laid at the root of the tree, and then he added, 'Every tree, therefore, that bringeth not forth good fruit shall be cut down and cast into the fire.' The words of the Baptist seem to be a warning against trusting to any external privileges which men may possess, and not to the practice of virtue and the keeping of the commandments of God, for he had said just before, 'Think not to say within yourselves, we have Abraham for our father. For I tell you that God is able of these stones to raise up children to Abraham.'[5] What His Forerunner thus applies universally, though still with a special reference to the Pharisees and others, who must above all men have prided themselves on being the children of Abraham, our Lord now applies to the false teachers of whom He has been speaking. He said afterwards of the Pharisees, when He was told that they were scandalized at His teaching, 'Every plant which My Heavenly Father hath not planted, shall be rooted up.'[6] And now, in the same way, He adds the sentence of destruction on the false teachers and their systems, having already sentenced them to incapacity in producing any good fruit. Not only are they to be thus sterile of good and prolific of bad fruit, but they are to be cut down and cast into the fire, not, as the words run, for producing bad fruit, but because they have not borne good fruit. 'Every tree, therefore, that bringeth not forth good fruit shall be cut down and shall be cast into the fire.' And, as a matter of history, this sentence has been executed, even in this world, in a variety of ways, for such teachers are cast out of the Church of God, and they are very frequently indeed punished in a remarkable manner, even temporally, in this life: they lose their credit and influence, their sup-

[5] St. Matt. iii. 9, seq.   [6] St. Matt. xv. 13.

porters turn against them, or sometimes, in the very heyday at their apparent triumph, they are cut short by some sudden and appalling death. The same thing happens in due course of time to the systems which they originate and the communions which they found. They carry in their bosom the poison which is in the end to destroy them, and if they do not dissolve into discordant fragments at once, it is usually because they are supported by the State, which exacts, as a condition of its support, a certain measure of apparent and outward cohesion. One after another they lose the detached fragments of truth which they carried away with them when they broke off from the Catholic Church, their religious life dries up, learning and activity decay, and then perhaps, the State, of which they have become the bondslaves, grows wearied of them, or a political convulsion ensues, which sweeps away the State and them together. Never do they live long, never do they stand the storms of adversity, never do they remain what they were at their beginning, never can they retain the respect and the affection of the nations on which they have imposed themselves, though their best chance of apparent life is to identify themselves as far as may be with those nations, and so to exist by virtue of the national spirit, which is the great antagonist of the Catholic spirit in the Christian world.

'Therefore,' our Lord concludes, 'by their fruits you shall know them.' You shall know them at once, by the fruit of disobedience to the Church, of separation from unity, of rebellion against authority, which will be the one universal note of their false teaching from the beginning. You shall know them by the moral and spiritual effects which their doctrines will produce in their own lives and in the lives of their unhappy dupes, effects which issue in the denial of all truth, in the degradation of the Christian standard of morality, and in a thousand social evils which will vitiate human life and human civilization. And you shall know them by the terrible fruits which their miserable trade will produce for themselves, the blighting and withering up of all that is good, the loss of the truths which they still desired to retain, the sins into which they are allowed to fall, the contempt and hardness with which the world will visit their servility to itself upon them, and by the just and conspicuous judgments which will so often fall upon their persons and on their works, on whatever they may attempt to construct in the way of a religious society, on whatever system of doctrine they may have endeavoured to substitute for the theology of the Catholic Church.

CHAPTER XVII.

Profession and Practice.

St. Matt. viii. 21—23; *Vita Vitæ Nostræ*, § 36.

THE first of the warnings of which this last portion of the Sermon on the Mount consists, is addressed to all Christians, and especially to all who are called to serve God in perfection, in the observances of the Evangelical Counsels, and the like. This is the warning or instruction contained in our Lord's words about the narrow gate. Thus the first great principle of Christian security, of which this closing part of the Sermon speaks, is the principle of the due estimate and practical view of the end which we have to gain and the difficulties which beset it, chiefly on account of our own great frailty, blindness, and carelessness. The second warning or instruction which our Lord gives in the same place is that which we have just been considering—the truth of the continual danger to the souls of the faithful from false teachers and false doctrines. Two more remain to be considered, to which, as to those of which we have already spoken, our Lord afterwards recurs in other portions of His teachings. These two warnings are first, that against profession without practice, to which this chapter will be devoted, and the other against hearing and not acting on the word of God, which will be considered in the next.

The exhortation against profession without practice, as a common danger into which a great number of

Christians will fall, is twofold, and may be considered as addressed, in the first place, to all the faithful in general, and in the second place, to those in particular who have any teaching or ministerial office in the Church. 'Not every one that saith to Me, Lord, Lord, shall enter into the Kingdom of Heaven, but he that doeth the will of My Father Who is in Heaven, he shall enter into the Kingdom of Heaven.' These words, as has been hinted, are altogether general in their application, for all Christians call on our Lord in their professions of faith and acts of religion, and all Christians are called upon to do the will of the Father in order to enter into the Kingdom of Heaven. But the next words seem more particular in the persons of whom they may be supposed to speak. 'Many will say to Me on that day, Lord, Lord, have we not prophesied in Thy Name, and cast out devils in Thy Name, and done many miracles in Thy Name? And then will I profess unto them, I never knew you,' 'Depart from Me, you that work iniquity'[1]—which last words are taken from the Psalms.

It is not difficult to see how these exhortations or warnings grow one out of the other. Our Lord first touches our internal weakness in order to deliver us from the blindness as to our danger in the struggle for salvation which that weakness might engender. But, in the next place, He seems to add, that much as we may strengthen ourselves, and firm as may be our resolution as to the gaining salvation even at a great cost, we shall be often in danger of being led astray from the narrow path by false guides. But then, even after that danger has been provided against by the use of the test which our Lord is so careful to furnish, after we are safe in the one true fold and are fed upon the pure doctrine

[1] Psalm vi. 9.

of the Church, there arises another danger which may be as fatal as either of the former. We may take the confession of the Catholic faith and the practice of Catholic worship for the whole of the religion of Jesus Christ, whereas a true faith is indispensable to salvation, but it is not all-sufficient for salvation, and even the external worship of God is not enough without the service of a life free from sin. We shall see hereafter how the last of these great notes of warning is connected with that which is now before us.

We shall have in a future chapter to draw out the features in this Divine Sermon which may have been before the mind of the Evangelist when he speaks at the conclusion of the whole, of the great appearance of authority in this teaching of our Lord. Here, however, we must notice in passing the very lofty tone which He adopts in this warning. 'Not every one that saith to Me, Lord, Lord, shall enter into the Kingdom of Heaven.' He has not told them anywhere to pray to Him, or to adore Him, or to use language towards Him which declares that He is the object of their worship, and yet His words in this place may fairly be taken as implying all this without any hesitation or limitation. No one could ever imagine that entrance into the Kingdom of Heaven could be secured by the use of the language of which our Lord speaks to a simple man, a prophet or teacher, of however high pretentions and rank in God's Kingdom. Such language may be used in a lower sense of earthly dignitaries, but then it could never be supposed that such homage as that which is conveyed by it could be a passport to salvation. It could only be as addressed to a Divine Person that it could ever be considered as such. Our Lord, therefore, is here distinctly speaking of Himself as the Object of worship, and therefore, as God made Man. And He tells us plainly that even this homage paid to Him will not be enough, unless those who pay it are also observers of the commandments of God. There is another great claim contained in the words which are used in the second clause of this passage, about the Day of Judgment, on which we shall have presently to dwell.

Our Lord's words in the verse before us must undoubtedly be understood of a true profession of faith and worship. He tells us, that such a profession is not enough. If it were otherwise, we should have had something about hypocrisy in the use of the words, Lord, Lord, and the antithesis in the second half of the sentence would not have mentioned the doing the will of the Father as the condition of salvation, but the true and hearty invocation of our Lord. Thus our Lord here seems to anticipate the false doctrines about faith and its profession which arose in the Church so many centuries after this time. St. Paul, the great champion of the truth as to the justifying power of a true faith in our Lord, such as that which was preached by the Apostles, was to say, 'If thou confess with thy mouth the Lord Jesus, and believe in thy heart that God hath raised Him from the dead, thou shalt be saved, for with the heart we believe unto justice, but with the mouth confession is made unto salvation. For the Scripture saith, Whosoever believeth in Him shall not be confounded. For there is no distinction of the Jew and the Greek.' Here the Apostle touches the particular error which He has been combating in his Epistle. 'For the same is Lord over all, rich unto all that call upon Him, for whosoever shall call upon the name of the Lord shall be saved.'[2] A comparison of these words with the text before us shows us how the Catholic doctrine must be gathered from the whole of Scripture, and how a single

[2] Rom. x. 9—13 ; Isaias xxviii. 16 ; Joel ii. 32.

text may be abused in contradiction to the analogy of the faith. The hearty profession of the true faith, according to St. Paul, is the essential condition of salvation, for he is contending against those who would add thereto, as a further condition, the observance of the Mosaic Law. It was not to his purpose to speak, in the passage just now quoted, of the necessity of the observance of the commandments of God—what our Lord calls doing the will of His Father Who is in Heaven. Without faith and the profession of faith, Heaven cannot be entered, but it must be faith that is productive of good works, as St. Paul says to the Galatians: 'In Christ Jesus neither circumcision availeth anything, nor uncircumcision, but faith that worketh by charity.'[3] And so St. James adds, that 'faith without works is dead.'[4] This is exactly the doctrine of these words of our Lord. And it is most remarkable that St. Paul, the Apostle of the Gentiles, has to vindicate the prerogative of faith against the Judaizing teachers who insisted on the necessity of the works of the Law, while, on the other hand, St. James, the great Christian teacher of the circumcision, as Bishop of Jerusalem, where there were so many thousands of Jewish converts, 'all zealous for the Law,' as St. Paul was told, as it seems, by St. James himself,[5] has to vindicate the necessity of the addition of good works to faith in order that the latter may not die. It seems as if the fault which St. James had to correct was very much the same with that against which our Lord here speaks in prophecy.

It seems only fair to think that there was something which predisposed men to this fault in the highly external character of the Jewish religion as our Lord found it in practice. This was the great charge which He made against the Pharisees and their teaching—that they con-

[3] Galat. v. 6.   [4] St. James ii. 20.   [5] Acts xxi. 20.

sidered it enough to be the children of Abraham, to hold the true faith, and to practise a multitude of external acts of religion. The idea which we derive from the Gospels of the prevalent practice is that it tolerated very largely the separation of morality from religion. We know from other sources that there was immense depravity, even among the priests and the higher clergy, and this seems to come to the surface in the story of the woman taken in adultery. Our Lord reproached the Pharisees with tithing mint and anise and cummin, and leaving the weightier matters of the Law, judgment and mercy and faith. He said that they made clean the outside of the cup and of the dish, but that within they were full of rapine and uncleanness. They were like whited sepulchres, 'which outwardly appear to men beautiful, but within are full of dead men's bones, and of all filthiness: so likewise they appeared to men just, but inwardly were full of hypocrisy and iniquity.'[6] A population among whom this kind of religion was in honour might under some circumstances be tempted to join themselves to the new Teacher, especially as He was magnificently bountiful in His miracles, and yet retain some of their former ideas concerning the sufficiency of external observances and the like. We cannot doubt that when our Lord sent people away, as He sometimes is recorded to have done, without admitting them to His own company, this tendency to a shallow external religion may have been one of the motives for their rejection.

This tendency, however, cannot be confined to the Jews of our Lord's time, or to those nominal Christians who afterwards caught their spirit and carried on their traditions. It is not, indeed, very likely that, when the Church is under persecution or struggling with other

[6] St. Matt. xxiii. 23—28.

difficulties, there should be very great temptation to such a resting in externals, for the mere pressure of adversity would make it likely that those whose religion was so hollow would fall off altogether from the profession of the faith. But the Church has had her times of outward prosperity and wealthiness, when she has had great temporal prizes to distribute to her ministers, when her bishops have become great State officials, and when some kind of observance has been either fashionable or imposed by law, authority, or custom. And in all times there must be numbers among her children whose religious practice has withered away under worldliness or internal impurity, and these may wish to persuade themselves that their outward profession will count in the scales of God's justice when they come to be tried. Such is also the danger of Catholics who live in the midst of heretics, and on whom the controversy as to the Church is continually forced. They may get to maintain the Catholic cause and the Catholic doctrines, without uniting to their profession the practice of a Catholic life. There have ever been conspicuous literary defenders of Catholicism in times like our own, who have nevertheless passed almost their whole lives in the neglect of prayer and the sacraments, and in the moral faults to which such neglect usually leads, and by which it is explained.

The second part of this warning, as has been already pointed out, may be understood in reference more particularly to teachers and ministers of the Church. 'Many will say to Me in that day, Lord, Lord, have we not prophesied in Thy Name, and cast out devils in Thy Name, and done many miracles in Thy Name? And then will I profess unto them, I never knew you; depart from Me, you that work iniquity.' Here then our Lord implies that He is to be the Judge at the Last

Day. This would be all the more remarkable, if we could be certain that up to this time He had never spoken to them of the Judgment. But the teaching of St. John Baptist about our Lord pointed to the judgment which He was to execute, as when the Baptist described Him as One Whose fan was in His hand, and He will thoroughly cleanse His floor, and gather His wheat into the barn, but burn up the chaff with fire unquenchable.'[7] But it is certain that the people at large must have been unprepared for the truth that our Lord was to judge the world, a truth on which, a few weeks later than this time, He chose to dwell with great emphasis in His dispute with the Jews after the miracle at the Probatic Pool.[8] And yet our Lord speaks as if what He said could not fail to be intelligible. At that terrible Day of Judgment, then, He says, many will come to Him as if to remonstrate at their rejection, and remind Him that they have preached or even prophesied in His Name, and cast out devils and performed miracles in His Name. It may be understood that this remonstrance will not be made publicly, but in their own hearts, and that our Lord's language is meant to convey this graphically, just as we find, in His description of the Last Judgment at the end of His Preaching, that the good are said to ask Him when they have done so much mercy to Him as He speaks of, and the wicked, in the same way, will ask when they saw Him in need and did not relieve Him. It may be supposed that the clear sight of all their lives in the light of God, which is a part of the process even of the Particular Judgment, will remove all self delusion from the minds even of the wicked, and that they will be perfectly convinced, not only of the justice of their doom, but that God has been far more merciful to them than they

[7] St. Matt. iii. 12.   [8] St. John v. 25—29.

deserve. But yet it is not to be forgotten that the wicked are confirmed in their wickedness at death, and that they may become brazen-faced, as it were, and as insolent as the demons themselves in their complaints against our Lord. And, if this can happen in any case, it may be more likely to happen in the case of those of whom our Lord speaks than in that of any others. There is nothing so incorrigible and blinding as the interior impurity and hypocrisy of a minister of religion, who is given up to ambition and worldliness and the hatred of men who may seem to thwart him or stand in his way, while his soul is in truth dead to God. And the same truth is very obvious in the case of men who are leading impure lives while they are ministering at the altar or in the pulpit. In the case of such persons, their perpetual familiarity with sacred things, the constant administration to others of the means of grace which are so useless to themselves, the repeated preaching of truths and maxims which they have given up all attempt to practise, may produce a blindness in the soul which may enable it to think that it is hardly dealt with when the condemnation of its hypocrisy falls upon it.

The men whom our Lord adduces as instances of this miserable delusion, are those who have had the very highest favours bestowed upon them in their ministrations to others, such as the graces which theologians call *gratis data*, that is, graces which do not necessarily sanctify the persons in whom they reside, but which are given to them for the sake of the Church. The most conspicuous of these graces are the gifts of prophecy, of casting out devils by exorcisms, and of miraculous cures. It is beyond all question that Catholic theologians do not speak of a merely speculative evil when they tell us that gifts like these are compatible with a state of the soul of the person who possesses them, from which sanctifying grace is absent. But our Lord may mention these as the strongest, or, at least, as the most conspicuous cases of this terrible self-delusion, and may mean us to fill up other details of the picture for ourselves from our own experience. The gift of prophecy, the power which is shown in exorcisms and in miraculous cures, are gifts which cost the persons on whom they are bestowed nothing, though they expose them greatly to the dangers of vanity and pride. There are other gifts and other services, gifts which seem closely connected with interior sanctification, services which cannot be performed without self-sacrifice, and yet even of these it is certain that they may often be found without the true principle of holiness. St. Paul mixes up the two heads of gifts together, in his famous passage about charity: 'If I speak with the tongues of men and of angels, and have not charity, I am become as sounding brass or a tinkling cymbal. And if I should have prophecy, and should know all mysteries and all knowledge, and if I should have all faith, so that I could remove mountains, and have not charity, I am nothing. And if I should distribute all my goods to feed the poor, and if I should deliver my body to be burned, and have not charity, it profiteth me nothing.'[9] These words are the condemnation of all the teachers and preachers outside the Church, however great may be their seeming gifts, however great their self-sacrifice. They have not charity, because, as one of the Fathers says, if they had, they could not tear the seamless Robe of Christ. But the same words are the condemnation of all the ministers and servants of the Church, the highest as well as the lowest, if their zeal is guided by ambition and self-seeking, if their hearts are dead to charity on account of some

[9] 1 Cor. xiii. 1, seq.

Profession and Practice. 319

jealousy or animosity. They are the condemnation also of a thousand external workers of good for the service of the Church, preachers whose eloquence shakes great cities, missionaries who cross the seas and brave death to spread the Gospel, doctors and teachers and controversialists and confessors and superiors alike, if their own consciences are neglected while they are labouring for the good of others. Every now and then the Church at large, or some portion of the Church, is startled by a conspicuous fall, the news of which pierces the hearts of the devout people of God as with a sword of ice. But for one such fall that is known to the public, there are a score that are known in secret but to a few, and for a score that are hidden from the public eye, though known to some, there are perhaps hundreds that are known to God alone, and that will never be revealed until the day comes of which our Lord here speaks, when He will say to many who have worn the mask to the very end, 'I never knew you. Depart from Me, you that work iniquity.'

The words of our Lord seem to imply that, at the time of which He speaks, when all that is hidden will be manifested, not only to those immediately concerned, but to all the world beside, the revelation of the truth concerning such persons as these will be made by a public declaration of His own. Just as He says elsewhere, that He will confess or deny before His Father Who is in Heaven those who confess Him or who deny Him upon earth, so now He says that He will profess unto those who have taught and done wonders in His Name without keeping His commandments, that He never knew them; that is, as it seems, He will not only say to them that He knows them not,[10] as He will say to those who are represented by the foolish virgins in

[10] St. Matt. xxv. 12.

one of His last parables, meaning that at the time at which they are found unprepared they are outside His grace, but that all the time during which these others were preaching and performing miracles in His Name, He was not with them, He never knew them. The knowledge of which our Lord here speaks is not, of course, knowledge in its simplest sense, in which sense our Lord knows the wicked as well as the good, the fallen angels themselves, as well as the Seraphim around His Throne and His dearest saints, but that kind of knowledge of which Sacred Scripture speaks in many places, and which signifies that loving gaze with which His eyes rest upon those in whom He delights. Thus St. Paul says, 'If any man love God, the same is known of Him;'[11] and again, 'The sure foundation of God standeth firm, having this seal: The Lord knoweth who are His, and let every one depart from iniquity who nameth the Name of the Lord'[12]—words which seem in some measure an echo of the passage on which we are commenting. And the sentence of banishment which follows, the words of which are taken from the first of the penitential Psalms, in which they seem to have reference to the enemies of the soul who have been tempting and tormenting the penitent, especially, perhaps, to despair, are taken up into the mouth of the Judge Himself, as if our Lord had before Him the terrible sentence, 'Depart from Me, ye cursed, into everlasting fire,' but chose rather to use the words of the Psalm which furnish the reason for the eternal banishment, which is in itself the greatest of curses, and which is to fall on some who have ceased to be His servants and the ministers of His grace. The reason is that they have been 'workers of iniquity,' self-seekers, ambitious, envious, uncharitable, wearing the appearance of a piety

[11] 1 Cor. viii. 3.   [12] 2 Tim. ii. 19.

and a devotion to which their hearts were altogether strangers, being filled with the idols of avarice and pride, or with the still fouler images on which the sensual mind is fed.

CHAPTER XVIII.

The Two Foundations.

St. Matt. vii. 24—27; *Vita Vitæ Nostræ*, § 36.

THE prophetical warning against profession without practice, which our Lord has just given, both to the faithful in general and to the ministers of His Divine Word and Sacraments in particular, very naturally leads on to the next and last warning of which we are now to speak, and with which the Sermon on the Mount closes. The preaching of the Gospel truths and rules of conduct brings on a terrible hardness and blindness in the souls of those ministers of the Church who do not practise what they preach, or live up to their high profession of faith. These are the 'workers of iniquity,' who have had the words of virtue and purity in their mouths, day after day, for the benefit of others. But what if those to whom these saving words are addressed hear them and do not keep them and practise them? Our Lord tells us that it is as dangerous to hear and not keep to His words, as it is to preach them and not to practise them. The spiritual state of such persons is like the bodily state of men who take into their mouths the food which is necessary for their sustenance, but who are unable to swallow it, digest it, or to assimilate it. It is given them for the support of their life and strength, and it contributes nothing to either. In the case of the body, this may be the effect of a disease or of some

V 24

secret decay of the natural forces, over which the will of the sufferer has no control. In the case of the spiritual food of the Word of God, it is not the same. The Word of God is always accompanied by grace, which knocks at the heart of the hearer at the same time that the accents of the preacher or teacher fall upon his ears, and it must be in consequence either of the levity or of the malice of the soul to which this grace addresses itself in vain that the fruit is not produced. The great danger which is thus generally stated is the subject of this last admonition of our Lord, in which He uses a parabolical form of expression, with something more of fulness of detail than we have as yet found in His discourses. He is preparing, as it were, for His teaching in parables, and it may be said that this last passage of the Sermon on the Mount is in a double sense a connecting link between His former teaching and His parables. In the first place, it forms such a link on account of the fulness of the imagery which it contains, the house built on the rock or on the sand, the rains, the floods, the winds, by which that house is assailed, and the issue of the assault, in the one case, firm resistance, in the other, a great and lamentable ruin. In the second place, this passage is directly connected with the parables by reason of its subject-matter, which is very much the same with that of the first parable, to which reference has already been made, and which describes the various ways in which the Word of God is received in different souls.

'Every one, therefore, that heareth these My words, and doth them, shall be likened to a wise man that built his house upon a rock. And the rain fell, and the floods came, and the winds blew, and they beat upon that house, and it fell not, for it was founded upon a rock. And every one that heareth these My words and doth them not, shall be like to a foolish man that built his house upon the sand. And the rain fell, and the floods came, and the winds blew, and they beat upon that house, and it fell, and great was the fall thereof.' Here we have the same strain of warning against imprudence and folly, such as reasonable men who are awake to the circumstances under which they live would never think of being guilty of. The folly of building a house upon the sand is like that of the virgins in one of the very last parables of our Lord, who did not take care to provide oil for their lamps. So that, here again, we may suppose our Lord to intend us to note that our blindness to the dangers and risks of our position is in itself the greatest of those dangers and risks. The fundamental cause of this blindness in us, as to the point in question, is a false estimate as to the difficulty of perseverance and stability in the service of God, which false estimate rests on ignorance of the weakness of our nature, of the persistency and power of temptations to evil, and of the absolute and constant necessity of Divine grace. This, however, in itself, would only be a form of that want of appreciation of the truths concerning our position which has already been touched by Him in the first of these closing warnings of His at the end of this Sermon, when He speaks about the narrowness of the gate which leads to life. In this last warning, our Lord dwells more particularly on the danger of carelessness in hearing His Divine words, in whatever form or manner they may be addressed to us. This folly may be connected with and founded on the false estimate as to our dangers, but it contains in itself fresh elements of mischief to our souls. For it involves disrespect to God, it implies an irreverent treatment of the most precious gifts which He bestows upon us, which are not only the most precious of gifts in themselves, but also the chosen means by which He has appointed that our progress and security in His service shall be provided for. Those who neglect to put in practice the Divine lessons which are addressed to them by God, act in the manner of which St. Luke speaks when He says of the Scribes and Pharisees,[1] the rulers and teachers of the Jews, that they despised the counsel of God for their good, by refusing to accept the penitential teaching of St. John Baptist, which was the Providential preparation by which it was intended that they should be made fit to receive our Lord. In consequence of this refusal, they were unable to become disciples of our Lord, and were punished with a judicial blindness, which was the cause of their enormous crime in bringing about the Passion, and their own ultimate destruction and perdition. In the same way, the careless and disrespectful treatment of the words of our Lord is certain to lead to disaster in the soul, which is deprived thereby of the strength which it most sorely needs, while at the same time it is in itself a fault deserving of punishment. The soul cannot live without the strength which can come to it only from Him, and when it practically despises the means by which that strength is communicated, it is liable to be abandoned to the assaults of its enemies and allowed to meet them with its own powers, or its own feebleness, alone.

The immense importance which our Lord attaches to this truth of the duty of that careful and reverential attention to His Word which shows itself in the performance of what that Word recommends or enjoins, will be easily seen when we consider the pains at which He has been to insist upon it. It is certainly something very significant that He should keep this piece of instruction for the last in this Divine Sermon. We have already alluded to the connection between the closing sentences of the Sermon on the Mount and the earliest of the parables.

[1] St. Luke vii. 30.

The Two Foundations.

It is quite clear that the subject-matter of those parables is the reception and treatment of the Word of God by various classes of souls. Moreover, the adoption by our Lord of that new method of teaching is distinctly attributed in the Gospels to His sense of the dulness and hardness which had grown upon the people to whom He had then been for some time preaching. It seems as if He had a double motive in His change of method, the motive of withdrawing truths from persons who had shown themselves unworthy of them, and the motive of refraining from obtruding truths on persons who were not prepared to receive them, and whom they might thus even injure—as if He was acting, in this respect, on His own principle of not casting pearls before swine. St. Matthew tells us that the disciples, at this time, asked our Lord why He spoke to the people in parables? ' Who answered and said to them, Because to you it is given to know the mysteries of the Kingdom of Heaven, but to them it is not given.' And then He adds the reason, which seems to consist in the bad reception which the people had given to the truths which had already been put before them—'For he that hath, to him shall be given, and he shall abound; but he that hath not, from him shall be taken away that also which he hath. Therefore do I speak to them in parables, because seeing they see not, and hearing they hear not, neither do they understand.' And our Lord then goes on to apply to the people the prophecy of Isaias: 'Hearing you shall hear, and shall not understand; and seeing you shall see, and shall not perceive.'[2] And He added at the same time the blessing on the faithful hearers: 'Blessed are your eyes, because they see, and your ears, because they hear.' The two other Evangelists, St. Mark and St. Luke, mention in the same con-

[2] St. Matt. xiii. 10, seq.; Isaias vi. 9, 10.

nection some other very similar words of our Lord, when, having said, 'He that hath ears to hear, let them hear,' He added, 'Take heed what, or how, you hear. In what measure you shall mete, it shall be measured to you again, and more shall be given to you.' Here we have another instance in which a familiar image is used by our Lord, with an application different from that which had been formerly given to it. He no longer means us to understand that as we treat our neighbour so God will treat us, but rather that God will treat us, in regard of the truths which He will impart to us, according to the measure of our faithfulness to those truths which we have already received : 'For he that hath, to him shall be given; and he that hath not, that also which he hath—or which he thinketh he hath—shall be taken away from him.'[3] And we find the account of the first series of parables closed by the Evangelists with the remark that, 'With many such parables He spoke to them the Word, according as they were able to hear. And without parables He did not speak unto them; but, apart, He explained all things to His disciples.'[4]

It is quite clear that the principle of withholding truths and points of sacred teaching from persons who would not profit by them was very largely acted on by our Lord, and that it is, indeed, necessary in order to explain His line of action towards the Jewish rulers as well as the multitudes. In His last discourse to His disciples, after the celebration of the Blessed Eucharist, He said of the Jews, 'If I had not come and spoken to them they would not have sin, but now they have no excuse for their sin,' just as He said of His miracles, 'If I had not done among them the works that no other man hath done they would not have sin; but now they have

[3] St. Mark iv. 24, 25 ; St. Luke viii. 18.
[4] St. Mark iv. 34.

both seen and hated both Me and My Father.'[5] That is, their indifference both to the teaching of our Lord and to the witness of the miracles was not a mere indifferent piece of idle carelessness, which had no moral character beyond that of inadvertence. It amounted to a display of hatred against our Lord and against the Father Who sent Him.

It may be supposed that this would be the strongest case of culpability, and that not all who did not act on our Lord's teaching would deserve so severe a censure. There is a point up to which simple heedlessness may be pleaded as the reason for inattention, though, in the case of the word of God, even heedlessness is not only dangerous but blameworthy. St. James seems to allow for this to some extent in the passage in which he uses the image of a man looking into a mirror. He seems to have the same thought in his mind as to the very great importance of hearing faithfully the Divine Word. 'Every best gift and every perfect gift is from above, coming down from the Father of Lights, with Whom is no change nor shadow of alteration. . . . Let every man be swift to hear, but slow to speak and slow to anger.' Then he seems to dispose of the dangers to faithful hearing which arise from the strength of passions and concupiscences. 'Casting away all uncleanness and abundance of naughtiness, with meekness receive the ingrafted word, which is able to save your souls. But be ye doers of the word, and not hearers only, deceiving your own selves. For if a man be a hearer of the word and not a doer, he shall be compared to a man beholding his own countenance in a glass, for he beheld himself and went his way, and presently forgot what manner of man he was.'[6] 'But,' he adds, subjoining the other side of the picture, as in the contrast which our Lord draws

[5] St. John xv. 22, 24.   [6] St. James i. 17. 19—21, 24.

in the passage before us between the house built on the rock and the house built on the sand, 'he that hath looked into the perfect law of liberty, and hath continued therein, not becoming a forgetful hearer but a doer of the work, this man shall be blessed in his deed.' It seems as if St. James would represent the word of God to us as a mirror in which we see ourselves, our characters, our duties, our capabilities, and our needs, and which thus furnishes us with the most proper light for our guidance in all emergencies; light by which we know just what to do, and how and by what means to do it. It may be that the Apostle is speaking more directly of the word as preached to us, but his doctrine applies to reading, or to the lights we may receive in meditation, the inspirations that come to us in prayer, the instruction that we gain from the example of others in circumstances like our own—that is, to all the manifold ways fn which God conveys practical light to the soul. All this practical knowledge vanishes at once from the soul of the inattentive hearer, who is then left to cope with all the difficulties which may arise before him without any Divine assistance. His work will be, at the best, natural, and he can expect no special blessing upon it.

Again, our Lord's words suggest that we shall have need of every kind of strength, and of all the manifold manifestations of grace, in consideration of the danger by which the stability of our spiritual edifice will be tested.| It is not for nothing that He takes pains so great to furnish us with the instructions conveyed in the Sermon on the Mount, of which He seems to be directly speaking, and in other great monuments of His wisdom and intelligence, the substance of which is put before us so constantly by the Church. Not one item of all this treasury of spiritual lore but is necessary for us for the

The Two Foundations.

conflicts in which we may be engaged. In these circumstances this last warning of the Sermon on the Mount goes beyond the others which have preceded it, in which we have had no mention of external assaults except those which are made, under the guise of friendly teaching, by the false prophets, who wear the clothes of sheep while they are in truth wolves.

In the present passage, however, our Lord seems to take it for granted that all kinds of trial will test the strength of His children's virtue. The time had hardly come for speaking in detail of the persecutions which were in store both for Himself and for them, but they are sufficiently foreshadowed in His words about the rains, and floods, and winds. Indeed, many commentators consider that the description here given is meant rather to signify the internal temptations from the three great concupiscences, sensuality, which softens and dissolves virtues, as the rain, anger or pride, which rages like the rising flood, and covetousness or worldliness, which acts by the power of a false persuasiveness, like the wind. However this may be, the general sense of the passage remains much the same, and it is certain that no external persecution or violence can have much effect upon the soul, except through its weakness on the side of one of the three concupiscences. They alone enable any outward assaults which may be made to fasten themselves on us in any way, and with any hope of success.

As the only strength of the soul lies in its union with God, so the weakness of the soul consists only in its separation from Him. This separation may be entire, as when the soul is in a state of mortal sin, or it may be something short of entire, as when the soul is at a distance from Him, when it feels instinctively that He has something against it, that it has refused Him something which He has asked of it, or has treated Him with coldness and unfaithfulness. In such a state the soul cannot expect much from Him, and, what is perhaps the worst feature of all, it has no confidence in Him, for it does not feel as if it had any right to have recourse to Him with freedom, to open to Him its troubles, and to rest upon Him for guidance and deliverance. But anything like habitual inattention to our Lord's words, in all the various ways in which they can be addressed to us, is the natural and inevitable cause of coldness, distance, feeling of separation and of disgrace with Him, and in such states the soul is already disarmed before the assault is made upon it, whether from without or within. Its recourse to our Lord is cut off by its sense of its own unfaithfulness. And, of course, the case is still worse if, as is most probable, the passions have become strengthened by the neglect of vigilance, if the habit of prayer has died out, and the practice of virtue has come to rest in the external performance of religious duties.

Considerations such as these enable us further to understand the very great contrast which our Lord here draws between the two classes of hearers of whom He speaks. There may be men standing, as it were, side by side in the Church, as the two houses of which the parable speaks may have been seen side by side on the same piece of ground. Their position, their gifts, their dignity, their reputation and credit may be alike, and yet all the time the one may rest only on the sand, the foundations of the other may be pushed down to the solid rock. The difference between them is in this alone, that is, according to our Lord's interpretation, the one may be faithful to the teaching and guidance of God as far as he knows them, and the other may be what St. James calls 'an unfaithful hearer.' In consequence of this difference all the storms of temptation and persecution will be seen to sweep in vain against the one, while the other, under trials no heavier, or even lighter, will fall with a great fall. These last words of our Lord's cannot be used by Him without some special purpose. It may be that He allows such persons to be assailed by great and original temptations, and that the fall corresponds to the violence of these. It may be that those who have great opportunities, such as those to whom the Sermon on the Mount, full as it is of counsels of perfection and maxims of the most sublime spirituality, was addressed, are likely to fall very conspicuously and very grievously if they are unfruitful, and that for them there is no comparatively slight ruin. It may be that the sense of their own unfaithfulness, bursting upon them after a season of blind presumption but of instinctive separation from God, fills them with despair, and so drives them headlong down the path of destruction without stop or let till they reach the lowest abyss. So certainly it is sometimes found to be with men who, up to a very short time before the catastrophe which has proved the hollowness of their virtue, have been considered as models of excellence, trees full of fruit, columns in the temple of God.

We may thus see that this last warning may apply to all Christians, both to those who are called upon to teach and to those who are taught by them. We are all, in the first instance, hearers of the words of our Lord, though we have not all the further commission to hand them on to others. But the punishments of which He speaks, in connection with those two last warnings, are different. The punishment of the preachers and ministers of the Church who have been, all the time, workers of iniquity, is rejection by our Lord at the last day. From this we may gather, not indeed that such persons can never be brought to repentance before death, but that it is very difficult so to bring them, and that, if penitence does not intervene, their punishment will be that of rejection by our Lord as their Judge. He says that they who are thus to be treated at the last day will be many. The punishment of those who hear our Lord's words and do them not, is that they will be allowed to fall in time of trial and temptation. Such a chastisement, unlike the other, may be permitted in God's great mercy, as the only means or the natural means of arousing such souls from their irreverent and presumptuous folly, and opening to them the door of restoration by means of great and conspicuous humiliation. Happy indeed are those who find the grace thus to profit by their fall!

CHAPTER XIX.

Teaching with authority.

St. Matt. vii. 28 ; *Vita Vitæ Nostræ*, § 36.

AT the conclusion of his account of the Divine Sermon of which we have been speaking, St. Matthew places the remark that 'when Jesus had fully ended all these words, the people were in admiration,' or wonder, 'at His doctrine,' or manner of teaching, 'For He was teaching them as One having power, and not as the Scribes and Pharisees.' The words of the first Evangelist might leave us in uncertainty, whether the 'teaching,' at which the multitudes marvelled on the ground which has been mentioned, was the teaching of the Sermon on the Mount in particular, or the general tone and style in which our Lord taught. The similar passages in the other Evangelists, St. Mark and St. Luke, who notice the impression which was produced by this feature in our Lord's manner, occur in places where they are not relating the Sermon on the Mount, but are speaking of our Lord's teaching in general. Nor, indeed, are there any features in the Sermon on the Mount which are not to be found elsewhere. That Sermon may be the most solemn and formal act of what we may call moral and spiritual legislation on the part of our Lord of which we have any record, if indeed we are not right in considering that it occupies a position altogether of its own and without any exact parallel in the whole course of His preaching. But there is very good reason for thinking that the authority and power of which St. Matthew here speaks were characteristics of His teaching as such, qualities which could not but mark it, inasmuch as He was what He was, and came to do the work for which He came. But the mention of the marvel of the people on this occasion by St. Matthew may well suggest to us some thoughts on this general characteristic of the teaching of our Lord, of the nature of which we have already spoken in an earlier chapter of this work.

The statement of the Evangelist comes to this, that our Lord's teaching was distinguished by its power and authority, and that in this it presented a contrast to the teaching of the Scribes and Pharisees, which made a wonderful impression on the people. The word which in our version is rendered 'power,' signifies that kind of power which involves inherent authority or sovereignty in those in whom it dwells, as distinguished from mere force or ability, and this holds good even when the power or authority is communicated, as when St. John says in the beginning of his Gospel of our Lord : 'As many as received Him He gave them power to be made the sons of God'—that is, He communicated to them the right, which belonged to His own Divine Person, of being in that relation to God, as far as their nature permitted it. The full signification of the expression is not, therefore, reached if we understand it in the passage before us and in others like it, of the force, might, efficacy, persuasiveness, or commanding influence of the language and method of our Lord's teaching. All these qualities might be found in the eloquence or declamation or logical cogency of merely human speech, in cases where the speaker was arguing to a conclusion or advocating a cause. Nor again, is it enough, in order to understand the full force of the word before us, to consider it as representing that kind, even of authority, which is to be found in the utterances of a judge who declares and administers the law which he has not made, and which he has no power to exceed or change or modify in any respect. Such a man may give an authoritative decision, from which there is no appeal, and yet his function may be simply ministerial, almost as much as that of an ambassador or a messenger. The difference will be clearer if we contrast our Lord's authority with that of others who had taught the chosen people of God before He came.

It has already been said that the Scribes and Pharisees, as our Lord said to the people, sat in the seat of Moses, and that in this sense their teaching was to be regarded as authoritative and followed as such. Yet it was just the difference between their manner of declaring the Law and the manner in which our Lord taught, that caused the wonder of the people which has been carefully recorded for us by the three Evangelists who have been named above. For the Scribes and Pharisees alleged the authority of the Law or the interpretations and traditions of the 'elders,' and did not claim for themselves any higher office than that of the guardians of these traditions and interpretations. They could not speak with the authority of the Lawgiver, nor were they themselves the sources of the Law, nor did it derive its binding powers from them. They were below the Law and after the Law, not above it and before it. Yet this last is the true relation between the Lawgiver and the Law. Now it is just this kind of sovereign and inherent authority which breathed in all our Lord's teaching, as it characterized also His manner when He dealt with the devils, or with diseases, or with the elements of nature, the winds, and the waves. In all these cases, He spoke as absolute Master in His own Name, and we find the same expressions of astonishment at His so doing recorded for us by the Evangelists. We cannot doubt that this was one of the grounds on which men were meant, in the Providence of God, to conceive that faith in His Divinity which was expressed by St. Peter in his famous confession. All these instances of authority on His part formed portions of that teaching of the Father in Heaven concerning Him, of which He Himself spoke to His chief Apostle on the occasion when that confession was made. It was evident that He assumed Divine authority, and it was evident that He could not possibly assume it without having it. Thus is the account to be given of the full meaning of the words which the Evangelists use when they speak of the 'power' with which He taught.[1]

The language and style of authority, therefore, and of authority of the very highest kind, were to be discerned in all that our Lord taught and in all that He did, and we cannot understand St. Matthew as signifying that the Sermon on the Mount was more remarkable in this respect than any other of His utterances, except inasmuch as it was itself distinguished among those utterances for its singular solemnity and majesty. But it may help us in our contemplations of this feature in our Lord's demeanour and manner of proceeding if we remind ourselves of the many instances thereof which are furnished to us in this single Sermon. The Beati-

[1] The use of the word ἐξουσία may be studied in other places as well as those referred to, *e.g.*, St. Matt. ix. 6—8, St. Mark ii. 10 (of the power to forgive sins). x. 1 (authority over devils) comp. St. Mark i. 27, St. Matt. xxi. 23, 24, 27 (where it is the word used in the question put to our Lord about His authority) comp. St. Mark xi. 28, 29, 33, St. Luke xx. 2—8. St. Mark iii. 15 (power of healing) ; vi. 7 (power over the devil committed to the Apostles) ; St. Luke iv. 6 (the power over this world falsely claimed by the devil) ; iv. 36 (power over the devils) ; ix. 1, x. 19 (same power communicated to the Apostles) ; St. Matt. xxviii. 18 (all power in Heaven and on earth given to our Lord) ; St. John v. 27 (authority to be the Judge of all given to Him) ; St. John xvii. 2 (power over all flesh given to Him by the Father) ; Acts i. 7 (the Father keeps the time and seasons in His own power) &c.

tudes themselves are not perhaps, in their form alone, examples of the language of authority such as might not have been found in the mouth of a human teacher. At least, we find the form in which they are cast in other parts of Sacred Scripture, as in the Psalms and elsewhere. But the series of the Beatitudes, their position at the beginning of the Sermon, which reminds us so much, as has been said, of the Commandments which were given to Moses on Mount Sinai, the magisterial and sovereign allotment of the rewards which correspond to each, rewards which are conveyed in the language of Divine promise—all these are circumstances which certainly enhance the appearance of sovereign authority in their delivery. There is something of the same kind in the intimation to the Apostles that they are to be persecuted like the prophets for the sake of our Lord, that they are commissioned to be the salt of the earth and the light of the world. The same character is observable in the language of the passage which immediately follows, in which our Lord, first of all, assures His hearers that they are not to think that He is come to destroy the law or the prophets—as if so to do would not have been beyond His powers if He had been so minded—and then goes on to correct, with the highest appearance of authority, a number of false or inadequate interpretations of various parts of the Divine Law which were then current among the Jews. Who could this Teacher be but the Lawgiver Himself, if He could require justice so far higher than that of the Scribes and Pharisees, and could set right so many of these received heads of practical doctrine? Again, if we examine closely the language on the point of divorce, we see in it an anticipation of that further declaration on the subject which our Lord afterwards made, and which amounted to nothing less than a withdrawal of the toleration and indulgence which Moses had been allowed to sanction. There is the same air of authority about the assurances given that all our debts are to be fully exacted in Purgatory, if they are not cancelled at once here, which follows on the explanation given of the commandment which prohibits anger.

The Sermon soon passes, after these sublime explanations of the Divine precepts, to heads of doctrine which modify and elevate, with the same unearthly purity and the same penetrating spirit, the common rules about the ordinary actions of religion, almsdeeds, prayer, and fasting. Just as, in the explanations given of the Commandments which regard our neighbours, our Lord goes at once to the very heart and kernel of the principle concerned, tearing out, as it were, the very roots of anger or lust from the most hidden recesses of the heart, so, in regard to the duties of religion, He casts aside as comparatively worthless all that is only external, and requires the most perfect homage of the heart and its intentions in anything that is to be fit to meet the eye of God. This is the principle which runs through the series of precepts which relate to the three great works above-named. It receives its most complete and sublime exemplification in the petitions which are put into our hearts and mouths in the Lord's Prayer. Here again, as with the Beatitudes, it may be said that the form does not go beyond what might be found in the teaching of an earthly Sage or Scribe, for it appears that the Masters among the Jews composed forms of prayer for their disciples. But there is certainly a Divine authority manifested in the arrangement of the petitions, and, it may be said, even especially in those of which no trace has been found in the Jewish formularies, the petition for daily bread, which seems to anticipate the later portion of the Sermon, in which we are told to take no anxious care for the morrow, and that in which our forgiveness is asked of God on the condition, as it were, of our forgiveness of others, and in which we seem to touch the secret power of the Atonement on the Cross, as giving us a right to such forgiveness in the name of Him Who teaches us this prayer.

In much the same way, it is not difficult to discern this tone of authority in the instructions which follow after the Lord's Prayer and the passage in which fasting is dwelt upon. There is no appeal at all made to Sacred Scripture or to any other authority, and yet promises are made which, as it were, pledge to us the faithfulness of God Himself and open to us the most secret counsels of His government. Even the Apostles, in laying down such precepts as those of which we speak, would assuredly refer to Scripture for their authority and security. There is nothing of the sort here. The precepts about absolute confidence in God, about not being solicitous for the morrow, about not casting pearls before swine, and about the duty of prayer, are of such a kind as to require warrant. But our Lord gives none, but the all-sufficient security of His own words. The summing up of the Law and the Prophets in the maxim of doing to others all things that we would they should do unto us, wears the same stamp of authority. It is easy to see, also, with what a sovereign knowledge of the ways of God and of man the warnings with which the Sermon closes are marked. In these our Lord speaks with the most absolute knowledge of the future issue of the work which He has come on earth to begin, and, as has been already remarked, in the course of these warnings He introduces Himself as the object of Christian worship and of the profession of Christian faith, as well as the appointed Judge of the great Day of account.

All through this Sermon there is no citation of authorities, no argument from this or that text or acknowledged fact to render an assertion more acceptable. It is true that our Lord reasons from the character of His Father as the Creator and Preserver of the world, as He that feeds the birds and clothes the lilies of the field with beauty. This reasoning is not so much aimed at the establishment of a truth, as at the facilitating an heroic confidence, by the means of the considerations on which His own Sacred Heart was never weary of dwelling. With this constant thought of His Father running through the whole discourse, our Lord always speaks in His own Name and legislates on His own authority. Accustomed as we are to the teaching of the Church, and knowing as we do the value in the sight of God of the faith and obedience which correspond to that teaching, it is not perhaps easy to us to understand at once the fulness of wonder and admiration which this kind of teaching must have created. It is the privilege of Catholics to be guided by authority, and their faith rests on that authority with so much implicit simplicity, that reasonings and arguments and deductions and the balancing of authorities are superfluous to them, as well as absolutely insufficient to engender that 'joy and peace in believing,' of which the Apostle speaks,[2] and the manner in which the Church takes up the tone of our Blessed Lord in this respect is to them one of the evidences of her Divine mission and of her perpetual union with Him. In this, as in so many other endowments and prerogatives of His Sacred Humanity, the Church has taken His place and speaks in His name. The Synagogue, as may be gathered from our Lord's words, already referred to, about the Scribes and Pharisees, could teach with a

[2] Rom. xv. 13.

certain authority on practical matters, and in this respect the people were able to obey their teachers. But, as has been said before, the Synagogue did not claim even to unfold the truths which lie hid in the deposit which it had received, and for any new emergency which might come in the case of fresh questions or heresies, it was content to wait for the coming of a future prophet. This is exactly the case with Christian communities in which the principle of the ever-living *magisterium* of the Church has been abandoned. They look back to the past, and interpret 'antiquity' for themselves, in defiance of the living Church from which they have separated themselves, or they look forward to the future, a future which cannot possibly touch them in their present rebellion, and appeal to a General Council of which they must themselves settle the conditions and the qualifications. Anything will satisfy them but the voice of the present Church, the only voice which they can hear, the only voice which can disturb them in their mutilations of truth and condemn their novelties. That is, they cast away the very greatest of the privileges which our Lord has provided for His children in the ever-abiding presence of the Holy Ghost in the Catholic Church, which secures for them the blessings which the multitudes in Galilee hailed with so much wonder, when they marvelled at our Lord because He spoke as One Who had authority, and not as the Scribes and Pharisees.

It is not without significance that this notice of the authority, which was so marked a feature in the teaching of our Lord, should have been inserted by St. Matthew at the end of the account which he gives of the Sermon on the Mount. We are accustomed to consider that the great purpose for which God has conferred on His Church the infallible and everliving authority which has been acknowledged in her by all her true children from the very beginning, must have been the security of an unerring standard of faith and doctrine. That is undoubtedly true, but it is not less true that the moral and spiritual teaching of our Lord and of His Church, that is, such teaching as is promulgated in this Divine Sermon, requires, no less than the doctrines of faith themselves, the foundation of an authority which is raised above all question or doubt. The Beatitudes, and all the glorious chain of instructions which follow on them, are addressed, in the first instance, to faith, and those who have carried them into practice most perfectly, have been those of whom most of all the words of which St. Paul was so fond come true, that the just live by faith. The faith by which, as the same Apostle tells us in the Epistle to the Hebrews, we believe that the world was framed by the 'word of God,'[3] the faith by which we grasp the sublime truths of the Creed concerning the Ever Blessed Trinity of Persons in the Divine Unity, and the like, takes the intelligence of man captive, and elevates it, by its submission, to a knowledge of truths which it could never of itself have even conceived. But the faith which enables men to carry out the practice of the virtues which are crowned in the Beatitudes, by means of which men like ourselves become poor in spirit, hungering and thirsting after justice, clean of heart, mourners and peacemakers in the world, and the rejoicing and exulting victims of persecution, rules over man not only in his intelligence, but in his will, his affections, his natural desires; it makes him triumph over nature and self and all that is earthly 'by the power of an indissoluble life,' by a spiritual might which drinks its inspiration from an intuition which seems little short of the clear vision of God. The whole history of Christian

[3] Heb. xi. 3.

perfection in the Church, is the history of the observance of the teaching of this Sermon. Not the Beatitudes alone, but the precepts which follow, which require the utmost purity of heart, the most entire charity, the most perfect detachment from earth and self, the most childlike trust and openness with God, are to be traced in the formation of the first Church in Jerusalem as described by St. Luke, they are exemplified in the lives and in the Epistles of the Apostles, and since their time, age after age, they have been the guiding stars and moving impulses of thousands upon thousands of holy lives, of which the greater part have been open only to the eye of God, but which have still been so powerful in their external influences and manifestations as to modify the whole character of society and to give birth to scores of religious institutes moulded on their example. All this could never have been the issue of teaching which did not speak with the authority of God, which could not lift the veil which hides Him, His character, His promises, His rules of action, from the eyes of earth, which could not declare authentically what pleased Him most, unfold the delicate accuracy of His judgments, whether in crowning or in punishing, and speak with equal right of the tender watchfulness of His Providence and the searching severity of His anger. Just as the Christian Creeds fall to dust, as soon as they are considered to be the deductions of even the most enlightened human wisdom from reason, or Scripture, or history, so would the teaching of the Sermon on the Mount give way under the weight of its own requirements, if it were made to rest on its intrinsic beauty, ineffable as that is, or its adaptation to spiritual needs, wonderful as that may be, or on any other foundation whatsoever, except the Divine authority of Him Whose word it is.

APPENDIX.

Harmony of the Gospels.

§ 29.—*Beginning of the preaching in Galilee, and call of four disciples.*

Matt. iv. 12—22.	Mark i. 14—20.
Now when Jesus had heard that John was delivered up, he retired into Galilee. And leaving the city Nazareth he came and dwelt in Capharnaum on the sea-coast, in the confines of Zabulon and of Nephthalim : that what was said by Isaias the prophet might be fulfilled : the land of Zabulon and the land of Nephthalim, the way of the sea beyond the Jordan, Galilee of the Gentiles : The people that sat in darkness saw great light : and to them that sat in the region of the shadow of death, light is sprung up.[1] From that time Jesus began to preach, and to say : Do penance, for the kingdom of heaven is at hand.	And after that John was delivered up, Jesus came into Galilee, preaching the gospel of the kingdom of God, and saying : The time is accomplished, and the kingdom of God is at hand : repent, and believe the gospel.
And Jesus walking by the sea of Galilee, saw two brothers, Simon who is called Peter and Andrew his brother, casting a net into the sea (for they were fishers). And he saith to them : Come	And as he walked by the sea of Galilee, he saw Simon and Andrew his brother casting nets into the sea (for they were fishermen). And Jesus said to them : Come after me, and I will make you to

[1] Isaias ix. 1, 2.

Matt. iv. 19—22.	Mark i. 18—20.
after me, and I will make you to be fishers of men. And they immediately, leaving their nets, followed him. And going on from thence, he saw other two brothers, James the son of Zebedee, and John his brother, in a ship with Zebedee their father, mending their nets : and he called them. And they immediately, leaving their nets and their father, followed him.	become fishers of men. And immediately, leaving their nets, they followed him. And going on from thence a little farther, he saw James the son of Zebedee, and John his brother, who also were in the ship mending their nets. And forthwith he called them. And they left their father Zebedee in the ship with his hired men, and followed him.

§ 30.—*The Sabbath at Capharnaum.*

Matt. viii. 14—17 ; iv. 23—25.	Mark i. 21—39.	Luke iv. 31—44.
	And they came into Capharnaum ; and forthwith on the sabbath-day, going into the synagogue, he taught them. And they were astonished at his doctrine : for he taught them as one that had authority, and not as the Scribes. And there was in their synagogue a man with an unclean spirit; and he cried out, saying : What have we to do with thee, Jesus of Nazareth? art thou come to destroy us? I know who thou art, the Holy one of God. And Jesus threat-	And he went down into Capharnaum, a city of Galilee, and there he taught them on the sabbath days. And they were astonished at his doctrine : for his word was with power. And in the synagogue there was a man who had an unclean devil, and he cried out with a loud voice, saying : Let us alone; what have we to do with thee, Jesus of Nazareth? art thou come to destroy us? I know thee who thou art, the Holy one of God. And Jesus

*W 24

Matt. viii. 14—16.	Mark i. 25—31.	Luke iv. 35—40.
	ened him, saying: Speak no more, and go out of the man. And the unclean spirit tearing him, and crying out with a loud voice, went out of him.	rebuked him, saying: Hold thy peace, and go out of him. And when the devil had thrown him into the midst, he went out of him, and hurt him not at all.
	And they were all amazed, insomuch that they questioned among themselves, saying: What thing is this? what is this new doctrine? for with authority he commandeth even the unclean spirits, and they obey him. And the fame of him was spread forthwith through all the country of Galilee.	And there came fear upon all, and they talked among themselves, saying: What word is this, for with authority and power he commandeth the unclean spirits, and they go out? And the fame of him was published in every place of the country.
And when Jesus was come into Peter's house, he saw his mother-in-law lying, and sick of a fever: And he touched her hand, and the fever left her, and she arose and ministered to them.	And immediately going out of the synagogue, they came into the house of Simon and Andrew, with James and John. And Simon's wife's mother lay sick of a fever: and forthwith they tell him of her. And he came and lifted her up, taking her by the hand; and immediately the fever left her, and she ministered unto them.	And Jesus rising up out of the synagogue, went into Simon's house. And Simon's wife's mother was taken with a great fever, and they besought him for her. And standing over her, he commanded the fever, and it left her. And immediately rising, she ministered to them.
And when evening was come they	And when it was evening, after sun-	And when the sun was down, all

Harmony of the Gospels.

Matt. viii. 17; iv. 23.	Mark i. 32—39.	Luke iv. 40—44.
brought to him many that were possessed with devils; and he cast out the spirits with his word: and all that were sick he healed. That it might be fulfilled, which was spoken by the prophet Isaias, saying: He took our infirmities, and bore our diseases.[1]	set, they brought all to him that were diseased, and that were possessed with devils. And all the city was gathered together at the door. And he healed many that were sick of divers diseases: and he cast out many devils; and he suffered them not to speak, because they knew him. And rising very early in the morning, going out he went into a desert place; and there he prayed. And Simon, and they who were with him, followed after him. And when they had found him, they said to him: All men seek for thee. And he saith to them: Let us go into the neighbouring towns and cities, that I may preach there also; for to this purpose am I come.	they that had any sick with divers diseases, brought them to him. But he laying his hands on every one of them, healed them. And devils went out of many, crying out and saying: Thou art the Son of God. And he, rebuking them, suffered them not to speak: for they knew that he was Christ. And when it was day, going out he went into a desert place, and the multitudes sought him and came unto him: and they detained him, that he should not depart from them. And he said to them: I must preach the kingdom of God to other cities also: for therefore am I sent.
And Jesus went about all Galilee, teaching in their synagogues, and preaching the gospel of the kingdom; and healing all diseases and infir-	And he preached in their synagogues, and in all Galilee, casting out devils.	And he was preaching in the synagogues of Galilee.

[1] Isaias liii. 4.

Matt. iv. 24, 25.	Mark i.	Luke iv.
mities among the people. And his fame went throughout all Syria; and they brought to him all sick people that were taken with divers diseases and torments, and such as were possessed by devils, and lunatics, those that had the palsy, and he healed them: And great multitudes followed him from Galilee, and from Decapolis, and from Jerusalem, and from Judea, and from beyond the Jordan.		

§ 31.—*The Eight Beatitudes and the Light of the World.*

Matt. v. 1—16.

Now Jesus seeing the multitudes, went up into a mountain: and when he had sat down, his disciples came to him.

And opening his mouth he taught them, saying:

Blessed are the poor in spirit: for theirs is the kingdom of heaven.

Blessed are the meek: for they shall possess the land.

Blessed are they that mourn: for they shall be comforted.

Blessed are they that hunger and thirst after justice: for they shall be filled.

Blessed are the merciful: for they shall obtain mercy.

Blessed are the clean of heart: for they shall see God.

Blessed are the peacemakers: for they shall be called the children of God.

Blessed are they that suffer persecution for justice' sake: for theirs is the kingdom of heaven.

Blessed are you when men shall revile you, and persecute you, and shall say all manner of evil against you falsely, for my sake; Rejoice and be exceeding glad, because your reward is very great in heaven: for so they persecuted the prophets, that were before you.

You are the salt of the

Matt. v. 13—16.

earth. But if the salt lose its savour, with what shall it be salted? It is then good for nothing, but to be cast out, and to be trodden upon by men.

You are the light of the world. A city that is set on a mountain cannot be hid. Neither do men light a candle, and put it under a bushel, but upon a candlestick, that it may give light to all that are in the house. Let your light so shine before men, that they may see your good works, and glorify your Father who is in heaven.

§ 32.—*Evangelical Justice.*

Matt. v. 17—48.

Think not that I am come to destroy the law, or the prophets: I am not come to destroy, but to fulfil. For Amen I say unto you, till heaven and earth pass, one jot or one tittle shall not pass from the law, till all be fulfilled. Whosoever, therefore, shall break one of these least commandments, and shall teach men so, he shall be called the least in the kingdom of heaven: but whosoever shall do and teach the same shall be called great in the kingdom of heaven.

For I say to you, that unless your justice abound more than that of the Scribes and of the Pharisees, you shall not enter into the kingdom of heaven.

You have heard that it was said to them of old: Thou shalt not kill.[1] And whosoever shall kill, shall be guilty of the judgment. But I say to you, that whosoever is angry with his brother, shall be guilty of the judgment. And whosoever shall say to his brother, Raca, shall be guilty of the council. And whosoever shall say, Thou fool, shall be guilty of hell fire. Therefore, if thou offerest thy gift at the altar, and there shalt remember that thy brother hath anything against thee; Leave there thy gift before the altar, and first go to be reconciled to thy brother; and then come and offer thy gift.

Make an agreement with thy adversary quickly, whilst thou art in the way with him: lest, perhaps, the adversary deliver thee to the judge, and the judge deliver thee to the officer, and thou be cast into prison. Amen I say to thee, thou shalt not go out from thence till thou pay the last farthing.

You have heard that it was said to them of old: Thou shalt not commit adultery.[2] But I say unto you, that whosoever looketh on a woman to lust after her, hath

[1] Exod. xx. 13. [2] Exod. xx. 14.

Matt. v. 28—48.

already committed adultery with her in his heart. And if thy right eye cause thee to offend, pluck it out, and cast it from thee; for it is better for thee that one of thy members should perish, than that thy whole body should be cast into hell. And if thy right hand cause thee to offend, cut it off, and cast it from thee; for it is better for thee that one of thy members should perish, than that thy whole body should go into hell.

It hath also been said: Whosoever shall put away his wife, let him give her a bill of divorce.[3] But I say to you, that whosoever shall put away his wife, excepting for the cause of fornication, causeth her to commit adultery: and whosoever shall marry her that is put away, committeth adultery.

Again, you have heard that it was said to them of old: Thou shalt not forswear thyself;[4] but thou shalt perform thy oaths to the Lord. But I say to you, not to swear at all; neither by heaven, for it is the throne of God; nor by the earth, for it is his footstool; nor by Jerusalem, for it is the city of the great king: Neither shalt thou swear by thy head, because thou canst not make one hair white or black. But let your speech be, Yea, yea;

No, no: for whatsoever is more than these, cometh from evil.

You have heard that it hath been said:[5] An eye for an eye, a tooth for a tooth. But I say to you, not to resist evil: but if any man strike thee on thy right cheek, turn to him the other also. And if any man will go to law with thee, and take away thy coat, let him have thy cloak also. And whosoever shall force thee to go one mile, go with him other two. Give to him that asketh of thee, and from him that would borrow of thee, turn not away.

You have heard that it hath been said:[6] Thou shalt love thy neighbour and hate thy enemy. But I say to you, love your enemies: do good to them that hate you: and pray for them that persecute and calumniate you: That you may be the children of your Father, who is in heaven: who maketh his sun to rise upon the good and the bad, and raineth upon the just and the unjust. For if you love those that love you, what reward shall you have? do not even the publicans the same? And if you salute your brethren only, what do you more? do not also the heathens the same? Be you, therefore, perfect, as also your heavenly Father is perfect.

[3] Deut. xxiv. 1.
[5] Exod. xxi. 24.
[4] Num. xxx. 3.
[6] Levit. xix. 18.

§ 33.—*Alms, Prayer, and Fasting.*

Matt. vi. 1—18.

Take heed that you do not your justice before men, that you may be seen of them; otherwise you shall not have a reward from your Father, who is in heaven.

Therefore, when thou doest an alms-deed, sound not a trumpet before thee, as the hypocrites do in the synagogues and in the streets, that they may be honoured by men. Amen I say to you, they have received their reward. But when thou doest alms, let not thy left hand know what thy right hand doeth: That thy alms may be in secret, and thy Father, who seeth in secret, will repay thee.

And when you pray, you shall not be as the hypocrites, who love to pray standing in the synagogues and at the corners of the streets, that they may be seen by men: Amen I say to you, they have received their reward. But thou, when thou shalt pray, enter into thy chamber, and having shut the door, pray to thy Father in secret: and thy Father, who seeth in secret, will reward thee.

And when you are praying speak not much, as the heathens do: for they think that they are heard for their much speaking. Be not you, therefore, like them. For your Father knoweth what you stand in need of, before you ask him. You, therefore, shall pray in this manner:

Our Father, who art in heaven, hallowed be thy name.

Thy kingdom come. Thy will be done on earth as it is in heaven.

Give us this day our daily bread.

And forgive us our debts, as we forgive our debtors.

And lead us not into temptation. But deliver us from evil. Amen.

For if you forgive men their offences, your heavenly Father will also forgive you your offences. But if you will not forgive men, neither will your Father forgive you your sins.

And when you fast, be not, as the hypocrites, sad: for they disfigure their faces, that to men they may appear fasting. Amen I say to you, they have received their reward. But thou, when thou fastest, anoint thy head, and wash thy face: That thou appear not fasting to men, but to thy Father, who is in secret: and thy Father, who seeth in secret, will reward thee.

§ 34.—*Confidence in God our Father.*

Matt. vi. 19—34.

Lay not up for yourselves treasures on earth; where the rust and the moth consume, and where thieves dig through and steal. But lay up for yourselves treasures in heaven: where neither the rust nor the moth doth consume, and where thieves do not dig through, nor steal. For where thy treasure is, there is thy heart also.

The light of thy body is thy eye. If thy eye be simple, thy whole body will be lightsome. But if thy eye be evil, thy whole body shall be darksome. If, therefore, the light that is in thee be darkness, how great will the darkness itself be?

No man can serve two masters: for either he will hate the one, and love the other; or he will hold to the one, and despise the other. You cannot serve God and mammon. Therefore I say to you, be not solicitous for your life, what you shall eat, nor for your body, what your shall put on. Is not the life more than the food, and the body more than the raiment? Behold the fowls of the air, for they sow not, neither do they reap, nor gather into barns: yet your heavenly Father feedeth them. Are not you of much more value than they? And which of you, by thinking, can add to his stature one cubit? And for raiment why are you solicitous? Consider the lilies of the field, how they grow: they labour not, neither do they spin. And yet I say to you, that not even Solomon, in all his glory, was arrayed as one of these. Now, if God so clothe the grass of the field, which to-day is, and to-morrow is cast into the oven; how much more you, O ye of little faith? Be not solicitous, therefore, saying: What shall we eat, or what shall we drink, or wherewith shall we be clothed? For after all these things do the heathens seek. For your Father knoweth that you have need of all these things. Seek ye, therefore, first the kingdom of God, and His justice: and all these things shall be added unto you. Be not, therefore, solicitous for to-morrow: for the morrow will be solicitous for itself. Sufficient for the day is the evil thereof.

§ 35.—*Against judging others, and of confidence in Prayer.*

Matt. vii. 1—12.

Judge not, that you may not be judged. For with what judgment you have judged, you shall be judged: and

Matt. vii. 2—12.

with what measure you have measured, it shall be measured to you again. And why seest thou a mote in thy brother's eye, and seest not a beam in thy own eye? Or how sayest thou to thy brother: Let me cast the mote out of thy eye; and behold a beam is in thy own eye? Thou hypocrite, cast out first the beam out of thine own eye, and then shalt thou see to cast out the mote out of thy brother's eye.

Give not that which is holy to dogs; neither cast ye your pearls before swine; lest they trample them under their feet, and, turning upon you, tear you.

Ask, and it shall be given you: seek, and you shall find, knock, and it shall be opened to you. For every one that asketh, receiveth: and he that seeketh, findeth: and to him that knocketh, it shall be opened. Or what man is there among you, of whom if his son ask bread, will he reach him a stone? Or if he ask a fish, will he reach him a serpent? If you, then, being evil, know how to give good gifts to your children: how much more will your Father, who is in heaven, give good things to them that ask him?

All things, therefore, whatsoever you would that men should do to you, do you also to them: for this is the law and the prophets.

§ 36.—*The narrow way to life.*

Matt. vii. 13—29; viii. 1.

Enter ye in at the narrow gate: for wide is the gate, and broad is the way that leadeth to destruction; and many there are who enter by it. How narrow is the gate, and strait is the way, which leadeth to life: and few there are who find it!

Beware of false prophets, who come to you in the clothing of sheep, but inwardly they are ravenous wolves. By their fruits you shall know them. Do men gather grapes of thorns, or figs of thistles? Even so every good tree yieldeth good fruit, and the bad tree yieldeth bad fruit. A good tree cannot yield bad fruit; neither can a bad tree yield good fruit. Every tree that yieldeth not good fruit shall be cut down, and shall be cast into the fire. Wherefore, by their fruits you shall know them.

Not every one that saith to me, Lord, Lord, shall enter into the kingdom of heaven; but he that doeth the will of my Father, who is in heaven, he shall enter into the kingdom of heaven. Many will say to me in that day: Lord, Lord, have we not prophesied

Matt. vii. 22—29; viii. 1.

in thy name, and in thy name cast out devils, and done many wonderful works in thy name? And then will I profess unto them: I never knew you: depart from me, you that work iniquity.[1]

Therefore, whosoever heareth these my words, and doeth them, shall be likened to a wise man, who built his house upon a rock. And the rain fell, and the floods came, and the winds blew, and they beat upon that house, and it fell not; for it was founded upon a rock. And every one that heareth these my words, and doeth them not, shall be like a foolish man who built his house upon the sand. And the rain fell, and the floods came, and the winds blew, and they beat upon that house, and it fell; and great was the fall thereof.

And it came to pass, when Jesus had fully ended these words, the people were in admiration at his doctrine. For he was teaching them as one having authority, and not as their Scribes and Pharisees. And when he was come down from the mountain, great multitudes followed him.

[1] Psalm vi. 9.

www.ingramcontent.com/pod-product-compliance
Lightning Source LLC
Chambersburg PA
CBHW020304240426
43673CB00039B/698